T0251446

Managing Spontaneous Community Volunteers in Disasters

A Field Manual

Managing Spontaneous Community Volunteers in Disasters

A Field Manual

Lisa Orloff

CRC Press
Taylor & Francis Group
Boca Raton London New York

CRC Press is an imprint of the
Taylor & Francis Group, an **informa** business

CRC Press
Taylor & Francis Group
6000 Broken Sound Parkway NW, Suite 300
Boca Raton, FL 33487-2742

International Standard Book Number: 978-1-4398-1833-6 (Hardback)

Library of Congress Cataloging-in-Publication Data

Orloff, Lisa.
  Managing spontaneous community volunteers in disasters : a field manual / Lisa Orloff.
    p. cm.
  Includes bibliographical references and index.
  ISBN 978-1-4398-1833-6 (hardback)
  1. Emergency management. 2. Voluntarism. I. Title.

HD49.O75 2011
363.34068'3--dc22   2011006789

Visit the Taylor & Francis Web site at
http://www.taylorandfrancis.com

and the CRC Press Web site at
http://www.crcpress.com

For my mother, who believed I could do anything, and my father, who taught me to never say "Uncle."

CONTENTS

FOREWORD

My life changed drastically the moment I decided to leave my home and find a way to help my fellow New Yorkers in the immediate aftermath of the attacks of 9/11. Where I wound up and how I helped was a toss of the dice.

Why I prevailed while others were turned away could be attributed to fate or a combination of fate and fortitude. It is a matter of record that thousands of others driven by the same need to help played a significant role in the 9/11 rescue-and-recovery effort.

For me, my role in the 9/11 relief effort and subsequent long-term recovery did not end when the pile turned into a pit, when the rescue turned to recovery, or when recovery turned to rebuilding. From spontaneous volunteer to founding board member of two community centers that served more than 45,000 individuals affected by 9/11 to curriculum developer turned author, my life has taken a different path, as I am sure it has for many before me, for those alongside me, and will be so for those long after me.

The lessons that I have learned through my own personal experiences, the experiences and stories of those whom we have helped through September Space Community Centers and of those professionals who have helped me cannot be contained in one book or in one manual.

I start here with *Managing Spontaneous Community Volunteers in Disasters: A Field Manual* in the belief that what we have learned, if put into practice, will better serve all of us—emergency managers, citizens, survivors, victims, and family members. I believe a structure that empowers the community in every step of the disaster management cycle must be embraced and championed. From preparedness to response and recovery, professional leadership must partner with community leadership and community leadership with its citizens.

ACKNOWLEDGMENTS

So many people have contributed to the development of World Cares Center, our programs and training, and the information contained in this manual. From the leaders who emerged during the 9/11 relief effort, to our international initiatives and everything in between, your influence is reflected not only in this book, but in everyday life, in our work, and in our volunteering. Without your contributions of time, knowledge, resources, and support, World Cares Center would not exist, this book would not be published, and disaster response in general would not be as effective in saving lives and communities.

A special thank you to Marilyn Shigetani, Bernadette Freker, and Susan Jensen for their inclusive mentorship; to Eric Ottaway, Ingrid Maritato, Diane Carroll, and Claudia Fitzpatrick for their friendship and faith; and to the board members, advisors, supporters, and volunteers of World Cares Center who together form the sum of who we are.

ABOUT THE AUTHOR

Inspired by her personal experiences in the field as a spontaneous volunteer managing 300 others like her in the immediate aftermath of 9/11, and as the founder of World Cares Center (WCC) along with fellow 9/11 spontaneous volunteers developing and managing the September Space Community Centers and working with communities post-Katrina and following the Haiti earthquake, author Lisa Orloff has evolved as a champion in the field of community empowerment and spontaneous volunteer management. Having researched the subject for nearly a decade, the author has gathered the experiences and expertise of seasoned responders in the field and academics, and has been called upon as a subject-matter expert by the Defense Advanced Research Projects Agency at the Department of Defense, the Joint Forces Command, and emergency management agencies around the nation and the world. As Joseph Catalino, private sector integration domestic initiatives coordinator for NORAD-USNORTHCOM,* states: "Lisa Orloff wrote the book on spontaneous volunteer management as she was responding herself."

Through her work at WCC, Orloff has trained responders from across the nation. Emergency managers are requesting WCC's Spontaneous Unaffiliated Community Volunteer Management training as a module to be offered to their graduated community emergency response teams (CERT), volunteer groups, and other communities of interest.

---

* NORAD: North American Aerospace Defense Command; USNORTHCOM: U.S. Northern Command.

INTRODUCTION

Picture yourself sitting in your house or office when, suddenly, you realize that something has occurred outside; power is cut off, phone lines are down. You open the door and see an emergency unfold before you. No official responder has arrived on scene as of yet. What do you do? Would you go back inside your home or office and do nothing? Would you step outside and assess the situation and help?

I would guess that you would step outside and see if there was some way you could help. Your response would be the same as that of a majority of your fellow citizens, an instinctual reaction to take action: fight or flight. The difference between citizen volunteers and official responders lies in the combination of training, experience, connection to official resources, and the authority to conduct operations, not in the willingness to help.

Acknowledging that success in disaster response is based on the knowledge and resources that are immediately available, take into consideration that citizens also have a cultural understanding of the affected community that outside official responders will not. Community members also have the ability to connect to local resources that are immediately available, both material and human.

The gap between those who hold important local and cultural knowledge, coupled with a willingness to help, and those with professional disaster management training and resources must be bridged to improve response and to address the mistakes that we have seen cost lives and property in the not-so-distant past.

Taking these issues into account, the intent of this manual is twofold: (a) to give emergency managers and community leaders the tools to safely and effectively manage spontaneous community volunteers and (b) to provide guidance to managers and community leaders on ways to empower citizens to take a proactive role in their community's preparedness and response efforts.

Sharing these situations experientially helps to further paint the picture of interaction between community and official responders in a catastrophic disaster response. From Haiti to Indonesia to New Orleans to post 9/11 New York City, citizens emerged as responders after every disaster, and history has documented the lack of a coordinated effort to make use of this vital resource.

NEW YORK CITY, SEPTEMBER 11, 2001

It may be difficult to estimate the exact number of spontaneous volunteers who came out to help during the 9/11 relief effort in New York City alone. In several documents, it is stated that over 40,000 volunteers came out to help within their community; that supply chains emerged at the Jacob K. Javits Center, a convention center on 34th Street that spans four city blocks (Figure I.1); and that the Park Avenue Armory and Stuyvesant High School in Lower Manhattan, across the street from the former site of the twin towers, became an impromptu triage site for those who needed minor medical care. All of these locations had two things in common: They emerged spontaneously through the leadership of the citizens who lived and worked in the area, and they were "staffed" and managed by community members themselves.

Because the New York City Office of Emergency Management was housed in the World Trade Center, their offices were destroyed. In the first

Figure I.1 Post-9/11 response at the Jacob Javits Center, New York City. (Photo credit: Tom Sawyer.)

two weeks of response, much of their time was spent setting up a replacement command center. This left a gap that community members filled. Their efforts were by no means perfect, and many mistakes were made. However, the positive side of human nature prevailed, and out of chaos, communities that had never met before worked side by side to form a productive rescue-and-recovery workforce. What was learned in this process was that most of the challenges that emerged could be attributed to the lack of training and guidance on how to utilize the world's greatest resource—people.

What we did see in these extreme circumstances were leaders emerging from within agencies and from communities, developing and adapting management structures to suit the immediate needs of the situation at hand. There was no manual to follow. Such leaders included Captain Sweet of NYC's Manhattan South police unit, Sergeant First Class Jay Kaczor of the Army National Guard, and the leadership at the Jacob Javits Center, Chelsea Piers, Chelsea Market, and others who should be commended for their willingness to be flexible in utilizing the resources that appeared before them, including spontaneous unaffiliated community volunteers (SUCV).

From within the Federal Emergency Management Agency, Voluntary Agency Liaisons Marilyn Shigetani, Susan Jensen, and Bernadette Freker created a structure that was inclusive and empowering, and which greatly contributed to this book. Seeing the needs that would exist for months and years, community volunteers collaborated in an effort to assist in FEMA outreach programs, eventually leading to the formation of World Cares Center (WCC) and its September Space Community Centers. These centers provided long-term recovery support well beyond the lifespan of the national support systems that were beginning to plan their departure only a few short months after the attack.

NEW ORLEANS, HURRICANE KATRINA, 2005

In "Heralding Unheard Voices: The Role of Faith-Based and Non-Governmental Organizations during Disaster" (2006), the Department of Homeland Security took a huge leap forward with its after-action report that chronicled all of the services that the community-based and faith-based local groups performed in the aftermath of Hurricane Katrina in 2005 (see Figure I.2). The report found that thousands of faith-based organizations (FBOs) and nongovernmental organizations (NGOs) stepped in, often as

Figure I.2 Damaged harbor in the wake of Hurricane Katrina, New Orleans. (Photo credit: Lisa Orloff.)

the primary provider of services. Relying on their specific expertise and on their knowledge of the community, they demonstrated numerous best practices, such as effective partnering among NGOs and faith-based organizations, to provide essential services and in maintaining family unity in the shelters. Small organizations, without a specific mandate in disaster response, and often suffering their own effects from the storm, still managed to shelter thousands of evacuees, and many are continuing to serve in the long-term recovery and rebuilding efforts today. Their effectiveness was attributed to their people-centered missions, their closeness to the community they were serving, and their unique resources, among them the volunteerism of their members and networks. The same organizations that were formed on an ad hoc basis in the response to Hurricane Katrina sprang into action during the BP oil spill, or the Deepwater Horizon oil spill, which began with an oil well blowout April 20, 2010.

But "Heralding Unheard Voices" also outlines many of the hurdles these groups faced. As groups that had not been included in prior government plans for emergency response, they were rarely consulted, and the government and its officials did not coordinate with these groups, even though they were providing the bulk of services. In addition, few of these organizations had prior training or experience in providing services, especially at the magnitude that Katrina necessitated. The human cost of intensive service provision led to staff burnout and volunteer fatigue. These and other lessons lay the groundwork for an initiative to help communities become more effective in disaster preparation, response, and resilient recovery. WCC worked closely with the University of New Orleans, holding community assessment meetings with local and faith-based leadership and lending its expertise in the development of community-based centers in both New Orleans and Baton Rouge. Its methodologies were applied in developing the Welcome Home centers in these locations, which housed many of the agencies and organizations providing resources to Katrina victims, including federal assistance services, disaster childcare, and counseling services.

The lessons learned since 9/11 have never before been used to develop a comprehensive training program, facilitate predisaster coordination efforts, and standardize procedures for use by other emergency managers and community leaders and citizens alike. It is these lessons— combined with hundreds of others collected from personal experiences in response to 9/11, Hurricane Katrina, the 2010 Haiti earthquake, and other disasters—that form the methodology behind this manual, a plan that can work for your agency and help build a resilient community and society. Extensive research has been conducted on existing plans, training regimens, and programs from a diverse range of authorities. The methodologies that are used are not strictly from emergency management or humanitarian assistance practices, but are combined with social empowerment philosophies. We have integrated the perspective of Robert Putnam* on relational organizing and the power of small groups and how empowering small groups within a community has a positive impact on the community as a whole. We have also incorporated recent psychosocial research that explores why involvement in disaster response has a positive impact on an individual's and a community's resilient recovery. In some cases, modifications have been made to existing charts and guides to incorporate the shared experience and expertise of the entire responder

---

* Robert Putnam, Lewis Feldstein, and Donald J. Cohen, *Better Together: Restoring the American Community* (New York: Simon and Schuster, 2003).

community, including the military, emergency services, volunteers, and risk managers as well as faith-based and community leadership.

THIS FIELD MANUAL: HOW IT WORKS

Anyone who considers himself or herself someone who would lead constituents in times of need is encouraged to read this book and take action. This manual lays out the rationale and process by which emergency managers and community leaders can take stock of the wealth of resources that exist in their neighborhoods and commit the time needed to cultivate a culture of collaboration and respect with these groups and individuals through outreach and training. For these leaders, this manual is designed to be a useful tool to safely and effectively prepare for, respond to, and recover from any scale of disaster or emergency within their communities.

Whether the process involves spontaneous convergent volunteers or solicited first-time volunteers who are new to your organization, assigning them "just in time" to fulfill essential roles and tasks requires a process that will: (a) assess your agency's needs and challenges, (b) build a plan for managing SUCVs by developing internal and external protocols, (c) develop spot screening and interviewing methods, and (d) engage community members in an information-sharing and outreach campaign. Each of these steps is distributed across the chapters that follow, each building upon the previous chapter's lessons with snapshots of templates that can be used as is or modified to suit your particular needs and conditions. At the end of each chapter, review questions will guide in the development of your plan. The appendix to this book contains all the templates that will form the core of your spontaneous-volunteer management plan.

Managing Spontaneous Community Volunteers in Disasters: A Field Manual should be suggested reading for all levels of community leaders as well as emergency, volunteer, and risk managers. In addition, the author hopes that this book may be of help to faculty and students who are part of the growing number of emergency management university programs that have grown exponentially since the mid-1990s, and particularly since 9/11.

1

The History of Spontaneous Volunteerism in Disaster Response

Along the harbor front and throughout the north end, those still alive and able tried to free others, or searched desperately for family whose fates they were afraid to imagine.... People from outlying communities poured in to help as soon as a way was cleared.

Janet Kitz*

Immediately after the first shock, there was an enormous response and solidarity among the city population of 18 million people. Ordinary citizens organized brigades to help with rescue efforts and to provide food, clothing and emotional support to the homeless. Untrained, spontaneous volunteers saved 800 people. However, 100 people lost their lives while attempting to save others. This is a high price to pay and is preventable through training.

Guillermo Julio Soberon and Jaime Sepulveda†

---

* Janet Kitz. Shattered City: The Halifax Explosion and the Road to Recovery (Halifax, NS: Nimbus, 1989). This book is about the 1917 munitions ship explosion in Halifax, NS, Canada.
† Guillermo Julio Soberon and Jaime Sepulveda, "The Health Care Reform in Mexico: Before and after the 1985 Earthquakes." AJPH 76, no. 6 (1986): 673–680.

IN THIS CHAPTER

- The History of Spontaneous Volunteerism in Disaster Response
- Lessons Learned from Spontaneous Volunteerism in Disaster Response
- The Ecosystem of Supportive Partners in Disaster Response
  - National Government Initiatives
  - National or International/Nongovernmental Organizations
  - Businesses
  - Local Faith-based and Nongovernmental Organizations
  - Ordinary Citizens, Good Samaritans, and Local Assets

HISTORY OF SPONTANEOUS VOLUNTEERISM IN DISASTER RESPONSE

The fact that citizens come out spontaneously to help in the aftermath of disaster is not something new. Throughout history, there is documentation of neighbor helping neighbor. Such examples can be seen as early as 1859, when Henry Dunant organized civilian care for the wounded after a battle in the northern Italian town of Solferino that left tens of thousands of wounded soldiers without medical attention. Dunant, with the memory of the horror of what he had seen, worked to establish a society for the aid of those wounded in battle that would be neutral in their provision of care. That establishment is known today as the International Committee of the Red Cross.

Another example of spontaneous volunteerism can be seen in the aftermath of the Great Chicago Fire of 1871 that destroyed nearly 20,000 buildings and seventy-three miles of street, when architects, ordinary citizens, and firemen worked nonstop to rebuild the city, while cities all over the world sent supplies, money, and even books. In three months, this tremendous citizen effort led to the construction of 300,000 buildings, including the largest public library of its time.

Likewise, after the 1994 earthquake in Kobe, Japan, when communication lines were down and backup facilities lost, massive spontaneous aid emerged in the form of an estimated 630,000 to 1.3 million volunteers.* Most of the rescue work was conducted by local inhabitants, as official

---

* K. J. Tierney, Emergency Response: Lessons Learned from the Kobe Earthquake. Disaster Research Center, University of Delaware, 1997.

Figure 1.1 Oklahoma City bombing. (Source: Wikipedia Commons.)

responders only found about a quarter of those who were saved, while volunteers found the greater remainder of survivors.*

One year later, in Oklahoma City, the bomb that destroyed the Alfred P. Murrah Federal Building (Figure 1.1) led to an outpouring of assistance and donations, including the Compassion Center, established within seven hours of impact, which provided essential information services,

---

* O. Hiroi, "Earthquake Disasters: The Need for Robust Emergency Information and Transportation Networks," The Wheel Extended 93 (1995): 5.

mental health counseling, and comfort to bereaved family members. It was staffed and supported by voluntary organizations, pastors, chaplains, and mental health professionals throughout the area, state, and nation.* More recently, the devastating earthquake of 2008 that took place in China's Sichuan Province brought out more than 150,000 volunteers who helped to provide reconstruction assistance and provide refugee education and health services. It is undoubtedly true that without the efforts of these hundreds of thousands of volunteers, immediate response and long-term recovery would not have proceeded at the pace it did nor had as high a rate of success.

In the years following the attacks of 9/11, the international community has experienced disasters on a scale not seen in previous history, from the magnitude of the South Asian tsunami to the earthquake in Sichuan Province, China, and the Gulf Coast hurricanes. In all of the response efforts, we have seen a growing number of average citizens stepping up and becoming proactive responders, along with community leaders who are taking the initiative to guide their constituencies. What these individuals lack in formal emergency management training, they make up for in their commitment to their neighbors, fellow citizens, and community.

LESSONS LEARNED FROM SPONTANEOUS VOLUNTEERISM IN DISASTER RESPONSE

Lessons learned show us that just-in-time volunteers can provide cost- and time-saving services. Florida has led the effort in engaging citizens in postdisaster efforts. Two Florida counties have demonstrated that it is not only possible, but extremely cost effective to harness community volunteers, organizing and empowering this resource to effectively serve communities struck by major disasters.

When a rare F-4 tornado ripped through Osceola, Orange and Seminole Counties in late February 1998, tearing apart homes, businesses, and lives, calls from people offering assistance immediately began to pour in, and the voluntary agencies organized these citizen helpers, resulting in substantial savings in time and money, as seen in Table 1.1, which shows the results using volunteers compared to engaging a contractor.

---

* Oklahoma Department of Civil Emergency Management. "After Action Report."

Table 1.1 Time and Savings from the Use of Volunteers, Osceola County, FL

Initial cost for contractor	$8 million	Estimated time for contractor	90 days
Cost using volunteers	$1.4 million	Actual time for volunteers	55 days
Total cost savings	$6.6 million	Total time savings	35 days
Cost savings	83 percent	Time saved	39 percent

Source: Volunteer Florida.

In the United States, only recently has the Department of Homeland Security (DHS) extensively documented the positive roles that communities and community leaders played in disaster response and the challenges they face.* As the United Nations Office for the Coordination of Humanitarian Affairs (OCHA) recommended in a 2005 framework for building national capacities to manage disasters (the Hyogo Framework for Action), governments need to "develop specific mechanisms to engage the active participation and ownership of relevant stakeholders, including communities, in disaster risk reduction, in particular building the spirit of volunteerism."†

Understanding that citizens tend to respond as helpers rather than as victims is a crucial piece of information for those planning to manage these emergent citizens. When official responders find themselves faced with these citizen responders without a plan that includes the management of this resource, the result can be confusion, chaos, and ill will between community members and official responders. The additional burden that is put on official responders to manage both spontaneous volunteers and spontaneous donations often leaves them resenting the initial outpouring of good will and looking for simple black-and-white solutions. To date, there are limited frameworks in place to achieve a comprehensive and manageable process to ensure the most effective and safe response with the aid of spontaneous volunteers. When spontaneous unaffiliated civilian responses have been documented, the literature tends to reflect only

---

* U.S. Department of Homeland Security, "Heralding Unheard Voices: The Role of Faith-Based Organizations and Nongovernmental Organizations during Disasters," Homeland Security Institute, Arlington, Va., 2006. http://www.homelandsecurity.org/hsireports/Herald_Unheard_Voices.pdf.

† ISDR, "Hyogo Framework for Action 2005–2015: Building the Resilience of Nations and Communities to Disasters," International Strategy for Disaster Reduction, United Nations, New York, 2005.

on the challenges of volunteer convergence, while the positive experiences and aspects are left to sidebar conversations.

In some cases, due to the lack of planning and misperceptions about the efficacy of spontaneous volunteers, emergency managers will focus on how to dissuade individuals from assisting altogether. This approach has proven time and again to be ineffective. Studies have shown that disasters and emergencies from natural and human-made causes can have a negative effect on the human psyche, resulting in a sense of disempowerment and a loss of connectivity and purpose as well as a loss of faith.

In the face of disaster, the "fight or flight" response is triggered, and many individuals naturally seek ways to become reconnected. This initial reaction may not even be conscious or deliberate. Volunteering helps individuals to regain a sense of control to connect with each other and find hope post-tragedy. To eliminate this experience is to eliminate the community's ability to rebound from its disempowering experience of disaster.

In addition, research finds that an influx of volunteers can quickly restore a sense of equilibrium in an affected community. The fact that there are often more nonvictims than victims in a seriously impacted area allows the community to adjust itself into recovery.* The International Federation of the Red Cross and the Red Crescent Societies have found that it is also important to acknowledge posttraumatic growth, defined as "the perception of positive change and increased strength that an individual may feel upon experiencing a trauma and in responding to a disaster, and not just the negative aspects of volunteering in disaster situations."† A person's sense of social support is a significant factor in posttraumatic growth, and a supportive social network developed through volunteering can restore a volunteer's sense of mission and a sense of security and trust, which may have been lost in the initial impact of the disaster. A study of differences between volunteer and nonvolunteer survivors of a 1999 earthquake in Marmara, Turkey, showed that volunteers had more active and problem-solving coping strategies than nonvolunteers, contributing to their posttraumatic growth.‡

---

* K. J. Tierney, "The Social and Community Contexts of Disaster." In Psychosocial Aspects of Disaster, ed. R. Gist and R. Lubin, 11–39 (New York: Wiley, 1989).

† International Federation of the Red Cross and Red Crescent Societies, "Taking Volunteers Seriously: Progress Report 1999–2007." Geneva, Switzerland, 2007, p. 21.

‡ Nuray A. Karanci and Acarturk, "Post-Traumatic Growth among Marmara Earthquake Survivors Involved in Disaster Preparedness as Volunteers." Traumatology 2005 (11): 307–323.

The common lessons learned throughout these examples of citizen response, regardless of the national context, are:

1. Civilian volunteer involvement and leadership in emergency and disaster response is not only inevitable, but critical.
2. Effective disaster response requires preplanning that integrates SUCVs.
3. Officials must cultivate community volunteers before emergencies so that they are available to respond effectively when needed.
4. Good management and self-care of community volunteers is crucial to ensure a resilient volunteer workforce and responder community by reducing the incidence of harmful physical and mental effects.

The history of volunteerism in disaster response and the lessons learned from experience clearly reveal why spontaneous-volunteer management—from assessing needs to developing management techniques—is a key skill to have as a community leader, volunteer, or emergency manager.

THE ECOSYSTEM OF SUPPORTIVE PARTNERS IN DISASTER RESPONSE

Much like an ecosystem, the world of grassroots disaster responders is interlinked and interdependent, and connects across many different scales with a wide range of actors and environments. Coming to terms with the broad and diverse groups of disaster responders on the ground can seem overwhelming at first and might seem too difficult to effectively manage. However, thinking carefully about how these groups function and relate to each other helps to integrate them into your agency's response plan. The following descriptions provide an overview of some of the key groups of responders that emerge as assets in the majority of disasters and emergencies.

National Government Initiatives

A number of government-led programs that were implemented to form and train coordinated groups of citizens to respond to disasters started as far back as 1939. There are also many valuable stand-alone models that have been developed in an effort to cultivate affiliated volunteers.

Initiatives to empower citizens to prepare for military attack and practice evacuation plans started during World War II, as the Civil Defense Preparedness Office in the Department of Defense established state offices to prepare American citizens for attacks by Axis Forces.

The Citizens Corps, developed in January 2002 under President George W. Bush, has many features and motivations that are kindred to the values of the Civil Defense Office. In 2003, President Bush called on the Citizens Corps Council to develop the national Community Emergency Response Team (CERT) program as well as the Medical Reserve Corps (MRC), Fire Corps, USA on Watch, and Volunteers in Police Service (VIPS). The CERT concept was originally developed and implemented by the Los Angeles City Fire Department (LAFD) in 1985. Currently, CERT is a national program that encourages citizens to become part of a team that receives training in the skills needed to support local emergency responders in providing disaster relief and ensuring community safety.

Initiatives such as the Citizens Corps Council's Community Emergency Response Teams (CERT) and the Medical Reserve Corps (MRC) programs are great assets to emergency managers and are much-needed programs. Unfortunately, these programs have been mistakenly identified as *the* answer to spontaneous-volunteer issues. However, the CERT program has not yet produced any training or framework to manage or utilize spontaneous volunteers. The CERT and MRC curricula contain no materials to teach basic skills relating to volunteer management or the more complex issues of managing spontaneously emergent resources. For this reason, many states have come forward and requested the curriculum contained in this manual to be delivered as an adjunct module to the original CERT and MRC curricula. The intent is for the state and local Offices of Emergency Management to train their CERT and MRC members to manage spontaneous volunteers under the guidance of this program while integrating local protocols.

National or International Nongovernmental Agencies

National or international nongovernmental agencies may fall into the category of humanitarian relief, reconstruction, or development. Some may focus on a particular cause, such as finding the cure for cancer or alleviating hunger, or may focus on child-related issues. Some may have agreements in place with local, state, or federal governments, or may be entrusted with official aid relief duties. Operating on a larger scale than local organizations, they may become especially effective partners in mobilizing national or even global volunteer efforts in disaster response based on the site or the need that emerges from the disaster.

Businesses

Businesses range from local grocers who have developed trusted relationships within the community to international corporations with local branches that can leverage their parent company's resources, facility or warehouse space, distribution capabilities, and database management systems, as well as their pool of human resources.

Businesses welcome collaboration based on respect and teamwork to leverage their assets, such as their supplies, locations, and particular fields of expertise. In addition, they may have significant human resources to offer, from senior business executives that can help enhance the nation's security to local business owners who are experienced at leading essential operations, such as feeding, sheltering, or construction. All of these groups, and more, have the potential to emerge to help in the aftermath of disaster. The question is whether they will respond in separate silos or work collaboratively.

The immediate aftermath of a disaster is not the ideal time to pass out business cards and build collaborations. It must be done beforehand, prior to a disaster and, preferably, with any and all potential response partners. One such example is the Society of Food Service Managers (SFM), whose members used their connections to help provide food for first responders immediately following the attacks of 9/11. Bob Whitcom of Whitson's Culinary Group recounts his team's involvement:

> In the early stages, we were just providing food as needed with little coordination. It was not precise; however, it was a help. Later we began to organize, calling in our fellow SFM members to help us provide the 30,000 meals that the Salvation Army was to deliver to the responders on an ongoing basis. Once coordinated, our efforts became tighter and smarter. There was better coordination between the Salvation Army and our teams. After we became coordinated, our next challenge was the burnout that our staff who volunteered around the clock for two solid weeks experienced. We began to pull in people from the community that wanted to help, including family and friends. Through our partnerships we were able to provide "just in time" training and put to work our extended community.

Thus, relying on the skills and relationships already developed through the business of food service, one corporation was able to effectively leverage its human resources and its motivation to provide coordinated and sustainable efforts.

Local Faith-Based Organizations and Nongovernmental Organizations

Local faith-based organizations (FBOs) and secular nongovernmental organizations (NGOs) provide a network of both preestablished, pre-trained responders and preestablished, untrained groups that are capable of responding in times of need to serve their community. Often, differing terminology describes the same players. Along with FBOs and NGOs, alternative terms frequently used are *independent sector, volunteer sector, civil society, grassroots organizations, private voluntary organizations, self-help organizations,* and *non-state actors.*

Generally, these groups have a community-oriented focus and address a variety of issues, ranging from religious issues, emergency aid, and humanitarian affairs to the problems of homelessness and disease prevention. Local organizations such as food banks, social clubs, youth groups, and similar groups represent a component of the community that can serve as a useful resource, depending on how they are cultivated. While these groups may not have a mission of disaster response, they have responded time and again in disasters and emergencies as spontaneous responders, shifting their daily charity work to serve those affected by disasters.

These groups have strong links within their communities and thus can mobilize community action through volunteerism, donations, and the provision of services. These relationships are developed over time through groundwork and consistent presence in the community, an asset that cannot be developed as easily or as quickly by outside organizations or governments. Thus, these groups are the resources that hold the key to receiving and distributing trusted information, gaining the essential "buy in" of the community and accessing community resources.

In terms of the interface between these organizations and official response systems and agencies, the findings of "Heralding Unheard Voices" were consistent with data gathered from previous disaster-response efforts: In every case, FBOs, secular NGOs, and community groups faced significant challenges because official systems did not allow for the integration of these local resources. Yet time and again, these local groups emerged, evolved, and became an effective force through specialization in their fields of expertise, cultural knowledge, and the ability to partner effectively with each other.

Ordinary Citizens, Good Samaritans, and Local Assets

SUCVs were defined briefly in the Introduction, but here we will delve into their definition and features more thoroughly. SUCVs are individuals who come out of their homes to help neighbors and are often able to arrive first at the scene because of their proximity to the site. They have homes in the area, local knowledge, and cultural competency, and they know where resources are and speak the language of the community, whether literally or figuratively. These individuals may or may not have disaster-response training, but have proved to be an invaluable resource time and time again. It is essential that we do more to engage and empower this first-tier community of responders as a resource.

Recent research on volunteer management system design asserts, "The biggest myth is that firefighters and the police are first responders. They are official responders. The *real* first responders are ordinary folks."[*]

SUCVs may first emerge as unaffiliated individuals but will quickly and efficiently form into ad hoc networks and effective working groups using local relationships and assets. These groups may be associated with local leaders, or leaders may emerge spontaneously. In either case, they offer a point of contact for responding officials.

END-OF-CHAPTER QUESTIONS

- In the aftermath of disaster, how have you traditionally responded to the emergence of spontaneous volunteers?
- Why do volunteers emerge to help? What are their motivations or reasons?
- Are you part of an ecosystem of responders in your community or locale?
- Who or what agencies do you work most closely with?
- Who can you begin reaching out to now?

---

[*] Lee Clarke, Mission Improbable: Using Fantasy Documents to Tame Disaster (Chicago: University of Chicago Press, 2001).

CONCLUSION

The history of spontaneous volunteerism in disaster response shows us that, time and time again, individuals will emerge to help in the aftermath of disasters and emergencies, and that this is an instinctual response that has not changed for centuries. Our lessons learned tell us that spontaneous volunteerism is often a huge asset in disaster response. However, when left unmanaged or mismanaged it can pose challenges. We have seen that the lack of planning and resource allocation for the management of these volunteers poses a significant burden on emergency managers. Lastly, we have briefly outlined how an ecosystem of supportive responders that may already exist in your community can provide the resources, advantages, and potential partnerships for effective disaster response. I would hope that we have exposed the fact that we cannot change the human desire to help one another and that there exists a whole ecosystem that, with a little planning and coordination, can help manage all of the good will that emerges in disaster response.

2

Exploring the Unique Challenges of Today's Disaster Response

It struck me as to how many people we would have to bring in when responding to a catastrophic disaster—when they will get there, two maybe three weeks to stabilize the area with maximum mutual aid. With this in mind, I believe that we must change how we think about people. In my whole history in disaster response, we have looked at the public as a liability. Our perspective was that we need to take care of everyone. We cannot sustain this approach. There are not enough resources for recovery. What is left is everyone else. The public is not a liability, but a resource.

William Craig Fugate
Administrator, FEMA

IN THIS CHAPTER

- Public Challenges
  - Public Apathy
  - Communications
  - Diverse Populations and Cultures
- Internal Capacity Challenges
  - Lack of Staff and Partner Expectations
  - Liability

- A Typology of Disasters: Traditional Hazards and Threats
  - Terrorism
  - Pandemics
  - Natural Disasters
  - Human-made Disasters

Today's environment poses unique challenges for emergency managers. Surge-capacity needs must be filled, and limited staff is pulled in many directions, reducing internal capabilities. In this chapter we will be looking at each type of potential disaster and how each of them can create a different set of challenges for you, your agency, and your community. This section, starting with this chapter, sets the foundation for the first portion of this manual, which is dedicated to conducting essential internal assessments.

As the well-known proverb from the ancient Chinese military strategist, Sun Tzu, states, "It is said that if you know your enemies and know yourself, you will not be imperiled in a hundred battles; if you do not know your enemies but do know yourself, you will win one and lose one; if you do not know your enemies nor yourself, you will be imperiled in every single battle."* Therefore, we start with knowing our enemy—in this case, the unique challenges in disaster response today.

From financial disasters to political upheaval to climate change, present-day realities tip the scale between the impact disasters will have on our society and the ability our official responders will have to respond with additional resources. There is potential for great variation in how disasters and emergencies affect communities, based on their demographics and their unique set of geographic, political, social, and economic risk factors. How various disasters and emergencies affect each of our communities will affect the ability of emergency managers to respond to all needs in a timely manner. If the disaster has stricken a vulnerable population or combination of vulnerable populations, the complexity of achieving an effective and timely response will likely increase. If the disaster has impacted multi-ethnic neighborhoods, where many different languages are spoken, the need to share information between emergency managers and community members becomes more complicated. As communities and the larger reality of environmental change reconfigure and shift, the role of the emergency manager must accordingly evolve.

---

* From The Art of War, attributed to Sun Tzu, 6th Century B.C., China.

As standard procedure, emergency managers conduct an assessment process to determine what disasters will most likely impact their communities, where they are most at risk, and which conventional and unconventional partners reside within their communities. In this chapter, we will discuss three types of challenges that emergency managers face: public challenges, internal challenges, and the typology of disasters, both human-made and natural, that might affect any community. This review of challenges will be applied to the internal-assessments template housed in the guide. Once you have entered your information in the templates, they can be used to identify your agency's additional needs that may arise and can be addressed through the proper selection and management of spontaneous volunteers.

What are the types of disasters that emergency managers and community leaders like you are most concerned about? In 2008, World Cares Center, in partnership with the Harvard School of Public Health, conducted a survey of emergency managers to explore the more traditional concerns of emergency managers in relation to what they might be responding to. In 2009, World Center conducted an open-ended survey, asking the same questions but allowing emergency managers to fill in their own responses. The results of the two surveys were drastically different.

The first survey in 2008 revealed that emergency managers were concerned with the following possible disaster situations as likely to happen in their communities and jurisdictions:

- 59 percent were concerned about natural disasters
- 55 percent were concerned about a pandemic flu
- 63 percent were concerned about the likelihood of other infectious diseases
- 52 percent were concerned about chemical agents
- 50 percent were concerned about radiological agents

The second set of surveys in 2009 gave us a deeper understanding of organizational and community concerns. In these surveys, managers mentioned concerns and challenges beyond the traditional hazards, including such issues as public perception and dealing with partnerships and other organizations involved in response.

Guided by these results, this chapter consists of three sections, addressing:

Public challenges
Internal capacity challenges
A typology of traditional hazards and threats

Review the information in conjunction with the checklists of challenges provided with an eye toward how all of these possible occurrences and their particular challenges will affect your organization's ability to carry out its mission, function, roles, and tasks. In many cases, surge-capacity needs will leave gaps in the ability to serve, and ultimately these gaps should be filled in part with spontaneous volunteers.

PUBLIC CHALLENGES

There are several challenges that emergency managers face when engaging the public in disaster preparedness and safety measures. Among the three main factors—public apathy, communication, and diverse populations—additional considerations should be taken into account as factors that exacerbate existing problems, including the spontaneous and large-scale convergence of volunteers postdisaster, the attrition of volunteers once they are trained, and in some responses, the lack of volunteers all together.

Public Apathy

The findings from "Personal Preparedness in America: Findings from the Citizens Corps Survey of Four Urban Areas (2009)" probe the public's perspective on why they are not more prepared. The factors include the following:

- 37 percent of the public thinks that emergency responders will help them
- 27 percent report that they do not know what to do in case of disaster
- 24 percent report that they haven't had the time to take steps toward disaster preparedness
- 17 percent say it costs too much
- 17 percent say it would not make a difference
- 13 percent say they do not think they will be able to take preparedness steps

Additionally, in the same report, the public shared the barriers to taking preparedness training:

- 16 percent cite a lack of time
- 15 percent have not thought about it
- 15 percent say it is too difficult to get information on what to do

5 percent don't think it is important
2 percent cite a lack of money
2 percent do not think it will be effective
53 percent responded "other"

As you can see from the survey results, 37 percent of the public polled believed that responders would come in time to save them. This public apathy to personal preparedness may be addressed by changing the way we discuss our own challenges and limitations with the public. Within emergency management circles, for instance, we discuss the commonly known fact that responders may not be able to help within the first 72 hours after the impact of a disaster, even though most lifesaving occurs in this vital window of time. How many public messages have you seen that clearly state this fact? If you are going to publicize the reality and challenges of official response to the community, it is also your responsibility to combine this public information with a disaster-preparedness program that works with the neighborhoods to build their preparedness. Many agencies and organizations have valuable programs that foster citizen preparedness in disaster. However, we see that the number-one reason individuals are not taking preparedness training is the lack of time, and these programs require a sizable time commitment that not everyone can afford to give.

The unique challenges that public apathy poses for emergency managers include:

- Citizens and workplaces fail to develop individual and family preparedness plans.
- Lives are lost, injuries are more severe, and property is lost.
- Public information, preparedness trainings, and warnings are ignored.
- Citizens are unprepared for evacuation or other vital steps for survival.
- In the event of a disaster, the majority of the public does not know what to do and waits for outside assistance.
- The damage and recovery costs are far higher than if preparedness plans had been activated by communities and citizens.

Communications

Communication issues remain a challenge both among emergency managers and between agencies and the public they serve. They include:

17

- Incompatible technologies or communication channels (such as band-wave frequencies)
- Use of different terminology within specialized fields
- New Web 2.0 technologies

The issue of incompatible technologies exists between agencies or jurisdictions that find they cannot communicate across technological divides. This can be demonstrated by townships that may purchase a set of equipment that communicates on a certain frequency, but during disaster response, they may need to communicate with another township whose equipment is not compatible with their own. This kind of problem can have serious consequences, as seen in the immediate 9/11 response effort, when the warning to evacuate was transmitted to police twenty-one minutes before the remaining South Tower collapsed, but never reached the firefighters responding in the building. Not only was the firefighters' radio network unreliable that morning, but more critically, it was not linked to the police system's. While most of the police in that tower managed to survive, out of the 341 firefighters who perished on 9/11, 121 firefighters, most of whom could have made it out in time, died in the second tower's collapse.* Figure 2.1 illustrates an exercise in which participants sync their computers to the same network, a practice that could save lives in the event of another 9/11.

Regarding the second communication challenge in differing terminology, one example is when emergency medical response teams use terminology that is used differently by responding law enforcement or fire personnel as well as different from lay citizens' usage of and understanding of those terms. For example, emergency medical technicians refer to the ambulance as a "bus," which differs from how other official responders refer to their vehicles. In addition, their reference to a bus also differs from how the general public understands the term.

Communicating with the public is another challenge that emergency managers and agencies must contend with, especially in the era of Web 2.0 technologies, which can be both a blessing and a curse. The Internet has not only allowed for unheralded information dissemination, but it has created a new space for communication across communities that can be linked up to the federal and state levels. While old Web sites were designed to share static information, today's Web 2.0 is about sharing and exchanging resources and ideas. Social networks on

---

* Jim Dwyer, Kevin Flynn, and Ford Fessenden, "9/11 Exposed Deadly Flaws in Rescue Plan," New York Times, July 7, 2002.

Figure 2.1 Lisa Orloff serving as a logistics officer for an integrated disaster response demonstration, Strong Angel III, Operation Shadowlite, in San Diego. Participants are synching up their computers to connect to the same network. (Source: Lisa Orloff.)

the Web allow groups to be formed on common issues and for relationships to develop without having to leave your room, your building, your neighborhood, or for that matter, your country. When utilized correctly, social interface tools offer countless opportunities for citizen empowerment by providing training, knowledge, and connectivity. While we may find that, with Web 2.0 technologies, we may be more connected than ever, there are still challenges associated with this newfound and instantaneous communication.

First, the digital divide—the gap between those who do and do not have effective access to the Internet—is still a reality in the United States and in international settings. Paper mail, or so-called snail mail, is still a necessary form of communication and is especially useful for transmitting information to special-needs populations that are not Internet savvy or may not have the means to afford a computer and Internet access in their homes. Yet paper mail is often a time-consuming and expensive form of information dissemination.

In addition, for all the excitement about Web 2.0 connectivity, the potential for confidential, inaccurate, or damaging information to be posted on Facebook or Twitter—for all to see with little ability to control what goes out and how many people will view it—is a significant risk that must be proactively addressed ahead of time by emergency managers. In addition, the need to apply Web 2.0 technologies to disaster preparedness and response communication is challenging for many smaller to mid-sized agencies who have little to no budget to develop and manage multiple information sharing sites while also dedicating a watchdog to monitor the communication flow. However, because this is becoming an increasingly important part of communicating with the public, the final chapter in this book includes important considerations and examples of the successful use of Web 2.0 in disaster response and recovery.

The unique challenges in communication that emergency managers must face include:

- The still-existing digital divide means that not all citizens or communities can access information online.
- Certain populations still need to receive information by snail mail, which is only a one-way path of information.
- Web 2.0 technologies require new standards or procedures for confidentiality, security, and verification of information.
- Not all agencies or groups, especially small or medium-sized organizations, can take full advantage of Web 2.0 social media due to the need for training or dedicated human resources.

Diverse Populations and Cultures

Many parts of the United States have upwards of seventy languages spoken in areas that would surprise you. Each community and population group has its unique culture and needs. Recognizing the needs of these unique communities is a challenge that can be exacerbated by language barriers and the resistance of certain communities to seek support from government officials or rely on agencies external to the community. In these cases, citizens from within certain cultures will turn to their local community and faith-based leaders first to seek and give help.

From predominantly senior populations or areas where there is a high proportion of schools or day-care facilities, each of these population groups presents a different need and requires a targeted method of engagement.

Where People Settle

The impact of natural disasters can vary widely, depending not only on the severity of the natural event, but also enhanced or mitigated by human factors such as diverse demographics and human settlement in hazardous zones. These complicate the job of the emergency manager. For example, both in the United States and internationally, hazard-prone areas such as coasts and river banks provide an attractive and available site for housing or businesses that are not already claimed by others. Unfortunately, this increases the exposure that already-vulnerable populations have to the risk of natural hazards and the disastrous consequences that may result.

Hurricane Katrina showed us not only the increased severity of a natural disaster, but what happens when we populate areas not meant for intensive human habitat. Looking at historical maps where the colonial French settled in New Orleans, it is evident that early settlers had heeded where the floodplains were and built in lower-risk areas. Even as late as 1949 (Figure 2.2), only a minimal amount of land development

Figure 2.2 1949 Map of New Orleans (www.shutterstock.com).

encroached on flood plains. Lay the 1949 map over a map of post-Katrina damage (Figure 2.3) and it is apparent that present day—for a variety of social, economic, and political reasons—there appears to be extensive settlement of high-risk areas by low-income communities. Clearly much of this land development has occurred in a relatively short period of time, from 1950 to the present.

The Carless Society

Secondly, the range in access to resources within and across communities can also complicate response and recovery to natural disasters. The accessibility of certain demographics to evacuate and to access forms of transportation or organization poses various unique challenges as well. For example, natural disaster response plans that require an evacuation phase are challenged by whether or not a community has access to private transportation. In the case of New Orleans* or the post-tsunami communities along the Indian Ocean coastline, citizens who had no means of private transport ended up waiting in vain for days, weeks, even months for much-needed disaster relief and services. Generally, among emergency response plans, consideration of what is commonly called "the carless society" is in fact lacking. For example, a 2007 study found that most evacuation plans do not take into serious consideration those communities without private transportation.† Similarly, a 2006 joint study by the Department of Transportation and the Department of Homeland Security found that plans for evacuating people with special needs were almost nonexistent. This is alarming, considering that many of the elderly and disabled would have to choose between remaining in place or evacuating without any assurance that their medical conditions will be treated in transit or where they are going. Moreover, the need to consider the elderly

---

* The State of Louisiana's Emergency Operations Plan, "Supplement 1C: Louisiana Shelter Operations Plan Assumptions" clearly states, "The primary means of evacuation will be personal vehicles. However schools and municipal buses and where available specialized vehicles will be used to transport hurricane evacuees who do not have transportation." As we learned, neither of these assumptions held true. This can be seen in the results of a 2002 study of evacuation planning in pre-Katrina New Orleans, "Planning for the Evacuation of New Orleans," which stated that of the 1.4 million inhabitants in high-threat areas, an estimated 200,000 to 300,000 people were assumed to not have access to personal transportation.

† Daniel Baldwin Hess and Julie C. Gotham, "Multi-Modal Mass Evacuation in Upstate New York: A Review of Disaster Plans," Journal of Homeland Security and Emergency Management 4, no. 3 (2007): Article 11. http://www.bepress.com/jhsem/vol4/iss3/11.

Figure 2.3   Image of New Orleans flooded post-Katrina. (Source: NASA.)

is likely to become an ever-increasing need, as the overall aging population is only growing due to medical advances.

Beyond special-needs populations, the carless society not only describes those without the means, but includes vast swaths of the population who live in cities. In New York City, 56 percent of households reported in the 2000 Census that they did not own a vehicle; in Washington, D.C., Baltimore, Philadelphia, Boston, Chicago, San Francisco, New Orleans, Miami, and Cleveland, more than 25 percent of households did not have access to an automobile in 2000.* Thus, preparing for natural disasters intersects with human patterns, the challenge of diverse demographics, and communications needs that must be addressed to effectively save lives and minimize damage.

Diverse demographics pose unique challenges for emergency managers:

- A wider range of linguistic and cultural needs must be addressed.

---

* John L. Renne, et al., "National Study on Carless and Special Needs Evacuation Planning: A Literature Review," University of New Orleans Transportation Center. http://planning. uno.edu/docs/CarlessEvacuationPlanning.pdf.

- Some cultures may not want or know how to rely on public agencies or emergency management organizations.
- The need to build cultural competency and relationships with cultural, faith-based, and community-based leaders must be addressed.
- Special-needs populations and certain age demographics require special assistance or unique planning procedures in disaster response and recovery.

INTERNAL CAPACITY CHALLENGES

Fortunately, there are not enough catastrophic disasters to build and sustain a robust enough pool of experienced and seasoned disaster volunteers to respond effectively when these events occur. Therefore we must stand ready to train, deploy, and sustain large numbers of spontaneous community volunteers during catastrophic disasters in the future.

Scott Graham
Chief Response Officer, The American Red Cross of Greater New York

Lack of Staff and Partner Expectations

In the surveys, many emergency managers raised concerns about internal capacity, ranging from lack of manpower and staff to being able to live up to the expectations of municipalities and partners. Both of these issues have been verified in workshops and real response cases. As World Cares Center delivers its trainings, groups are asked to list what partner agencies will be responsible for providing support in key areas. Inevitably, the same agencies are listed over and over by all participating agencies in the room, revealing an unrealistic dependency on a few large agencies to fulfill vital functions. Whether these commitments are formally in place and recognized, and whether these large agencies will truly have the capacity to respond and fulfill all of their expected functions in the event of a disaster, is another matter. In the workshops, agencies are able to make clarifications and adjust their expectations by culminating the lists of expected partner collaborations and sharing the results. At the end of the day, the adjustment often shows even more of a gap in staff and manpower than was originally understood.

Liability

The lack of reliable benefits may be a barrier for potential emergency volunteers. It may also discourage employers from assigning their employees to work as emergency volunteers, because the employer's workers' compensation insurance could be responsible if the employee is injured.

Citizen Corp Volunteer Liability Guide

Liability is a complicated challenge for emergency managers. According to FEMA's "Citizen Corp Volunteer Liability Guide," liability laws are difficult to understand, protection is inconsistent from state to state, nongovernmental agencies are not well protected, and to complicate matters further, some volunteers have multiple affiliations that blur the lines as to who is responsible for their protection. Lastly, unaffiliated volunteers are unlikely to receive liability protection or injury benefits unless steps are taken to register them.

Civil liability includes negligent acts and omits intentional acts, liability for the acts of others, and strict liability. In emergency management circles, the concerns about liability are broken down into two issues of potential risk: (a) being sued by a spontaneous volunteer whom you have relied upon to assist your agency and (b) being sued by a client injured, either unintentionally or intentionally, by a spontaneous volunteer, with the agency becoming liable for that volunteer's actions. Confusion exists about what laws are in place to protect everyone in consideration and what internal agency policies like insurance or worker compensation will cover. This issue often stands in the way of agencies moving forward on their spontaneous-volunteer management programs.

The answers to addressing liability issues are unique to each organization and are based on their location within jurisdictions. It will be necessary to research Volunteer Protection Acts, Good Samaritan laws, related statutes for your state or city, and your own agency's insurance policies. Depending on the region or municipality you serve and the relationship to the mayor's or governor's office, a city or county attorney may be a good place to start. It is likely that, at some point in your career, you will have to weigh the risk of exposing your agency to liability versus saving more lives and helping more people with volunteer assistance. You will be reminded in Chapter 4, "Assessing Internal Readiness," with a checklist for liability in your state along with your agency's policies.

The unique challenges that liability poses for emergency managers include:

- Confusing and complicated legal language of liability policies
- Exposure to lawsuits
- Jurisdictional differences in liability policies, which differ from state to state
- Uneven coverage of volunteers by other institutions or affiliations
- Difficulty in covering unaffiliated volunteers, which may require extra steps
- Balancing the need to protect clients versus the benefit of having helpful volunteers

A TYPOLOGY OF DISASTERS: TRADITIONAL HAZARDS AND THREATS

The unique challenges reviewed in the previous section only add to the difficulties in responding to the natural and human-made disasters that are discussed in the next section. These issues, when viewed as they are related to each other, compound and create new needs, new gaps, and new opportunities for people to help in disaster response.

In this section, we provide a list of the more traditional challenges that emergency managers are expected to prepare for and respond to. If your community has a history of exposure to certain threats that have not been listed, add them to the chart in Table 2.1 at the end of the chapter and compare how the unique challenges we face today can make response more difficult for your agency.

Terrorism

While there is no agreed-upon definition of terrorism at the United Nations, various conventions and resolutions do attempt to define terrorism, and they include: "All criminal acts directed against a State and intended or calculated to create a state of terror in the minds of particular persons or a group of persons or the general public";* and has been further expanded to "criminal acts intended or calculated to provoke a state of terror … for political purposes that are in any circumstance unjustifiable, whatever the considerations of a political, philosophical, ideological, racial, ethnic, religious or other nature that may be invoked to justify them."† What is

---

* League of Nations Convention, 1937.
† UN Resolution, 1999, GA Res. 51/210, "Measures to Eliminate International Terrorism."

common among definitions of terrorism is the intention—to incite a state of terror in the general public or directed toward a certain group, and as such, are often carried out and focused on the "innocent" and unsuspecting public.

When we say the word terrorism, our minds may immediately replay the scenes from the attacks of 9/11, or the conflict between Israel and Palestine. In this country, terrorism is thought to be an exception to the rule. Although many terrorist attempts are made, the public may never be made aware of them. Thwarted attempts that are not publicized have the potential to effect apathy in preparedness and vigilance. The fact is that terrorism is a persistent and recurring presence in American culture and history, evident in cases such as the 1995 Oklahoma City Bombing, both World Trade Center attacks in 1993 and 2001, and the attack on the military base at Fort Dix, New Jersey, in 2007 by five men. More recently, in late 2009, thirteen people were killed at Fort Hood military base when an army psychiatrist opened fire. Events that can be classified as terrorism extend to the spate of attacks on schools and civic institutions, including but not limited to the Columbine High School attack in 1999, the Virginia Tech massacre in 2007, and the 2009 shooting at the American Civic Association building in Binghamton, New York. Because there is often no public warning on the specific details of an impending terrorist act, the unsuspecting public has hardly any time to prepare for or prevent its impact, leading to confusion and an ad hoc response if the public is not trained beforehand. The area of the attack will be considered a crime scene and require special consideration for access to the site, conditions that will require more security and limited access for additional responders who, in other circumstances, may have access to help.

To elaborate further on the challenge that terrorism poses for emergency managers, there is the issue of convergence. We can look again to recent events in American history where terrorism in our country often sparks an unprecedented level of patriotism and good will. In the immediate aftermath of 9/11, citizens from around the globe could not do enough to show their support of Americans. The psychosocial need of individuals to reach out and make a difference was kicked into high gear. That outpouring came in the shape of people and donations, but, in many cases, our emergency management structure could not handle these surges of good will. In these instances there was no shortage of help. There was, however, a shortage of ability to manage this help. It is fortunate that, in almost all cases, there was no secondary threat that caused significant injury to those who came out to help. Thought should be given as to the potential targets and threats of terrorism in your community.

The unique challenges that terrorism poses for emergency managers include but are not limited to the following:

- No warning
- A crime scene limiting access
- Potential for secondary devices or follow-up strikes designed to harm first responders or on sites necessary for emergency operations (hospitals, police stations, etc.)*
- Need for special equipment or protective gear
- Need for mass decontamination of persons and property at the site of impact and related quarantine, evacuation, and traffic control needs
- Crowd control, which may be more of an issue than in a dispersed event
- Potential for overwhelming or damaging communication, information, logistical, and infrastructural channels
- Unique mental health and social well-being challenges due to fears for safety and traumatic impact
- Injury and death
- Property damage, rubble, and unsafe response environments
- Unique toxic and environmental risk factors, depending on the type of terrorism (especially if chemical or biological agents have been released)

Pandemics

According to the World Health Organization (WHO), a pandemic is "a worldwide epidemic of a disease which occurs when there are more cases of that disease than normal." In particular, a range of flu pandemics have traversed the globe. The WHO explains these types of pandemics as a situation when "a new influenza virus appears against which the human population has no immunity." Factors that increase the risk and speed of pandemic transmission include the increase in global transport, along with the rapid growth of cities and overcrowded conditions in some areas.

---

* James Jay Carafano, "Preparing Responders to Respond: The Challenges to Emergency Preparedness in the 21st Century," Heritage Foundation, Heritage Lectures, October 22, 2003.

As this field guide is being written, we are in the midst of experiencing a global pandemic of the H1N1 virus, otherwise known as *swine flu*. According to the World Health Organization, as of July 2009, the number of H1N1 cases is still increasing, and we have yet to develop a working vaccine.* Fortunately, we have not seen the same scale of impact that was characteristic of the Black Death that killed approximately a third of the populations of Europe along with unknown numbers in Asia and North Africa, peaking between 1348 and 1350.†

In the event of a catastrophic pandemic, the capacity and response efforts of the public health workforce are of significant concern, according to the *Journal of Emergency Medicine*. Emergency workers will not respond equally to all emergencies: 87 percent of emergency room workers said they would come to work in the event of an airplane crash, 72 percent would report to work in the event of a radioactive bomb, but only 54 percent said they would in a disaster involving a biological agent. Thus, the official responder community's reaction to a pandemic will be starkly different from that of other disasters that we have seen, and managers will be in great need of medical professionals and those who can assist in points of distribution, where vaccination is distributed to the public; in traffic control; in security; and more. We must create comprehensive, flexible plans for volunteer management in order to fill those gaps.

While points of distribution (PODs) and other plans to divert the burden from hospitals are implemented in some cities, counties, and states, the issue of how long these sites would be up and running and how many public health workers and volunteers would be needed to adequately staff a 24/7 POD leaves planners with the question as to how we will fulfill this surge need.

Here, we look not at the likelihood that well-intended citizens will emerge from their homes and places of work, but the exact reverse. In the event of infectious diseases, we are likely to see a shift from convergence of volunteers to a resistance to stepping into a potentially contagious environment. In this case, managing unaffiliated volunteers that you are reaching out to for help will have the same management challenges as well as the need to conduct outreach to these populations of potential helpers.

---

* World Health Organization, "Pandemic (H1N1) 2009 Briefing Note 4," Geneva, Switzerland, July 24, 2009.
† Encyclopedia of Death and Dying. http://www.deathreference.com/Bl-Ce/Black-Death.html.

The unique challenges that pandemics pose for emergency managers are as follows:*

- An increased need for licensed medical professionals
- Surge in need and number of health-care seekers at hospitals and clinics
- Security, crowd, and traffic control needs
- Evacuation, quarantine, vaccination, and medication-related challenges
- Travel restrictions that limit local volunteers who assist the home-bound and the elderly as home health-care workers
- Staffing needs at PODs that are unfilled or underresourced
- Increased workload on medical personnel while caring for the "worried well"
- Increased workload on medical personnel while addressing the mental health needs of those who are already vulnerable to mental illness as well as new cases of those with first-time mental health problems
- Lack or delay in providing timely, comprehensive, and accurate pandemic information
- Loss of life or illness and secondary trauma to caretakers due to fear, depression, stress, grief
- Vacancies at all places of work, including municipalities and public agencies
- Greater reliance on or mistrust of public officials

Natural Disasters

Natural disasters are defined as "the effect of a natural hazard (e.g., flood, volcanic eruption, earthquake, or landslide) that affects the environment and leads to financial, environmental, or human losses. The resulting loss depends on the capacity of the population to support or resist the disaster, and their resilience."†

Emergency managers do not have to look very far back into the past to see that natural disasters are occurring more frequently, with increased

---

* N.J. Department of Human Services, Division of Mental Health Services, "The Mental Health System Response to Avian and Pandemic Influenza." www.njdcisr.org/downloads/division_mental_health_services.pps.
† G. Bankoff, G. Frerks, and D. Hilhorst, eds., Mapping Vulnerability: Disasters, Development and People (London: Earthscan Publications, 2003).

severity, and with differing impacts on populations and countries based on levels of development and readiness of response. Climate change and urbanization are among the main forces intensifying the magnitude and severity of weather-related natural hazards such as floods, droughts, and tropical cyclones. The increased occurrence of and the increased severity of natural disasters and the reasons we are seeing an increase in both has been hotly debated. Of the ten disasters with the highest death tolls since 1975, half occurred in the most recent five-year period, 2003 through 2008, while four of the ten disasters with the greatest economic losses also occurred in the same period.* Moreover, disaster risk, which is a complex and accumulated set of conditions and interactions within each community, has also increased for most hazards. Global flood mortality risk, for example, has increased by 13 percent between 1990 and 2007, and economic loss risk has increased by 33 percent in the same period.†

Following later in this chapter, we have listed a number of natural hazards and the challenges they pose for emergency managers. This is not an exhaustive list. More information can be found at: FEMA: Natural Hazards. "Are You Ready?" (http://www.fema.gov/areyouready/natural_hazards.shtm) and the University of Colorado at Boulder, Natural Hazards Center (http://www.colorado.edu/hazards/resources/).

In this section, the natural hazards that we will review include:

Hurricanes and coastal storms
Landslides and mudslides
Floods
Tornadoes and windstorms
Tsunamis
Wildfires
Blizzards and ice storms

If there is a natural hazard specific to your area that appears in this list, please review that section.

Hurricanes
Hurricanes are defined as "a violent, spiraling tropical storm with fierce rotating winds and a calm central eye; usually develops over warm tropical

---

* United Nations, "2009 Global Assessment Report on Disaster Risk Reduction: Risk and Poverty in a Changing Climate."
† United Nations, "2009 Global Assessment Report on Disaster Risk Reduction: Risk and Poverty in a Changing Climate," Chapter 1, p. 5.

seas."* Few other storms are as destructive as a hurricane in terms of wind speed, size, and duration. They can cause massive flooding in areas that are low-lying or have poor drainage, and the walls of water pushed up by the storm can be incredibly dangerous.† Figure 2.4 shows New Orleans after the levee breach during Hurricane Katrina.

Coastal Storms

Coastal storms are the broader category of natural hazards that include hurricanes, but may also include northeasters and tropical storms. Northeasters are defined as "any reasonably strong wind blowing from the northeast for an extended period of time."‡ They are also capable of mild to severe coastal flooding and erosion.

Hurricanes and coastal storms pose unique challenges for emergency managers:

- Resistance to evacuation based on a false sense of security
- Need to evacuate vulnerable populations that lack means of private transportation
- Potential for jammed evacuation routes, which may require traffic control
- Potential for flooding and wind damage and associated public health needs
- Loss of life and mass injuries
- Potential for multiple hurricanes to strike during hurricane season, thereby exhausting resources

Landslides and Mudslides

Landslides are defined as "a sudden collapse of a large mass of hillside; the falling of masses of earth or rock"§ and can also be expanded to include "many types of downhill earth movements, ranging from rapidly moving catastrophic rock avalanches and debris flows in mountainous regions to more slowly moving earth slides and other ground failures."¶ Mudslides are defined as "a surge of water-saturated rock, earth and debris" that

---

* Natural and Environmental Disaster Information Exchange System (NEDIES). http://nedies.jrc.it/index.asp?ID=82.
† New York City government, "NYC Hazards: Coastal Storm Basics." http://www.nyc.gov/html/oem/html/hazards/storms_terms.shtml.
‡ Delaware Department of Natural Resources and Environmental Control, "What Is a Coastal Storm?" http://www.dnrec.state.de.us/soil/CoastStorm/StormWhat.htm.
§ Natural and Environmental Disaster Information Exchange System (NEDIES), 2009.
¶ United States Geological Survey.

Figure 2.4 New Orleans after the Hurricane Katrina levee breech. (Source: Shutterstock.com.)

develops after water rapidly accumulates in the ground.* They may occur as a consequence of changed conditions following the occurrence of other natural hazards, such as after heavy rains, droughts, earthquakes, or volcanic eruptions. Areas that are at high risk include those that have experienced loss of vegetation (such as after a wildfire), steep slopes, and areas at the bottoms of canyons or slopes, construction sites that have altered slopes, areas adjacent to rivers and streams, and areas that receive surface runoff. In the United States, landslides cause twenty-five to fifty deaths a year and $2 billion in damage.† In December 1999, Venezuela was threatened by thousands of landslides due to unprecedented heavy rains. The landslides affected eight Venezuelan states, leaving nearly 600,000 people without drinking water‡ and burying or dragging approximately 30,000 people out to sea.§ This disaster was among the largest landslide catastrophes to take place worldwide. Figure 2.5 shows a region affected by a mudslide.

Unique challenges that landslides and mudslides pose for emergency managers:

- Little to no warning
- Injury, loss of life, and damage to property
- Urgent window of opportunity for search and rescue of human lives
- Need for specialized equipment and specialists to move debris
- Blockage of transport routes hinders evacuation and first-responder access
- Vulnerable populations settled in steep slope, landslide-prone areas require additional and special assistance and recovery efforts
- Downed power or utility poles and lines and damaged infrastructure pose risks for life and property
- Mitigation measures that involve resettlement of populations in high-risk areas are unpopular
- Structural mitigation measures, such as building check dams and debris basins, are expensive to build and maintain

---

* Centers for Disease Prevention and Control, "Emergency Preparedness and Response: Fact Sheet on Landslides and Mudslides." http://www.bt.cdc.gov/disasters/landslides.asp.
† Centers for Disease Prevention and Control.
‡ "Disaster in Venezuela," a supplement to Disasters: Preparedness and Mitigation in the Americas, the quarterly newsletter of PAHO/WHO, January 2000, no.1: S-1. http://www.paho.org/English/DD/PED/ped100e.pdf.
§ USAID: Venezuela Factsheet, February 2000, USAID-Office of Foreign Disaster Assistance, 2000, p. 2.

Figure 2.5   Region affected by a mudslide. (Source: NOAA Research.)

Floods

Floods are defined as "the submerging with water of a normally dry area." Flood hazards include a particularly dangerous flood type, the flash flood, defined as "a faster, more dangerous flow of water that results from tropical storms, dam failures, or excessive rain and snow; the flooding of an area that occurs in a matter of hours." This hazard also includes coastal flooding, which is "seashore flooding caused by high tides usually brought about by storms."*

Floods are the most prevalent hazard in the United States. This high flood risk is compounded by the fact that many communities move back into or settle as new residents into flood-prone areas, only increasing the chance for a repeated cycle of disaster loss in the case of floods.† This increases the time required to evacuate, the likelihood that transit routes for evacuation may be overwhelmed, as well as the scale of the damage on human lives and property.‡ Another additional challenge is that the

---

* Center for Disease Prevention and Control, "Emergency Preparedness and Response: Fact Sheet on Landslides and Mudslides." http://emergency.cdc.gov/disasters/landslides.asp.
† Cigler, "Emergency Management and Public Administration," Report 86-12, University of North Carolina at Chapel Hill, 1986.
‡ Eric Auf der Heide, Disaster Response: Principles of Preparation and Coordination (St. Louis: Mosby Year Book, 1989).

presence of flood-control technologies, such as levees, dams, and sea walls, may give a false sense of security and encourage even greater density of settlement in an area, as well as make it difficult to convince people to evacuate in the event of a flood or hurricane warning.*

Unique challenges that floods pose for emergency managers include:

- Means of transport and transit are severely affected and damaged by high waters
- Destruction of property, weakened foundations of buildings and infrastructure
- Moving floodwaters pose ongoing risk
- Risk of contaminated drinking water and damaged sewage and septic systems pose public health risk
- Floodwaters may be electrically charged from downed or underground power lines
- Floodwaters may contaminate property and pose health risks due to sewage, chemicals, oil, gasoline
- Populations may continue to resettle in flood-prone areas during recovery process, complicating mitigation efforts

Tornadoes

Tornadoes are defined as a "violent and destructive funnel-shaped whirling wind, whirlwind, twister."† While they do occur in other parts of the world, they are most frequently found in the United States. One of the most extensive and deadly of 1999 in Oklahoma and Kansas consisted of a total of seventy-four tornadoes that broke out across both states in less than twenty-one hours, killing forty-six people, injuring 800, and causing $1.5 billion in damage.‡ Tornadoes are most commonly found east of the Rocky Mountains during the spring and summer months. They are commonly presented as among the most violent and destructive of natural storms, unfolding in unpredictable, rapid movements. Tornadoes are capable of moving at wind speeds of 112 miles/second (250 mph) or more, while the scale of damage may be more than 1 mile wide and fifty miles long.§

---

* Eric Auf der Heide, Disaster Response: Principles of Preparation and Coordination (St. Louis: Mosby Year Book, 1989).
† Babylon Online Dictionary. http://dictionary.babylon.com/.
‡ National Climactic Data Center Storm Data. http://www4.ncdc.noaa.gov/cgi-win/wwcgi. dll?wwevent~storms.
§ Subcommittee on Disaster Reduction, National Science and Technology Council.

Figure 2.6 Windstorm damage. (Photo credit: Shutterstock.)

Windstorms

A windstorm is defined as "a wind that is strong enough to cause at least light damage to trees and buildings and may or may not be accompanied by precipitation."* Wind speeds typically exceed thirty-four miles per hour. Although tornadoes and tropical cyclones also cause damage through wind speed and gusts, they are usually classified separately. Figure 2.6 shows windstorm damage.

Unique challenges that tornadoes and windstorms pose for emergency managers:

- Little to no warning
- Unpredictable path of storm
- Additional impact from windborne debris
- Possibility of emergency response sites destroyed along with other property
- Downed communication lines, street signs, site markers, and landmarks, causing disorientation and uncoordinated movements
- Damaged infrastructure and utilities systems; water, electricity, and the like must be brought into the site

---

* Encyclopedia Britannica.

Tsunamis

A tsunami is defined as "a series of enormous waves created by an underwater disturbance such as an earthquake, landslide, volcanic eruption or meteorite." Tsunamis move quickly, up to hundreds of miles per hour in the open ocean, and can collide with the shore in the form of 100-foot -high or larger waves. A tsunami can strike anywhere along U.S. coastlines. If an area is at less than twenty-five feet above sea level or within a mile of shoreline, it is at greater risk. Recent findings indicate that tsunamis are also possible along the Atlantic Ocean coastal area, including Virginia and North Carolina.

The Indian Ocean tsunami that struck in 2005 was among the most destructive natural disasters to occur since 1975, with 226,408 fatalities. Figure 2.7 shows the ruins of houses in Aceh, Indonesia, after the tsunami.

Unique challenges that tsunamis pose for emergency managers:

- Evacuation warning and other information may not be available in a timely manner

Figure 2.7   Ruins of houses in Aceh, Indonesia, after the tsunami.

- Disaster may cause difficulty in transit and transport due to flooding and destruction of transport paths and means of transport
- Loss of life and high rates of injury
- Contamination of drinking water
- Unique mental health challenges, including posttraumatic stress disorder
- Loss of property and continued hazard from destroyed gas lines, ruptured gas tanks, etc.
- Vulnerability of populations in disaster-struck areas may be higher than average, compounding the complexity of response efforts
- Difficulty in reconstruction and rebuilding

Wildfires

The wildfire is defined as "a fire, regardless of ignition source, which is unplanned, has escaped control, or is not authorized under state law or local ordinances."* The latter comment is meant to distinguish the wildfire as hazard from the wildland fires or prescribed fires† that the National Park Service or other agencies may manage in national parks and forested areas.‡ These and wildland fires, which are seen as a natural and cyclical occurrence, are fires "that occur near shrub, grass, forests, or other natural areas,"§ where there may be low population density. Wildfires, on the other hand, can be extremely destructive to life, property, and resources. Figure 2.8 shows wildfires burning near Los Angeles, California.

Nationally, the number of acres burned by wildland fires has increased greatly in the past five years. While annual totals of acreage largely stayed below 5 million in the 1980s and 1990s, since 2000, numbers have dramatically risen, such that within the 2004–2008 period, annual acreage affected by fires hovered between 8 and 9 million.

In the United States, conditions of prolonged drought and settlement in areas of high fire risk have led to destructive wildfire disasters.

---

* Nature Conservancy, "Wildfire Response Plan," Fire Management Manual.
† A prescribed fire is "any fire ignited by management actions to meet specific objectives. A written, approved prescribed fire plan must exist, and National Environmental Policy Act requirements (where applicable) must be met, prior to ignition." Based on National Wildfire Coordinating Group, Glossary of Wildland Fire Terminology. http://www.nwcg.gov/pms/pubs/glossary/n.htm.
‡ National Park Service, Fire and Aviation Management. "About Wildland Fire." http://www.nps.gov/fire/fire/fir_wil_about.cfm.
§ California Department of Forestry and Fire Protection. http://cdfdata.fire.ca.gov/incidents/incidents_terminology?filter=W.

Figure 2.8 Wildfires raging near Los Angeles, California.

Likewise, the wildfires that occur annually and seasonally in California also point to the intersection between hazards that occur naturally and the ways in which human settlements and planning do not take certain risks into account.

If you are located in or near a dense woodland, forest, or grassland area; have a high to extreme fire danger class; have experienced a prolonged dry period; or have experienced past wildfires, your community may be at risk.

Unique challenges that wildfires pose for emergency managers include:

- Changing weather and topography conditions that make it dangerous for first responders
- Fires, which can create their own dangerous weather conditions
- Difficulty in accessing sites that need fire suppression
- Need for specialized equipment and vehicles, such as helicopters
- Need for specially trained firefighting personnel or volunteers
- Evacuation and other information needed in a timely manner

- Fighting the fires taxes resources and supplies at a rapid rate
- Properties and landholdings that contain flammable fuels pose grave danger if caught in the path of the wildfires*
- Loss of property and extensive damage to woodlands and wildlands
- In the long-term, loss of vegetation may lead to erosion and lead to a second wave of potential risks, including flooding, landslides, and runoff in water supplies†

Blizzards, Ice Storms, and Severe Winter Storms

With the onset of winter, several types of snow and ice-related storms can affect entire regions and states. An ice storm "involves rain which freezes upon impact. Ice coating at least one-fourth inch in thickness is heavy enough to damage trees, overhead wires, and similar objects and to produce widespread power outages."‡

A blizzard is a "snowstorm with sustained winds of 40 miles per hour (mph) or more or gusting up to at least 50 mph with heavy falling or blowing snow, persisting for one hour or more, temperatures of ten degrees Fahrenheit or colder and potentially life-threatening traveling conditions."

Some regions generally expect ice storms of some severity in the winter. However, in 1998, the northern part of New York State was impacted by what later became known as the Great Ice Storm of 1998. One of the responders, a platoon sergeant of the New York Army National Guard Unit, Jay Kaczor, recalled that the freezing rain had stranded vehicles and people along the street and blocked residential areas from rescuers because the streets were completely blocked off by felled trees. Rescuers in these instances had to proceed on foot and be careful of live electrical lines in order to reach people stranded in their own homes. "We were constantly rotating men out of the field, and having them warm up inside of the running vehicle while out on search and rescue missions. I think dealing with the cold was probably the most challenging and difficult task that we had to deal with."

This storm impacted 1.4 million households and 3 million people, and the initial response period lasted eight days in two upstate towns.

---

* Nature Conservancy, "Wildfire Response Plan," Fire Management Manual. http://www.tncfiremanual.org/wildfire.htm.
† USDA Forest Service, "Burned Area Emergency Response (BAER) Background. http://www.fs.fed.us/biology/watershed/burnareas/background.html.
‡ Providence Emergency Management Agency. http://www.providenceri.com/pema/blizzard.html.

Unique challenges that ice storms pose to emergency managers:

- Risk of injury and death from hypothermia, traffic accident, and other conditions
- Makes walking and driving extremely dangerous, including for first responders
- Hinders transportation of people and goods from affected areas to shelters
- Low and subfreezing temperatures affect the functionality of equipment and communications systems
- The formation of ice may damage electrical lines, causing widespread power outages and leave communities without power or heat
- Outage of power causes reliance on generators; improper usage causes carbon monoxide poisoning
- Special-needs populations, like the elderly or disabled, especially vulnerable and need assistance in case of evacuation to shelters
- The thaws from winter storms may cause flooding
- Repeated occurrence during the winter season may tax supplies and resources

HUMAN-MADE DISASTERS

Human-made disasters are defined as "disasters or emergency situations where the principal, direct cause(s) are identifiable human actions, deliberate or otherwise." Apart from "technological" and "ecological" disasters, this mainly involves situations in which civilian populations suffer casualties, losses of property, basic services, and means of livelihood as a result of war or civil strife. For example, human-made disasters/emergencies can be of the rapid- or slow-onset types, and in the case of internal conflict, can lead to "complex emergencies" as well, in which hazards are compounded due to the nature of disaster, for example, combining chemical or industrial contamination with long-term natural-hazard effects. Furthermore, the nature of the human-made hazard has sometimes been found to lead to higher amounts of psychological distress in communities when compared to those disasters perceived as "natural disasters," depending on the population's familiarity with the human-made disaster agent, the speed of the disaster impact, and the length of the warning period.

Construction Accidents

Construction accidents are human-made disasters that happen at a site of construction, which may involve the improper use or maintenance of construction equipment or materials, improper or inadequate construction techniques, or the unintended collapse or malfunctioning of adjacent buildings or infrastructure that have been destabilized by construction. In metropolitan areas, where cranes work on half-finished buildings tens of stories above the sidewalks, construction crane collapses have caused the deaths of construction workers and extensive damage to adjacent property. In addition, the construction of buildings or infrastructure has, in some cases, affected the stability of nearby buildings or infrastructure, causing collapses or partial collapses that harm passersby and inhabitants. In many cases, the scene of the accident and the equipment involved must also be investigated for possible lack of adherence to legal codes and standards for construction. For example, a crane accident in New York that killed seven people in 2008 was found to be the responsibility of a rigging company using only half the amount of necessary slings to raise the crane (Figure 2.9). In 2007, a section of a bridge 1.7 miles

Figure 2.9 Building damaged by crane accident.

long under construction in Vietnam collapsed, killing sixty workers and injuring ninety-seven others. Many victims were trapped, and the use of specialized equipment was necessary. At the same time, conducting rescue efforts was risky business, as it increased the risk for further collapse of the bridge.*

Unique challenges that construction accidents pose for emergency managers:

- Little to no warning
- Loss of life, injury, and damage to property
- Need to save lives compounded by extremely heavy loads of materials
- Response efforts may lead to further collapse or damage
- Need to contain the area and protect passersby
- Requires the use of specialized skills and equipment to conduct rescue effort

Chemical and Industrial Hazards

Industrial disasters are defined as "mass disasters caused by industries, whether by accident, negligence, or incompetence."† Chemical hazards and industrial disasters can occur in the production, storage, transportation, use, or disposal of chemicals. Products containing hazardous materials are regularly shipped on the roadways and waterways and through the pipelines of America and globally. Hazardous materials may also be by-products of industrial processes that are not fully understood or fully regulated by public agencies. Such materials can interact with the environment or be absorbed or ingested by other plants and animals that humans consume. Chemical hazards may be present in the form of explosives, flammables, poisons, or radioactive materials. Not only the manufacturers of chemicals, but also everyday sites within your community, such as gas stations, hospitals, and waste sites, may be potential areas of chemical or industrial disaster.‡ Figure 2.10 shows an oil spill in the vicinity of South Pass, Louisiana.

---

* MSNBC, "Vietnam Bridge Collapse Kills 52 People," September 26, 2007. http://www.msnbc.msn.com/id/20986875/.

† Eric K. Noji. 1997. The Public Health Consequences of Disasters. New York: Oxford University Press..

‡ FEMA, "Hazardous Materials." http://www.fema.gov/hazard/types.shtm.

Figure 2.10   The oil spill seen here was investigated by the Coast Guard after it was reported in the vicinity of South Pass, Louisiana, April 6, 2010. (Coast Guard photo by Petty Officer 1st Class Jesse Kavanaugh.)

Transit of Hazardous Material through Your Town

In the 1980s, 4 billion tons of hazardous chemicals were shipped on the nation's highways, and approximately 10 percent of all trucks and 35 percent of all trains carried dangerous cargo. Every day, up to 76,000 tanker trucks carrying hazardous materials travel across the United States. A typical gasoline tank truck carries approximately the same amount of fuel as the planes that hit the World Trade Center.*

In addition, there is evidence that the shipment of hazardous materials poses a tempting target for terrorism. Between 1997 and 2000 alone, terrorists attacked surface transportation systems 195 times.† In addition, the United States has over 100,000 miles of rail track, and chemical products made up about 9 percent of the commodities carried by rail in 2002.‡ Trains also run very close to the heart of the nation's political center, passing within four blocks of the U.S. Capitol building. The 90-ton cars that regularly pass by the building contain enough chlorine to kill 100,000 people within thirty minutes and endanger 2.4 million people.§ Moreover, chemical companies have identified that if one of their 90-ton rail cars containing chlorine were to rupture, 3 million people could be endangered, and in California, the number is even higher, at 4 million. More seriously, the National Transportation Safety Board, in 2004, determined that more

---

* The Morning Call (Allentown), "Scrutinize Drivers of Hazardous Cargo," 2001.
† Government Accountability Office, "Rail Security: Some Actions Taken to Enhance Passenger and Freight Rail Security, but Significant Challenges Remain," 2004.
‡ Federal Railroad Administration, "Freight Railroads Background." http://www.fra.dot.gov/downloads/policy/freight5a.pdf.
§ Testimony of Dr. Jay Boris, Laboratory for Computation Physics and Fluid Dynamics, U.S. Naval Research Laboratory, before the DC City Council, October 6, 2003. http://www.greenpeace.org/usa/global/usa/report/2007/8/testimony-of-dr-jay-boris-u/. Rep. Ed Markey, letter to congressional colleagues, July 7, 2004.

than half of the nation's 60,000 rail cars carrying hazardous materials are too old to meet current industry standards and are thus at risk of breaking open after derailing. Some examples include a 122-car freight train in North Dakota that spilled nearly 150,000 gallons of ammonia, killing one person and injuring 333 people.*

Unique challenges that transit of hazardous materials pose for emergency managers:

- Little to no warning, especially in the case of an industrial accident
- Difficulty of immediately containing and blocking off affected areas
- Difficulty of first responders accessing the site because of damaged infrastructure
- Need for specialized hazmat teams
- Need for specialized equipment
- Need for medical personnel with specific expertise
- Need for antidote or specific neutralizing agents for a particular substance
- Increased spread of substances (as chemicals move downhill, downwind, etc.), depending on topographic conditions
- Mass emergency medical and mental health needs

Consider the impact of chemical, technological, and industrial disasters, which can range from small to large scale to the unthinkable: the 1956 discovery of large-scale mercury poisoning in Minamata, Japan; the 1979 Three Mile Island nuclear plant meltdown in the United States; the 1984 Bhopal industrial disaster in Central India, where the Union Carbide pesticide plant released forty-two tons of toxic gas, ultimately killing a disputed number of 25,000 citizens; the 1986 Chernobyl nuclear plant disaster in the Ukraine, where a nuclear power reactor exploded; the 1989 *Exxon Valdez* oil spill, in which 10.8 million gallons of crude oil was spilled into the Prince William Sound in Alaskan waters.

These real and potential threats differ from the terrorist threats of 9/11, the London subway, and similar human-made disasters. Chemical and industrial threats introduce the unknown effects of chemical and biological exposure both in the short and long term. In turn, based on the threat, the help that the community needs and the assistance it is willing to offer may shift. Unlike the challenge of managing an outpouring of

---

* Jonathan D. Salant, "Many Rail Cars Found Substandard," Associated Press, March 10, 2004. http://www.boston.com/news/nation/articles/2004/03/10/many_rail_cars_found_substandard.

citizen helpers, emergency managers may actually find themselves needing to seek the expertise of those within the community. The threat from
chemical and industrial threats may be ongoing, in contrast to single-event
natural disasters or single-strike terrorist events. Furthermore, based on
the urgency and immediacy of the threat, emergency managers who have
previously managed many aspects of a disaster may find themselves
focusing in a specialized area, leaving other duties unfilled. Emergency
managers may need to access additional human resource from within the
community, such as linguists and interpreters. Rather than deterring citizens from helping, emergency members can access to specialized equipment and supplies that the community possesses.

The unique challenges chemical and industrial hazards pose for
emergency managers include:

- Little to no warning, especially in the case of an industrial accident
- Difficulty of immediately containing and blocking off affected
  areas
- Damaged infrastructure may make it difficult for first responders
  to access the site
- Need for specialized hazmat teams
- Need for specialized equipment
- Need for medical personnel with specific expertise
- Depending on the substance, may need antidote or specific neu-
  tralizing agents
- Topographic conditions may increase spread of substances (as
  chemicals move downhill, downwind, etc.)
- Mass emergency medical and mental health needs
- Need to contain and block off affected areas
- Population may try to evacuate through or reenter site of contam-
  ination in a panic, blocking roadways or other means of entry to
  the site
- Possible contamination of groundwater, drinking water, air, and
  other essential supplies
- Need for decontamination before community can reenter their
  homes or workplaces
- Need for specialized disposal of waste and all contaminated
  materials
- First responders may be exposed to life-threatening conditions
- Unknown, chronic, or serious consequences of long-term exposure from leakage into groundwater, irrigation channels, etc.

- Materials may be flammable or otherwise have reactions with elements in the environment, further increasing harm and damage
- Mass communication and public notification needs
- Loss of life and property
- Unique mental health challenges
- People may not emerge to help

Finally, in the case of both natural and human-made hazards, and depending on the scale of the disaster, there is also the risk of disaster when the sites where evacuees or official responders are directed to are overwhelmed by a sudden increase in population. For example, after Hurricane Katrina, the city of Baton Rouge, Louisiana, was overwhelmed by a doubling of its population through the surge of evacuees from New Orleans, increasing from 150,000 to 300,000 residents. As tens of thousands of refugees flooded the city, and as thousands came to stay one year later, all municipal services and major institutions were taxed by this increased burden, from school systems and health-care facilities to roadways. Other cities such as Oklahoma City and Houston were also flooded with large numbers of storm survivors and had to scramble to get their basic infrastructure to manage this sudden large-scale need. Thus, even if your town or locale is not in the direct path of a natural or human-made hazard, if it is designated, officially or unofficially, as an evacuation destination, and your agency is involved in municipal or human services, chances are that your agency will be greatly impacted by an influx of evacuees and responders. In this case, it is also good to be prepared for the possibility of serving this role in disaster relief as a sanctuary or refugee relocation center, especially if your agency is in a mid- to large-sized city.

Now that we have reviewed the unique challenges of today's disaster response and explored how these interact with traditional hazards and disasters, use the worksheet in Table 2.1 to review and mark those challenges that you as an emergency manager or community leader face, and consider what gaps in human resources that your agency therefore needs to bridge.

Table 2.1   Worksheet: Organizational Challenges

	Gaps in human resources	Will affect agency's ability to provide following services
Public challenges		
❏ Public apathy	❏	_____
❏ Diverse demographics	❏	_____
Specify:	❏	_____
❏ Communications	❏	_____
Specify:	❏	_____
❏ Others: _____	❏	_____
Internal capacity challenges		
❏ Lack of staff	❏	_____
❏ Partner expectations	❏	_____
❏ Liability	❏	_____
Traditional challenges natural hazards		
❏ Hurricanes/coastal storms	❏	_____
❏ Tsunamis	❏	_____
❏ Landslides	❏	_____
❏ Floods	❏	_____
❏ Tornadoes and windstorms	❏	_____
❏ Wildfires	❏	_____
❏ Earthquakes	❏	_____
❏ Ice Storms	❏	_____
❏ Other: _____	❏	_____
Human-made challenges/hazards		
❏ Terrorism	❏	_____
❏ Cyberterrorism	❏	_____
❏ Pandemic	❏	_____
❏ Transit of hazardous materials	❏	_____
❏ Chemical and industrial hazards	❏	_____

Continued

Table 2.1 (*Continued*)   Worksheet: Organizational Challenges

	Gaps in human resources	Will affect agency's ability to provide following services
Specify:	❏	_____
❏ Other: _____	❏	_____

Challenge conclusion

END-OF-CHAPTER QUESTIONS

- What disasters could potentially affect your community?
- Of the disasters that have the potential of striking your community, which would your agency have the capacity to respond to?
- At what point would the size and magnitude of the situation overload your agency's capability and require outside resources?
- Do you have the equipment, technology, and systems necessary to complete your mission?
- Where is it likely these disasters will strike?
- What are the special needs of the communities that are affected?

CONCLUSION

As you can see, we are starting to break down the challenges that occur in disaster response and show how each should be dealt with to address a specific challenge. Public challenges, such as the general public's apathy toward disaster preparedness, must be addressed quite differently than when addressing the internal capacity needs of agencies that have the responsibility of responding to disasters. Yet they are all intertwined, and when one of these unique challenges is not addressed, it can exacerbate the emergency manager's abilities to respond quickly and effectively to the "traditional" hazards that may occur within a community. Take note of all the challenges that may apply to your specific circumstances, community, and locale. By looking at those challenges, you can begin to address internal capacity issues with forward thinking on how to fill the gaps in staff and resources.

3

Disaster Management Concepts Applied to Spontaneous Unaffiliated Community Volunteer Management

You don't manage a disaster—you watch your preparedness initiatives succeed or fail.

Walter Graham
Former Executive Director, Red Cross of New Jersey

IN THIS CHAPTER

- A Common Lexicon of Terms
- The Life Cycle of Disaster Response
  - Preparation
  - Response
  - Recovery
  - Mitigation
- The Incident Command System
- Integrated Communication Concepts
- Emergency Support Functions

Figure 3.1 World Trade Center disaster site. (Photo credit: Jay Kaczor.)

A COMMON LEXICON OF TERMS

Disasters tend to strike across jurisdictions and boundaries such that no single individual, agency, or institution responds alone. They bring agencies and managers out of routine communication and coordination scenarios into complex interagency and multilevel arrangements. As the research on disasters shows, communication problems surface as among the most consistent problems in disaster response and pose unique challenges for emergency managers.* We have found this to happen even amongst jurisdictions that are closely aligned and working together regularly.

Thus, one of the most prominent discussions in national and international circles of disaster response professionals, including emergency managers, the military in support of civilian authorities, nongovernmental

---

* D. Wenger, E. L. Quarantelli, and R. Dynes, "Disaster Analysis: Emergency Management Offices and Arrangements," Final Project Report No 34, Disaster Research Center, University of Delaware, Newark, 1986, cited by Eric Auf der Heide, Disaster Response: Principles of Preparation and Coordination (Saint Louis: Mosby Year Book, 1989).

organizations, and faith-based groups, is the need for a comprehensive and common lexicon of terms as well as standard operating procedures that are shared across boundaries. A lexicon is important so that emergency managers, community response teams, and civic leaders are all "speaking the same language" when working together for the first time. Standardizing terms is crucial to harmonize standardized operating procedures between agencies, clarify roles, and bridge the communication divide between them. Overall, this helps to bring each agency and emergency manager a sense of the big picture—not only satisfying one individual agency's needs for information, but communicating it strategically to the whole community of responding agencies and individual citizens.

In this manual, we take the federal framework for disaster management as a structure to translate and apply terms to be utilized at the community level. The National Incident Management System (NIMS), which is the United States' comprehensive, national approach to a collective and mutually shared *framework* for incident management, is applicable at all levels and across functional disciplines. The purpose of NIMS is to

- Be applicable across a full range of potential incidents and hazards, regardless of size or complexity
- Improve coordination and cooperation between public and private entities in a variety of domestic incident management activities

We also apply the disaster management concepts that are used every day by emergency managers. We review each for their relevance and application to management of spontaneous unaffiliated community volunteers (SUCV) as well as to create a foundation of common terminology that will be used in relationship to SUCV planning and management. We propose that you incorporate these concepts and terms into your SUCV management plan and teach the general public the same terms and procedures to follow.

If you are a seasoned emergency manager, please skim through this chapter as a review. You may also find new terms and protocols that other states and entities are using that may benefit your agency and partnering agencies.

For individuals who are reading this information for the first time, rest assured that terms will change and that these are not set in stone. However, to familiarize yourself with them further, there are multiple online sites available to you so that you may keep abreast of changing terms, functions, procedures, and so on. These sites include training at the Federal Emergency Management Agency (FEMA) Website (http://www.fema.gov/prepared/train.shtm) the IS100 and 200 online courses at *www.usda.gov/documents/ICS100.pdf,* as well as the CERT 101 course at http://www.citizencorps.gov/cert/training_mat.shtm.

THE LIFE CYCLE OF DISASTER RESPONSE

(Adapted from FEMA)

Emergency management can be understood as a life cycle of phases that follow each other in the event of a disaster. The life cycle is broken down into four segments within the disaster life cycle: Preparation, response, recovery, and mitigation (Figure 3.2). Some agencies may have responsibilities that lie in only one segment of the cycle, while others may encompass all four. Overall, a combination of actors that fulfill all phases of disaster response is necessary for healthy and diversified emergency management.

Preparation

Disaster preparation is a process that ensures that people and organizations are in a state of readiness to address the effects of a potential disaster in a way that will minimize loss of life, injury, and property, and have the ability to rescue, relieve, rehabilitate, and provide other services once disaster strikes. If and when disaster strikes, and in the case that essential services are not readily available, preparation ensures that individuals, communities, and organizations will have prepared for contingencies by

Figure 3.2 Life cycle of disaster response.

developing a plan, having practiced the plan, and then using the plan as a guide to their response efforts.

Preparation means different things for different communities. For individuals, preventing household accidents and mitigating and responding to disasters at home and at work is the first step, and this can be implemented through outreach and education programs. Ultimately, a prepared community is an educated community that reduces the burden on emergency managers in all phases of disaster and contributes to response as a force multiplier and resource. Preparation can include individual, family, school, workplace, and community readiness.

Effective preparation in the case of community engagement means developing plans and coordination to include robust outreach and education programs to educate and train your community. Including them in exercises while maintaining constant dialogue and a responsive relationship with them is also part of preparedness.

For an agency, preparation can take the form of registering individuals who may want to volunteer, thereby facilitating a credentialing process predisaster, as well as by encouraging citizens to become affiliated pretrained volunteers. The main focus in the task of preparation is that the system needs to be dynamic and provide options for everyone's lifestyles.

Plans should be devised to be fluid, as disasters are unpredictable. Instead of viewing the plan as the constant, it should be acknowledged that, in fact, change is constant, and a good plan encompasses a solid structure built to address multiple hazards and scenarios in such a way that each of those potential changes is well thought out and practiced. Thus, when there is a need to step out of the box, one can do so with many options to choose from.

Coordination with local groups and partnering organizations will play an important role in disaster response. Understanding what local groups will provide in disasters and how you might coordinate with each other or exchange services can be documented in a Memorandum of Understanding or Agreement. Such documents allow for groups to work through the processes of what, when, where, and how coordination will take place.

The Citizen Corps Council and Voluntary Organizations Active in Disaster (VOAD) are examples of groups that facilitate networking among agencies and nonprofit groups to prepare and train citizens in preparedness and response skills. Community engagement is not one-size-fits-all. Please explore the links provided in this book, and as always contact us with any questions. Additional means to engage your community are to include them in drills, exercises, and tabletops.

In Israel, citizen preparedness efforts for counterterrorism and disaster situations are extensive, taking the form of national-level annual civil defense drills.* Turning Point 3, a five-day exercise launched in 2009, included all citizens and many governmental offices in a variety of scenarios simulating war and attacks, with 252 local councils and municipalities opening "safe rooms" and responding to simulated emergency scenarios. Schools, employers, large organizations, and hospitals were engaged in the scenarios. New technologies for alerting citizens, such as nationwide cell phone alerts and special warning and evacuation systems for special-needs populations such as disabled children and the hearing impaired, were tested. While the context of Israel differs from that of the United States and other countries in many ways, the Department of Homeland Security found much to recommend from these and other citizen preparedness efforts by Israel, especially the extent to which the general public is included in efforts to prepare for disaster.

Response

Response begins as soon as a disaster is detected or begins to threaten. For emergency management agencies, the aim of response is to get people out of danger; provide needed food, water, shelter, and medical services; mobilize and position emergency equipment; and bring damaged services and systems back on line. Local responders, government agencies, spontaneous unaffiliated volunteers, and private organizations are all integral parts of the response. In the response phase, the emergency plan that has been developed in the preparedness phase—including a SUCV management plan—can now be put into practice to coordinate response. Response is further broken down into manageable time segments, most notably, in the first seventy-two hours. The most common planning segment is twelve-hour shifts and planning cycles. Depending on your plan and area of focus, planning can be broken down further. The closer one is to the immediate response, the shorter the planning cycles, as the situation will change rapidly. These phases reflect the recommendations and findings of emergency responders in the field.

---

* Yaakov Lappin. "Sirens Sound across Israel in Home Front Drill," Jerusalem Post, June 2, 2009.

Figure 3.3 Lisa Orloff, executive director of World Cares Center, taking part in Haiti earthquake relief efforts in 2010, conducting a needs assessment of a local orphanage that was destroyed in part by the earthquake. (Source: Lisa Orloff.)

The response phase is also when the most chaos can potentially occur, because officials may not have arrived yet or, when they do arrive, citizens have already begun to help, either by organizing themselves or by arriving in such large numbers that they create logjams in transit, communications, and supplies at the site of impact. This pocket of time and the lack of official direction can be referred to as a vacuum of authority. Official Incident Command is established and information needs to be gathered, verified, and validated, all while addressing the immediate needs of victims. This is where a robust SUCV management plan would relieve the most chaos for both emergency managers and civilians who are volunteering. You will also see the most selfless, philanthropic side of people during this time. It can be an exhilarating and humbling experience to see a mass of humanity coming out with a shared intent in mind—to help their fellow human beings. Contrary to the popular myth that civilians panic in disaster or may take advantage of the temporary disruption in law enforcement to behave in antisocial behavior or in looting, civilians affected by disaster tend to act rationally, are the first to respond, and seek out neighbors, relatives, and local groups.*

In most cases, the most urgent life-saving efforts must take place in the first seventy-two hours.† According to the Red Cross, the vast majority of those affected by disaster will die within seventy-two hours after impact, depending on a number of factors such as the type of injury, the temperature, and access to air and water. However, beyond the life-saving window of time needed in response, there may be occasions when the response phase is extended or changed based on the traumatic impact of a disaster and the emotional need of the affected community to maintain hope that lives can still be saved. During the 9/11 relief effort, for example, the response phase of the effort officially lasted for weeks. There was heated debate as to when the official call would be made to announce that the response phase of the effort aimed at life-saving would be turning to the phase of recovery and rebuilding. The magnitude of the disaster and the heightened state of emotions weighed heavily on authorities, making the decision as to when to shift from response to recovery an extremely difficult one.

Recovery

The goal of the recovery phase is to remove debris, restore the area affected by disaster to rebuild property, revitalize affected economies, and repair essential infrastructure.‡ It also involves a critical opportunity to implement mitigating measures that might otherwise not be accepted by citizens of the affected area.§ There are hundreds if not thousands of opportunity areas to help in recovery, from immediate needs such as sheltering and short-term housing to assistance centers such as New Orleans' "Welcome Home Centers" to offering long-term housing, health services, job training and job placement, and more.

The task of rebuilding after a disaster can take months, years, and even decades. Not only services and infrastructure, not only the facilities

* Perry, R.W., Lindell, M.K. (2003). Understanding Citizen Response to Disasters with Implications of Terrorism, *Journal of Contingencies and Crisis Management*, volume 11.
† Peter Walker, "International Search and Rescue Teams: A League Discussion Paper," League of the Red Cross and Red Crescent Societies, Geneva, 1991.
‡ George D. Haddow and Jane A. Bullock, Introduction to Emergency Management (Amsterdam: Butterworth-Heinemann, 2004).
§ David Alexander, Principles of Emergency Planning and Management (Harpenden, U.K.: Terra Publishing, 2002).

and operations, but the lives and livelihoods of thousands of people may be affected. Recovery not only deals with the physical effects of disaster, but the mental and emotional effects as well. Emotional recovery goes through its own cycle. The issues, effects, and mitigating behaviors are discussed further in Chapter 9.

The long-term recovery process as described in FEMA's "The Road to Recovery 2008" is "to restore or build a healthy functioning community that will sustain itself over time, while taking advantage of the opportunities to rebuild stronger smarter communities and mitigate against Future Disasters" (http://www.fema.gov/pdf/rebuild/ltrc/2008_report.pdf). In terms of managing the spontaneous volunteer response, one lesson learned through the 9/11 relief effort is that some agencies could not use the services of spontaneous volunteers during the initial hours, days, and even the first few weeks. But as the recovery period was extended, they did need the volunteers who came to help during the initial hours to come back and help during the long-term recovery process. Thus, even if you cannot utilize the manpower of those who come out to help spontaneously at the moment they arrive to volunteer, it is important to gather their names and contact information. Treat their offer of service with respect; thank them and ask them if they would be willing to help at a later date. We can again learn from the 9/11 response efforts, a "story" circulated amongst volunteers and responders that, at one of the armories, the names of those who were lining up to help were being taken, but at the end of the day, the lists were being thrown away as there was no role for the volunteers at that time. In the following weeks and months, those who had volunteered had to return to work, go home, or were burnt out and needed respite. At that time, many voluntary agencies, including World Cares Center, received calls asking for as many volunteers as we could find. In reaching out to find them, we discovered that they had either found other ways to help or were so disgruntled with the way they were treated that they refused to volunteer for some of the agencies who were at the armory.

Effective management strategies that were implemented on the spur of the moment are reflected by the experiences of Sodexo, a large-scale company providing food and facilities management services that responded to the needs of 9/11. President of Corporate Services Mark Bickford was receiving 1,000 e-mails a day with offers of help in the aftermath of 9/11. At that time, in the midst of rescue feeding operations, foreseeing that his staff would burn out quickly as they were working 24/7, he wrote back to these individuals, asking them to be available for rotations in three weeks. In this way, when those involved in the initial response began to feel the effects of what they had experienced and had to be transitioned out of their duties, he was able to tap those who had volunteered and who had been notified of an opportunity in the future.

How you treat potential future volunteers is an important consideration for the future, and especially for your process of long-term recovery and overall community relations.

Mitigation

Mitigation, defined as the ability to lessen the negative impact of an action, focuses on breaking the cycle of disaster damage. Mitigation efforts provide value by creating safer communities and reducing loss of life and property. A three-year independent study of FEMA mitigation efforts showed that, on average, in the face of all hazards, a dollar spent on mitigation saved society an average of four dollars.*

Although not stated directly, mitigation falls into each part of the disaster cycle, as each of the other phases aim to lessen the negative impact of disaster, albeit in more urgent or immediate ways. Preparation is the first step to mitigate the effects of any disaster. It may also prevent an everyday emergency from ever turning into a disaster.

Communities can take control of the mitigation process before a disaster strikes through preparedness and long after federal funding and resources are gone.

The following section describes disaster management concepts that are nationally and federally recognized as well as those adapted from lessons learned in the field. These concepts can and should be taught and implemented in all the phases of disaster response described previously.

THE INCIDENT COMMAND SYSTEM

NIMS employs the Incident Command System (ICS) as a system that integrates "a combination of facilities, equipment, personnel, procedures and communications operating within a common organizational structure"

---

* Multihazard Mitigation Council (MMC), National Institute of Building Sciences, "National Hazard Mitigation Saves: An Independent Study to Assess the Future Savings from Mitigation Activities," Washington, D.C., 2005. The study assessed savings from three mitigation programs: the Hazard Mitigation Grant Program, Project Impact, and Flood Mitigation Assistance Program.

for the purposes of incident management within the domestic context.* For the purpose of SUCV management, the ICS will be a focal point.

The Incident Command System (ICS) was developed in the 1970s following a series of catastrophic fires in California's wildland/urban interface. Property damage ran into the millions, and many people died or were injured. The personnel assigned to determine the causes of this disaster studied the case histories and discovered that response problems could rarely be attributed to lack of resources or failure of tactics. What were the lessons learned?

Surprisingly, studies found that response problems were far more likely to result from inadequate management than from any other single reason. Weaknesses in incident management were often due to

- Lack of accountability, including unclear chains of command and supervision
- Poor communication due to both inefficient uses of available communications systems and conflicting codes and terminology
- Lack of an orderly, systematic planning process
- No common, flexible, predesigned management structure that enabled commanders to delegate responsibilities and manage workloads efficiently
- No predefined methods to integrate interagency requirements into the management structure and planning process effectively

A poorly managed incident response can be devastating, costing lives and negatively impacting on our health, our safety, and on our economy. With so much at stake, we must effectively manage our response efforts. The ICS allows us to do so. ICS is a proven management system based on successful business practices. Therefore, we have focused on ICS as one of the primary tools to manage SUCVs.

We will utilize the incident command chart and the concepts included in developing a spontaneous volunteer management plan. If you have an incident action plan (IAP) or an emergency operations plan (EOP), standard operating procedures, or any kind of human resources manual, these can all contribute to your own Spontaneous Volunteer Management Plan. Our goal is to utilize these proven methods utilized by emergency managers and use them for volunteer management as well as share them with

---

* U.S. Department of Homeland Security, National Incident Management System, Washington, D.C., 2004.

community leadership to manage their constituency. Outlined below are the official descriptions of the ICS and chart, an IAP, and an EOP.

The ICS is a standardized, all-hazard incident management framework. ICS allows its users to adopt an integrated structure to match the needs and demands of single or multiple incidents without being hindered by jurisdictional or regional boundaries. ICS has considerable internal flexibility. It can grow or shrink to meet the diverse demands of a given incident. This flexibility is a very cost-effective and efficient management approach for both small and large incidents as well as a useful tool to manage SUCV. The ICS should be taught to the community, as it will help all citizens understand how disaster response can be managed. Figure 3.4 shows the basic executive functions that must be fulfilled under the incident commander. The positions within the ICS start with the incident command.

> *Incident command:* Sets the incident response objectives, strategies, and priorities and has overall responsibility at the scene of the incident or event.
>
> *Operations:* Conducts tactical operations to carry out the plan; develops the tactical objectives and organization, and directs all tactical resources.
>
> *Planning:* Prepares and documents the Incident Action Plan to accomplish the objectives, collects and evaluates information, maintains resource status, and maintains documentation for incident records.
>
> *Logistics:* Provides support, resources, and all other services needed to meet the operational objectives.
>
> *Finance/administration:* Monitors costs related to incident management and provides accounting, procurement, time recording, and cost analyses.

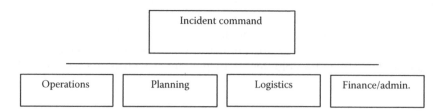

Figure 3.4   Incident command.

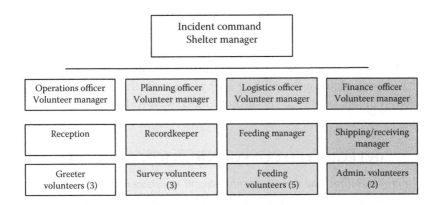

Figure 3.5   Incident command for managing a shelter.

ICS has been used for National Special Security Events, such as presidential visits or the Super Bowl, as well as other planned mega-events such as parades or demonstrations. It is good practice to see where you can implement ICS in your everyday life. At World Cares Center, we utilize an ICS chart and functions to manage the duties of our annual fundraiser. This serves to organize staff and volunteers while familiarizing everyone with a command-and-control environment and its benefits in a stressful setting.

As we delve further into its use for management of spontaneous volunteers, you can see how its structure can help volunteer managers. Figure 3.5 demonstrates how it may be used to manage a shelter.

An IAP is an oral or written plan that contains general objectives reflecting the overall strategy for managing an incident. An IAP includes the identification of operational resources and assignments and may include attachments that provide additional direction. Some emergency managers will choose to use an EOP. An EOP describes who will do what, as well as when, with what resources, and by what authority—before, during, and immediately after an emergency. This is a risk-based, all-hazards emergency operations plan addressing all of the hazards that threaten a jurisdiction in a single EOP, instead of relying on stand-alone plans.

EOPs can serve as the basis for effective response to any hazard that threatens a jurisdiction or organization. Through proper planning and preparedness, the plans facilitate the integration of mitigation into response and recovery activities. By sharing plans, coordination with the federal government during catastrophic disaster situations will be facilitated. Taking into consideration that all disasters are local and most response to those disasters will be by area groups and municipalities in the same way, an IAP or EOP will help municipalities plan and coordinate their resources to create a spontaneous volunteer management plan. Furthermore, sharing the EOP or IAP plans with the community predisaster will help to foster a community-integrated response.

INTEGRATED COMMUNICATION CONCEPTS

Interoperability: The use of *common communication plans* and technologies to ensure that responders and volunteers can communicate with one another during an emergency. This helps to improve the ability of everyone to understand a common language. Two things are often relied on. First, a set of common terms helps to resolve the confusion between the use of terms and the ways certain disaster-response fields or specialists may use those same words as acronyms or as part of their field's terminology. For example, for an emergency medical technician (EMT), the word *bus* is used to mean their vehicle, the ambulance. Therefore, when describing their needs amongst themselves, they will say they need a bus (ambulance) at such and such a location. Another responder from a different field or a citizen volunteer may take that word literally and order a school or commuter bus to the scene.

Then there is also a technical dimension of interoperable communication that centers on the types of technology and hardware that responding partners are using, with issues arising from whether they can work on the same frequency and therefore be able to reach each other, and whether different systems are compatible.

We will focus on the common terms utilizing some of the planning strategies offered through NIMS and the ICS.

Surge capacity: The ability to obtain adequate staff, supplies and equipment, structures, and systems to meet a sudden, unexpected rise in need following a large-scale incident or disaster.

Check-in: All responders and volunteers, regardless of agency affiliation, must report in to receive an assignment in accordance with the procedures established.

Span of control: Pertains to the number of individuals or resources that one supervisor can manage effectively during emergency response incidents or special events. Maintaining an effective span of control is particularly important in incidents where safety and account-ability are a top priority. Span of control is the key to effective and efficient incident management. The type of incident, nature of the task, hazards and safety factors, and distances between personnel and resources all influence span-of-control considerations.

Maintaining an adequate span of control with SUCVs is an important issue that we will explore in later chapters. For now, an effective span of control on incidents may vary from three to seven. A ratio of one supervisor to five reporting personnel or volunteers is recommended.

Chain of command: A designated line of authority within the levels of the organization.

Unity of command: Each individual involved in incident operations will be assigned to only one supervisor.

Resource tracking: Supervisors must record and report resource status changes as they occur.

Emergency operations center (EOC): EOCs are the locations from which the coordination of information and resources to support incident management activities takes place. EOCs are typically established by the emergency management agency at the local and state levels. In many cases, the EOC is in charge of activating many efforts such as CERT teams, volunteer reception centers, and other services in response to disasters.

Volunteer reception center or volunteer reception area: A model within emergency management for managing volunteers responding to help in a disaster or emergency. It is often a location that interested candidates are directed to that physically houses the processes involved with selecting, placing, and training volunteers. The volunteer reception area may be a smaller-scale version of the center.

Point of distribution (POD): In the public-health sector, a POD is a centralized location where vaccinations are administered by medical health professionals. The PODs are meant to reduce the burden away from hospitals. The term *point of distribution* may also be used more generally in reference to locations where the public picks up life-sustaining commodities following a disaster or emergency, such as shelf-stable food and water.

EMERGENCY SUPPORT FUNCTIONS

Emergency support functions (ESFs) involve the grouping of governmental and private-sector capabilities into an organizational structure to provide support, resources, program implementation, and services.

According to FEMA's "Developing and Maintaining State, Territorial, Tribal, and Local Government Emergency Plans Guide," CPG 101, March 2009 (http://www.fema.gov/pdf/about/divisions/npd/cpg_101_layout.pdf), there is no need for states to mirror the federal ESFs exactly: States have successfully used a hybrid approach. What is important is to share this language amongst all your stakeholders. For that reason, we have used the ESFs in a hybrid approach as well as a common language to ensure that local groups and managers of all levels are using the same terminology, thus eliminating confusion. If your state is using something different, it would be prudent to adapt the language you are using for your community.

If you are an established municipal agency, you will know which ESF you serve, as it will align with the mission statement of the municipal agency. If you are new to emergency management, such as a community group or a faith-based leader who serves a current need in the community and you plan to serve disaster victims by providing the same services in disaster response, you will use your mission to guide you.

Each agency serves only one ESF, although this may be confusing at first, as many of the ESFs mirror the needs you have within your agency. For instance, the ESF pertaining to "communication" is a necessary part of everyone's ability to complete their roles. A better way to look at defining your ESF is to ask yourself, "Are you providing these particular assets to another agency, or is it part of your internal ability to do your job?" If you are a TV station that is offering public service announcements in times of disaster, your ESF will most likely be "communications." However, if you are an agency that feeds the homeless and you will utilize public service announcements to advertise your location to the public, communications is an internal role within your organization, not the ESF you support.

The comprehensive ESF function list composed by World Cares Center (WCC) is a result of research and comparison among various emergency management organizations. By the time this guide is published and in your hand, there will no doubt be several updates to the ESF content. Therefore, we have listed the Web sites from which the research has come from for your reference, so that you can update the ESF functions to be compliant with FEMA's own listing. The ESF roles and tasks briefly outlined here will remain a useful guide on how to identify your agency's ESF and assign roles and tasks to staff and volunteers, which will be the focus of the next chapter.

Following is an overview of the ESFs:

1. Transportation
2. Communications
3. Public works and engineering
4. Firefighting
5. Emergency management
6. Mass care, emergency assistance, housing and human services
7. Logistics management and resource support
8. Public health and medical services
9. Search and rescue
10. Oil and hazardous materials response
11. Agriculture and natural resources
12. Energy
13. Public safety and security
14. Long-term community recovery
15. External affairs

Others:

16. Military support
17. Volunteer and donations management
18. Leadership

The following descriptions briefly explain the areas and roles fulfilled by each emergency support function.

ESF #1: Transportation

Assists federal agencies, state and local governmental entities, and voluntary organizations requiring transportation capacity to perform response missions following a major disaster or emergency. Also serves as a coordination point between response operations and restoration of the transportation infrastructure.

ESF #2: Communications

Ensures the provision of federal telecommunications support to federal, state, and local response efforts following a presidentially declared major disaster, emergency, or extraordinary situation under the federal response plan.

ESF #3: Public works and engineering

Provides technical advice and evaluation, engineering services, contracting for construction management and inspection, contracting for the emergency repair of water and wastewater treatment facilities, potable water and ice, emergency power, and real estate support to assist the state(s) in meeting goals related to lifesaving and life-sustaining actions, damage mitigation, and recovery activities following a major disaster or emergency.

ESF #4: Firefighting

Detects and suppresses wildland, rural, and urban fires resulting from, or occurring coincidentally with, a major disaster or emergency requiring federal response assistance. Duties may also include assistance to local authorities in fire suppression, and investigations of code compliance.

ESF #5: Information and planning

Information and planning collects, analyzes, processes, and disseminates information about a potential or actual disaster or emergency to facilitate the overall activities of the federal government in providing assistance to one or more affected states. Fulfilling this mission supports planning and decision making at both the field/regional operations and headquarters levels.

ESF #6: Mass care, emergency assistance, housing, and human services

Coordinates federal assistance in support of state and local efforts to meet the mass-care needs of victims of a disaster. This federal assistance will support the delivery of the mass-care services of shelter, feeding, and emergency first aid to disaster victims; the establishment of systems to provide bulk distribution of emergency relief supplies to disaster victims; and the collection of information to operate a disaster welfare information system for the purpose of reporting victim status and assisting in family reunification.

ESF #7: Logistics management and resource support

Provides logistical and resource support to other organizations through purchasing, contract, renting and leasing equipment, and supplies in a potential or actual presidentially declared major disaster or emergency.

ESF #8: Public health and medical services

Provides coordinated federal assistance to supplement state and local resources in response to public health and medical care needs following a major disaster or emergency, or during a developing potential medical situation. Resources will be furnished when state and local resources are overwhelmed and public health or medical assistance is requested from the federal government.

ESF #9: Search and rescue

Rapidly deploys components of the national search and rescue response system to provide specialized lifesaving assistance to state and local authorities in the event of a major disaster or emergency. Search and rescue operational activities including locating, extricating, and providing on-site medical treatment to victims trapped in collapsed structures.

ESF #10: Oil and hazardous materials response

Provides federal support to state and local governments in response to an actual or potential discharge or release of hazardous materials following a major disaster or emergency.

ESF #11: Agriculture and natural resources

Coordinates nutrition assistance and food safety and security. Also coordinates animal and plant disease and pest response, ensures protection of natural and cultural resources and historic properties, and the safety and well-being of household pets.

ESF #12: Energy

Helps restore the nation's energy systems following a major disaster, emergency, or other significant event requiring federal response assistance, as well as coordinates between energy industry utilities and makes energy forecasts.

ESF #13: Public safety and security

Coordinates facility and resource security, security planning, and technical resources; provides public safety and security support; and supports access as well as traffic- and crowd-control measures.

Provides security as well as traffic and crowd control in the event of an emergency or disaster. Also, fulfills the actual police functions normally associated with law enforcement activities, including riot control, explosive ordinance removal, prison watch, counterterrorism, etc. Further, this function assists in coordinating evacuations.

ESF #14: Long-term community recovery

Conducts social and economic community-impact assessment; provides and coordinates long-term community recovery assistance to states, tribes, local governments, and the private sector; and analyzes and reviews the implementation of mitigation programs.

ESF #15: External affairs

Coordinates emergency public information and protective action guidelines; undertakes media and community relations, congressional and international affairs, and tribal and insular affairs.

Adjunct ESFs

ESFs for other states and versions have at one time included:

Military support

Provides an orderly and continuing means of military assistance to state and local governments in their responsibilities to alleviate the suffering and damages that result from major disasters and emergencies.

Volunteer and donations management

Responsibilities include (a) expediting the delivery of voluntary goods and services supporting relief efforts before and after a disaster impact and (b) coordinating the use of persons and organizations who volunteer their services during a disaster or emergency.

Leadership

Leadership roles may not fit into any one category, but leaders have very important responsibilities and skills that can be utilized in the event of a disaster.

Begin to chart your agency and ESF that relates to your mission. Now you should be ready to jot down your mission and the emergency support function you fulfill (Table 3.1).

A note for nondisaster-response agencies: If you do not have a defined mission in disaster response, it is a good time to create one. For example, if your nondisaster mission includes a soup kitchen or shelter, you are best aligned with ESF #6: Mass care, emergency assistance, housing, and human services. Another key focus point is to assess your current capacity to fulfill the responsibilities to your daily constituency while adding on your new role to fulfill the needs of disaster victims. How will you continue to serve your regular constituents at the same time?

Table 3.1 Worksheet: Identify Your Agency's Mission and ESF

Agency name:

Agency mission:

(If not disaster organization, your mission in disaster response):

Emergency Support Functions Supported		Comment
1. Transportation	❏	_____
2. Communications	❏	_____
3. Public works and engineering	❏	_____
4. Firefighting	❏	_____
5. Emergency management	❏	_____
6. Mass care, emergency assistance, housing and human services	❏	_____
7. Logistics management and resource support	❏	_____
8. Public health and medical services	❏	_____
9. Search and rescue	❏	_____
10. Oil and hazardous materials response	❏	_____
11. Agriculture and natural resources	❏	_____
12. Energy	❏	_____
13. Public safety and security	❏	_____
14. Long-term community recovery	❏	_____
15. External affairs	❏	_____

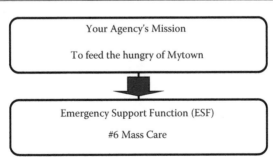

END-OF-CHAPTER QUESTIONS

- At what phase within the disaster life cycle will your agency provide services?
- What disaster management concepts will you apply to managing spontaneous volunteers or your constituents?
- What emergency support function does your agency fulfill as it relates to your mission?

CONCLUSION

In Chapter 2, we reviewed both the unique challenges of disaster response and the traditional disasters that you may be responding to that may create a surge capacity need. In Chapter 3 we covered disaster management concepts, including identifying the ESF your agency fulfills.

The next step in Chapter 4 is to identify or review the many roles that are needed to fulfill your agency's mission and ESF in disaster response. We will then assess your agency's readiness to fulfill all of the roles identified, and weigh the pros and cons of using SUCVs to fulfill these roles.

4

Assessing Internal Readiness

IN THIS CHAPTER

- Defining Agency Roles and Tasks in Disaster Response
- Assessing External Partner Support
- The Many Faces of Disaster Volunteers
- Identifying Spontaneous Unaffiliated Community Volunteer (SUCV) roles
- Weighing the Pros and Cons of Utilizing SUCVs
  - Checklist of Pros
  - Checklist of Liability Concerns

Now that we have reviewed disaster management concepts that will be used as tools in disaster response and identified your agency's emergency support function (ESF) in disaster response, we will proceed to assess what roles and tasks your agency must fulfill in response, where the gaps in human resources exist, and your agency's readiness and capacity to fill those gaps and provide the important services that the public is counting on you to provide. This chapter on assessing internal readiness begins to address the internal capacity challenges shared by emergency managers, including the lack of staff for surge-capacity needs and the challenge of either living up to partner expectations or clarifying them.

Volunteers may or may not come to you after a disaster has occurred. In some situations, they will come to your door; in others, you may need to reach out and solicit their help. Here are a few example scenarios of what may occur:

1. Mass convergence on your location
2. Mass convergence in an area you are arriving to serve in
3. Lack of resources altogether and the need to outreach to new and undeveloped volunteer resources

Each of these scenarios poses a different set of challenges; however, once you come in contact with the volunteers, the process will remain constant.

Likewise, a recent report by Trust for Americans' Health, "Ready or Not: Protecting the Public's Health from Diseases, Disasters and Bioterrorism," highlighted key areas of concern for America's public health sector that included

1. Strengthening leadership
2. Enhancing surge capacity and the public health workforce
3. Modernizing technology and equipment
4. Improving community engagement

These areas of concern, can also be extended to the entire disaster management field.

These key issues, when addressed, can improve surge capacity, or the ability of your organization to fulfill its mission when met with an increased need for services.

DEFINING AGENCY ROLES AND TASKS IN DISASTER RESPONSE

In this chapter, you will walk through the steps of assessing internal readiness of your agency to fulfill your area of responsibility. We will start with your emergency support function, subfunctions, roles, tasks that your agency will need to perform in each respective area.

Subfunction: Each of the major service areas or programs your agency provides that falls under the ESF your agency is aligned with.
Role: A responsibility required or expected of an individual or an organization in order to fulfill the aligned subfunction and the overall mission.
Task: An action or set of actions required to complete a role or responsibility.

Depending on your organization, there may be multiple roles to support, in which case you can expand the Incident Command System (ICS)

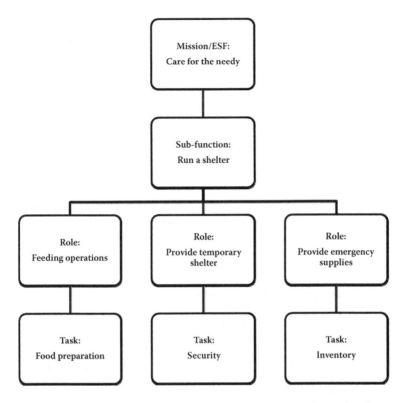

Figure 4.1 Example of an ICS to define agency mission to roles and tasks.

chart shown in Figure 4.1. The ICS chart in Figure 4.1 shows how the mission and ESF of an agency in disaster response (care for the needy) then leads to its agency's subfunction, which is to run a shelter. This subfunction is fulfilled by completing the roles and corresponding tasks of running a shelter, from food services to providing emergency supplies.

Now consider the blank ICS chart in Figure 4.2. Fill in your agency's mission and ESF in disaster response, your subfunctions, and the roles and tasks that are required to fulfill these subfunctions. Once you have comprehensively listed your subfunctions and roles, the next step will be to dig down even further. Under each role, you will list all the tasks that need to be performed to ensure that the subfunctions and roles are being fulfilled.

Using the blank chart in Figure 4.3, you may also list your agency's roles and corresponding tasks.

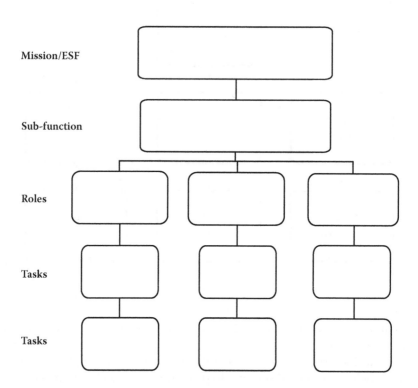

Figure 4.2 Worksheet: From agency mission to roles and tasks.

Mission/ESF:	
Sub function:	
	Role:
Task	
Task	
Task	
Task	
Task	
	Role:
Task	
Task	
Task	
Task	
Task	

Figure 4.3 Worksheet: Agency roles and tasks in list form.

Figure 4.4 Port Authority of New York and the New York City Police Department working together with construction volunteers in 9/11 response efforts. (Photo credit: Tom Sawyer.)

ASSESSING EXTERNAL PARTNER SUPPORT

One often-overlooked assessment is how agencies works with partners and other local organizations that provide services during emergencies and disasters. While taking stock of what your agency does, it is also prudent to check in with your partners, update them on your organization's capacity challenges, and learn about theirs.

Through our workshops, we have seen the result of addressing surge-capacity needs together with the partners that you depend on, and what an eye-opener that can be. Some of the questions that came up included:

- How many agencies are depending on the same nonprofit group to offer certain services in the event of a disaster?
- Are those agencies able to fill their own surge-capacity needs?
- At what point are those agencies unable to provide supportive services, e.g., provide 3,000 meals a day, without needing outside support?

- Do those agencies have an actionable plan to fulfill their surge-capacity needs?
- Does that surge-capacity need include your needs as well?

You will want to ensure that you are exchanging this type of information with your partners and identify whether there are any circumstances or unique challenges under which services cannot be offered. Many assessments have uncovered that the organizations you may depend on are themselves struggling with the same surge needs. As we noted, 80 percent of emergency managers will need new volunteers in the event of a catastrophic disaster.

One of the "tools" that can help organize some of the expectations amongst partners is a memorandum of understanding (MOU), which sets the parameters in which assistance will be provided and lays out the resources that you will respectively provide to each other in case of disaster. An MOU should list the specific duties that each agency will fulfill as well as list points of contact, release of liability, methods of reimbursement, and the terms of the agreement. Each agency representative then signs the agreement. Figure 4.5 is an example of an MoU.

Similarly, state agencies may have an agreement known as an emergency management assistance compact (EMAC), which is a mutual aid agreement developed out of the need to provide assistance and coordinate services across state borders in the event of disasters that exceed local response abilities. EMACs are between state agencies to expedite the process of requesting, mobilizing and deploying, receiving, and compensating partners for all the services and supplies they provide. However, this concept is also valid for other organizations that may have partners from other states that are willing and able to provide services and resources.

Now that your agreements with partner agencies are in place, you can focus on the crucial task of assessing who your volunteers are, beginning with a quick review of the range of disaster volunteers who may come to serve your agency and your community in times of disaster.

THE MANY FACES OF DISASTER VOLUNTEERS

How do you define a volunteer? There are many misnomers on what kind of volunteer is actually doing the good work. During the 9/11 relief effort, many emergency managers found it inconceivable that many of the spontaneous volunteers were not "affiliated" with an agency. How could they

MEMORANDUM OF UNDERSTANDING

Between

<u>***YOUR AGENCY***</u>

And

<u>***PARTNER AGENCY***</u>

* Note : All italicized text in this template must be specified.

Purpose: This MOU establishes procedures and policies regarding the following function area(s):_____

Parties to the MOU

YOUR AGENCY Organizational background:
Mission:
Address:
Phone:
PARTNER AGENCY Organizational background:
Mission:
Address:
Phone:

Duties and Responsibilities

- *YOUR AGENCY* agrees to:

- *PARTNER AGENCY* agrees to:

Communications

YOUR AGENCY Main point of contact will be: _____

Phone: _____ Cell: _____

Figure 4.5   Memorandum of Understanding.   *Continued*

Emergency or after-hours contact: _____

Phone: _____ Cell: _____

PARTNER AGENCY Main point of contact will be: _____

Phone: _____ Cell: _____

Emergency or after-hours contact: _____

Phone: _____ Cell: _____

Terms of the Memorandum

This agreement is in effect starting _____/_____/_____.

It may be terminated by either party given _____ days written notice.

The agreement will be reviewed and updated __*annually*___ .

All changes to the agreement must be written and agreed to by both parties.

The personnel of *YOUR AGENCY* deployed for these duties and responsibilities will be in good standing with the agency.

The personnel of *PARTNER AGENCY* deployed for these duties and responsibilities will be in good standing with the agency.

The personnel of *YOUR AGENCY* will abide by all federal, state, and local laws.

The personnel of *PARTNER AGENCY* will abide by all federal, state, and local laws.

Method of Reimbursement?

The following services will be reimbursed: _____ by *YOUR AGENCY* to *PARTNER AGENCY* if all requirements for reimbursement have been met. The rate of reimbursement will be:_____.

Requirement: The *PARTNER AGENCY* must provide detailed records of expenses and/or time spent by deployed staff or volunteers.

Liability Release and Covenant Not to Sue

YOUR AGENCY and PARTNER AGENCY understand the risks and hazards inherent in acting within these duties and responsibilities, and will assume all risk of loss, damage, and injury, including death, in

Figure 4.5 (*Continued*)   Memorandum of Understanding.   *Continued*

connection to performing the duties and responsibilities outlined in this Memorandum of Understanding.

YOUR AGENCY and PARTNER AGENCY will not bring a suit, claim, action or charge against the other party arising from fulfilling the duties and responsibilities outlined in this Memorandum of Understanding.

Activation

This agreement may be activated only by _____.

_____	_____
(Printed name)	(Printed name)
_____	_____
(Signed name)	(Signed name)
_____	_____
(Title)	(Title)
_____	_____
(Agency name)	(Agency name)
_____	_____
(Date)	(Date)

Figure 4.5 (*Continued*)   Memorandum of Understanding.

self-manage? Where did they get their training? The answer is: everyday life experience.

The following list is a typology of the many faces of disaster volunteers. Remember that unaffiliated volunteers—with training, experience, and familiarity with your management protocols—may transition into being your affiliated volunteers, a vital resource to utilize year-round.

> *Agency-affiliated volunteers*: This volunteer is a registered volunteer with your agency and has passed your agency's standards, including a background check, training, and credentialing as well as gained a history of volunteer service with your agency.
> *Registered volunteer*: This individual may be registered with your agency by having filled out a volunteer application, but may not have taken any of your agency's training or gained a history of volunteer service with you.

Figure 4.6 Volunteer working in the aftermath of the California wildfires. (Photo credit: Kim Guevara.)

> *Partnering agency-affiliated volunteers*: An example of this would be volunteers who have been trained by groups that you know in your community, such as faith-based organizations, the Boy Scouts, Lions Clubs, CERT teams, and PTA members. Affiliated volunteers with disaster management training may include those who volunteer for groups like the Salvation Army, United Way, Habitat for Humanity, and Doctors without Borders.
>
> *Spontaneous unaffiliated community groups*: Many nonprofit groups do not have a disaster-related mission, but they will find themselves and their constituency emerging to help in some way in the event of a disaster. Such groups may include faith-based groups, professional and trade associations, and clubs such as Rotary, Lions Club, Boy Scouts, as well as businesses within your community.
>
> *Spontaneous unaffiliated community volunteers (SUCVs) or just-in-time volunteers*: This volunteer is a citizen in your community. These volunteers have knowledge of the area and have ties to their community. They may or may not have training or experience in emergency response. Most volunteers do, however, possess skills from their everyday life experience, job experience, or experience

due to their responsibilities in running a household, managing volunteer responsibilities, etc.

IDENTIFYING SUCV ROLES

After filling out the Role and Task portions of the ICS chart and reviewing who the spontaneous volunteers are, begin to identify where you have staff to fill positions, where you would use affiliated volunteers and what agencies they are coming from, and where you could utilize SUCVs. Think about what kind of training your volunteers would need to effectively and safely fulfill their task and roles. In some cases, volunteers can apply their everyday experience to the roles you expect them to fill; in other cases, they will need either your agency's training or the training of a partner agency. What this process will produce is a well-rounded plan that allows tiered levels of experience to be utilized in disaster response.

From research and recent experience, you may also consider the following factors in considering what roles SUCVs may fulfill in your agency's disaster response plan.

Survey Results

World Cares Center conducted a survey in 2008 in which emergency managers listed the potential tasks that SUCVs could fulfill in the event of an emergency. The emergency managers listed transportation (62 percent), emotional support (52 percent), and communication (47 percent) as an area where they would place SUCVs to help their agencies. Other potential roles that emergency managers identified included: assisting in sheltering, security, warehousing, paper trail and tracking, mass care, physical clean up, shoveling, waste removal, and telephone messaging.

In the area of community response, the Department of Homeland Security's "Heralding Unheard Voices" outlined the services community groups provided during disaster response. These groups essentially fulfilled the roles of volunteers during disaster response. The following list identifies ten major service areas of faith-based and nongovernmental organizations during disasters:

1. Sheltering services
2. Food services

Task	Staff	Affiliated volunteer	SUCV
Receptionist	Gap	Gap	Potential task
Inventory manager	Gap	Gap	Potential task
Security	Filled Our agency	Filled Our agency	NO

Figure 4.7 How gaps may identify SUCV tasks.

   3. Medical services
   4. Personal hygiene services
   5. Mental health and spiritual health services
   6. Physical reconstruction services
   7. Logistics management and services
   8. Transportation management and services
   9. Children's services
  10. Case management services

In some cases, the work identified in the previous list can last years into the long-term recovery of a community, such as in the case of the Oklahoma City bombing of the Alfred P. Murrah Federal Building; Hurricane Katrina in New Orleans; the Indian Ocean Tsunami; the earthquake in Sichuan, China; and the attacks of September 11, 2001.

Figure 4.7 presents an example for the subfunction of running a shelter. In this case, it is evident that gaps in staff and affiliated volunteers for the role of receptionist or taking inventory can be fulfilled by an SUCV. Meanwhile, the task of security is not given to an SUCV to handle.

Table 4.1 is a blank worksheet. List where you require staff to fill positions; where you would use affiliated volunteers; and what agencies they are coming from and where you could utilize SUCVs. In the section for affiliated volunteers, be sure to mark if it will be your affiliated volunteers or another agency's volunteers, and go as far as to write down the names of those whom you think you will be assigning to each position. This chart will be used to define your agency's protocols in utilizing volunteers in each role.

Table 4.1 Worksheet: Assigning Roles and Tasks within Your Agency

		Staff	Affiliated volunteer	SUCV
Role	_____	_____	_____	_____
Task	_____	_____	_____	_____
Task	_____	_____	_____	_____
Task	_____	_____	_____	_____
Task	_____	_____	_____	_____
Task	_____	_____	_____	_____
Task	_____	_____	_____	_____
Task	_____	_____	_____	_____
Task	_____	_____	_____	_____

Staff: Paid employees

Affiliated volunteers: Preregistered and pretrained volunteers with experience in their role through your agency or through a partner agency that you have agreed to work with

SUCVs: People who are new to your agency at the time that they first volunteer

Tailoring Your Plan for Different Phases of Disaster

It is important to keep all phases of the disaster in mind, as roles and tasks will shift as you move from immediate response phase to recovery. For example, as you think through the challenges and begin to formulate the benefits of integrating community members into response when they arrive "just in time" to help, think through the essential and immediate roles that you would want to engage volunteers for in the response phase, such as interpreters for communities where English is their second language, or faith-based or community-based leaders that would organize community members for evacuation in a culturally sensitive and timely way. Another example is that, in the response phase, your agency may utilize volunteers for shelter feeding operations and for reception in order to fulfill its role of running a shelter. However, later in the recovery phase, as your agency's role may shift to providing essential human and health services to assist your community in finding temporary housing or other needed support, those same volunteers may then be needed and redeployed to man phone lines and file records, and trained professionals in mental health may be utilized to provide counseling on a volunteer basis.

Tailoring Your Plan for Anticipated Hazards

How might an event that causes a mass convergence of the hungry at your location differ from one that requires delivery of food to the homebound? While this manual is primarily framed within an all-hazards approach, it is also important to evaluate the specific hazards and challenges that your agency and your community historically or currently face, so that you can best prepare for the roles that SUCVs may fulfill. When planning SUCV roles, keep in mind that the nature of the hazard may necessitate different roles for affiliated and spontaneous volunteers. Make a note on what additional roles and tasks you may need and how they differ with each disaster you have identified as potentially affecting your community.

For example, fulfilling the role of food and water services during a flood hazard and a bomb threat hazard may cause you to designate tasks differently. During a flood, food preparation and water distribution may be fulfilled by SUCVs. However, in the case of a bombing or another violent human-made hazard that would render a site a crime scene, the distribution of water and food may only be entrusted to trained affiliated volunteers or staff rather than given to SUCVs.

Review all your work in this section and, if needed, revise your roles and tasks for SUCVs in the worksheet in Table 4.1. Make sure to fill in all the new roles for SUCVs that may have come up from the research listed above. Review your agency's plans to ensure that you have covered all roles and needs with the needed level of human resources.

WEIGHING THE PROS AND CONS OF UTILIZING SUCVS

As with any plan, emergency managers should carefully consider the pros and cons of utilizing spontaneous volunteers in their disaster response efforts, and specifically for the roles and tasks they have designated for SUCVs. You may define general pros and cons that apply to all SUCV positions or you may choose to go into the details of each position that you are considering for SUCVs and see how the pros and cons differ for each potential role. Applied in this way, weighing the pros and cons for each position may help you to decide if you will ultimately assign an SUCV to the position. As an example, in all of the workshops held by World Cares

Center, participants found that the cons of utilizing SUCVs in child care far outweigh the pros and decided not to assign SUCVs to those positions.

Pros

The pros involved in utilizing SUCVs come from the fact that these individuals and groups are experts about the neighborhood or community you are protecting and responding in, and possess cultural competencies and language skills that will greatly increase the effectiveness of your work. This is especially important in the immediate aftermath of a disaster, when you may need interpreters to extend services to diverse groups who are affected in your community. Moreover, before a disaster strikes and in the preparedness phase, SUCVs among community-based and faith-based leaders and organizations may be far more effective in the role of evacuating and getting buy-in on preparedness initiatives than your own staff or affiliated volunteers.

For some roles that require specialization or expertise, SUCVs also have skills and resources from their work or other volunteer experiences. Delegating such roles to SUCVs affords official responders access to a pool of additional skills and resources they may not have had access to within their own organizational circle or the official responder community at hand. Internationally, examples of the way in which volunteers add value include the response to disasters such as the Sichuan Earthquake of 2008, which flattened thousands of schools. Volunteers arrived from all over China and around the world to rebuild the schools, including architects who submitted new, more structurally sound designs.

Utilizing spontaneous volunteers in tasks that require little specialization also saves money and time by allowing official responders to do more advanced work and implement more programs.

In terms of recovery, utilizing SUCVs in roles where they feel they are making a difference also leads to benefits for the community at large in terms of emotional recovery and healing from trauma, as citizens who volunteer may regain a sense of control and safety through connecting with others. These individuals are able to identify themselves as volunteers and survivors, not as victims, and continue to be part of long-term recovery efforts and beyond.

Considering the pros of effectively integrating spontaneous volunteers in roles and tasks will maximize your agency's ability to efficiently utilize the vast levels of experience and resources volunteers possess. The following checklist reviews what we have considered thus far.

- Local experts
- Cultural competency
- Language skills
- Specialized skills and resources from work or other experience
- Official responders capable of doing more advanced work
- Official responders capable of assisting community in healing and emotional recovery process
- Savings in money and time

Cons

The cons of utilizing spontaneous volunteers include

- Liability
- Physical and emotional concerns
- The potential lack of internal readiness within agencies

Liability

Risk is inevitable. But the risk of relying on volunteers can be mitigated by implementing best practices such as effective volunteer screening techniques, training and orientations to properly prepare volunteers, and good management procedures for proper supervision. Comprehensively identifying the risks and managing them proactively will address the uncertainty of relying on volunteers, and in some cases can significantly reduce potential risks.

As we touched upon in Chapter 2, Exploring the Unique Challenges of Today's Disaster Response, the risks of being sued are abundant. Weighing past experience with the likelihood that you may be sued and the coverage that is available to you are factors in choosing where to place any staff or volunteer. The risks include coverage for a volunteer who is injured while volunteering under your guidance and organizational authority as well as whether a client might be injured by the volunteer you have chosen.

The high liability involved in using SUCVs in certain roles may become apparent and appear to be too risky when utilizing someone who is untrained or uncertified in roles or tasks that require complete confidentiality, working with vulnerable populations or requiring highly specialized skills that make the difference between life and death.

In the previous section of this chapter, you have aligned volunteers with roles based on need, the lack of staff, and needed skill sets. Much of the matching between roles and SUCVs you will do based on common sense. However, these must be documented in a plan for others to follow. Knowing what coverage you may have for volunteers and for your agency, and developing additional screening techniques and protocols for these roles, will further expand or contract those roles and develop a robust set of requirements.

At every conference, in every workshop and in all the discussion and planning sessions I have been in, there is always the issue of liability. Liability should not only be addressed in the legal sense but also in the physical and emotional sense. As we drill down into the details, walking through the steps of developing your agency-specific SUCV plan, you will identify the emotional and legal liabilities that each role and task exposes. Thinking through these potential liabilities, you will have to weigh the odds of leaving certain responsibilities unfilled versus utilizing volunteers, including SUCvs, and protecting your agency adequately from the liabilities. Matching the appropriate role to the appropriate volunteer is the key.

We can see an increasing recognition in the legal arena that expanding liability protection to organizations that provide voluntary services during disaster is necessary. As of the first half of 2009, a total of 28 state jurisdictions (including the District of Columbia) have passed laws that provide liability protection for business and nonprofit entities that assist their governments during emergencies.* About half of these states had passed their laws since 2007, perhaps with the increasing recognition that emergencies such as the H1N1 Swine Flu pandemic and other disasters require an increased level of cooperation with volunteers and community groups.

Partial checklist of liability concerns:†

- Does the state have a statute that provides immunity from civil liability for emergency management workers or disaster workers?
- Does the state have a statute that provides workers' compensation benefits for disaster workers and volunteers who are injured, become ill, or are killed?

---

* University of North Carolina Chapel Hill, "Six States Pass Entity Emergency Liability Protection in 2009," Public-Private Legal Preparedness Initiative. http://nciph.sph.unc.edu/law/ud_070909.htm.

† Adapted from FEMA, "Citizen Corps Volunteer Liability Guide: An Overview of Legal Issues and Approaches to Address Liability for Emergency Volunteers."

- Are disaster volunteers extended the same rights and immunities as state and local government employees providing similar functions?
- Is a disaster worker or volunteer required to have a current in-state license, certification, or permit to qualify for liability protection?
- Is a disaster volunteer required to take a loyalty oath to qualify for protection or workers' compensation benefits?
- Are authorized disaster volunteers included in the definition of *disaster worker* for statutory liability protection?
- What registration or acceptance requirements must an emergency management volunteer meet to qualify for liability protection or workers' compensation?
- Does the state or local government or agency provide authorized emergency management workers with a legal defense and payment of judgment if they are sued for authorized activities?
- Are nongovernmental entities protected from liability, or is it limited to individuals?
- Are individuals and nongovernmental entities protected from liability even if they receive compensation?
- Are volunteers protected from liability during planning, training, exercises, drills, and other authorized preparedness activities, or only during declared emergencies? Are they eligible for workers' compensation during these activities?
- Does the scope of protection include natural hazard events, human-made disasters, and public health emergencies caused by bioterrorist events or natural pandemic illness?
- Is the liability protection that is provided broad (civil liability or liability) or narrow (bodily injury, death, and property damage)?
- Are any activities in which volunteers might engage excluded from protection (e.g., driving a car)?
- Does the state statute protect from liability individuals and entities that permit the use of their real or personal property in emergency preparedness and response activities?
- Does the state limit the protection provided to volunteers under the Volunteer Protection Act of 1997?
- Does the state have a volunteer protection statute that protects volunteers from liability when they are engaged in activities unrelated to a declared emergency?

- Does the state have a Good Samaritan law that provides immunity from liability for individuals who try to help someone having a health emergency in a setting where there is no ready access to professional care?
- Does the state's Good Samaritan law limit its protection to people with first aid/CPR training or licensed medical training, or does it extend to anyone?
- To what extent does any statutory protection exclude gross negligence, willful and wanton misconduct, or reckless disregard for the safety of others?
- Does any government, agency or other entity provide liability insurance that protects emergency or disaster volunteers?
- Does the government, agency, or other entity with which the emergency volunteers work have an insurance policy that pays health-care expenses or other benefits to those who are injured?
- If the local governments and agencies with which disaster volunteers are affiliated provide workers' compensation benefits, are they required to provide these benefits by state law, or is it optional?
- What licensing, certificate, and permit requirements apply to workers who are required in emergency management, such as licensed health-care workers, architects, engineers, and commercial and regular vehicle drivers?
- Does any state to which emergency volunteers are deployed waive license, certificate, and permit requirements for emergency workers from other states, including volunteers who are not part of their state's EMAC forces or recognize licenses, certificates, and permits issued in another state?
- Do the state's professional licensure statutes include provisions for issuing a special license to retired health-care workers who register as emergency management volunteers?
- Does the law of any state in which emergency volunteers may respond provide civil or criminal penalties for practicing without a required license?
- Has the governor of a state affected by a disaster placed any restrictions or limitations on the recognition of out-of-state licenses, certificates, or permits?
- Does your program have a legal advisor?

- Does your program manage the risk of using volunteers by having a volunteer application; by maintaining a screening, selection, and termination process; by providing training and orientation; by maintaining activation and deactivation records; by providing supervision for volunteer work; and by ensuring that volunteers understand and obey the limits of their authority?
- Are activation and deactivation procedures clear, so that volunteers know when they are protected and when they are not?

Emotional and Physical Concerns

There are many positive emotional aspects of volunteering, as we have discussed previously. Many of these positive aspects motivate individuals to volunteer. However there are many risks involved with volunteering that individuals may not be aware of. It is important to keep in mind the full impact that disasters will have on volunteers and, correspondingly, on your agency and your constituents. Accordingly, certain tasks in disaster response may be associated with very high emotional burdens or risks that would not be advisable to assign to an SUCV. As a manager, however, you can ensure that volunteers are equipped to handle the everyday stress load of volunteering through self-care techniques. We will learn techniques to mitigate the potential negative impact on volunteers through proactive management and self-care in later chapters.

Physical risks can also pose challenges and need to be kept in mind and researched before sending a volunteer into a situation where he or she can be harmed. All precautions need to be taken to ensure that volunteers have the proper knowledge and equipment to protect them at the site where they volunteer. You may find that SUCVs can be experts in the fields that you need, or know how to operate certain machines or equipment in a nondisaster setting, but you will need to find out their capacity in a disaster response setting "on the spot."

Another dimension of both emotional and physical concerns regards those who may volunteer after being disaster survivors themselves or after having undergone great personal loss. When working with both the leadership and individuals from within the affected community, it is important to recognize that there is no one that remains untouched by what has occurred, including yourself. It is important to note that many individuals that have been the victim of certain events or circumstances will seek to help others as a way of giving back and healing. The experiences and insight they have can be of great value. However, it is important to recognize that, for those who have not fully healed from their experiences, there is a likelihood that, in volunteering, they themselves may be retraumatized or may inflict further unintended emotional harm on those who are seeking help or risk physical harm to themselves.

The emotional and physical risks of being both a disaster survivor and a volunteer in the aftermath of a disaster should be carefully weighed before simply assigning volunteers to a task. If you enter a situation with that understanding, it may be easier to identify and handle certain situations, and be equipped to better match SUCVs to the roles and tasks that will be rewarding and helpful for both them and your agency in the long run. It should be noted that this is something that should be monitored for managers and leaders as well. How events affect different people is often unknown until you are in the middle of response. Those in leadership should take time to reflect on how they themselves are being affected and whether their ability to manage others has been compromised.

Internal Capabilities: Staffing

As an emergency manager, you may feel excited about the prospect of utilizing SUCVs in various roles and tasks. However, you must stop to consider your internal staffing capabilities and readiness to screen, train, and manage SUCVs. Part of internal readiness is to assess the culture of your organization, the protocols you have set in place, the town you function in, and all the partnering organizations you work with as well as the community you are serving.

Some common internal readiness concerns include

- Limited paid staff to manage SUCVs
- Limited affiliated volunteers to work alongside or mentor SUCVs
- Lack of time to create a spontaneous volunteer management plan
- Lack of time to exercise the plan
- Language barriers between staff and the diverse communities served
- Agency culture

Table 4.2 is an example worksheet showing the pros and cons of using SUCVs in two different tasks. In the blank worksheet in Table 4.3, inventory the positions that need to be filled and where you might fill them with spontaneous volunteers. Write down the pros and cons of using volunteers in certain roles and tasks in order to indentify who (staff, affiliated volunteer, unaffiliated volunteer) is most appropriate in what area

Table 4.2 Example of the Pros and Cons of Utilizing SUCVs

Task	SUCV	Pros	Cons
Receptionist	√	Able to get more information	Must monitor emotional well-being
Inventory manager	√	Able to locate more supplies	Need to find the time to train

and what measures need to be put in place to mitigate the cons. This will also help you decide where you will eliminate the use of SUCVs in a position altogether as the cons far outweigh the pros. As mentioned previously, considering the specific skill sets of SUCVs may help you to identify which urgent and immediate needs can be filled by SUCVs. These include interpreters from within the community and those with managerial skills that can immediately be utilized to help manage certain processes.

END-OF-CHAPTER QUESTIONS

Revisiting the unique challenges and considering the different hazards, the different types of volunteers, and the phases of disaster for which you will need volunteers:

- Do you have a clear understanding of the roles and tasks your agency will perform in disasters and emergencies down to the level of individual volunteers?
- Do you have an understanding of where volunteer resources may come from within the community?
- Have you clarified the agreements you have with partner agencies?
- Have you identified the pros and cons of utilizing spontaneous unaffiliated volunteers for each role and task you have designated for them?
- Have you reviewed all the information to make a decision on where you will place SUCVs and where you will not?

CONCLUSION

By now you should have

- Charted the roles and corresponding tasks necessary to complete the agency's mission
- Identified (a) the gaps in fulfilling these roles and tasks and (b) where SUCVs can fill those gaps
- Identified the pros and cons of utilizing SUCVs as they relate to the roles and tasks required
- Identified urgent positions that should be filled immediately

Assessing internal readiness has taken you from identifying the roles your agency fulfills in disaster response to identifying what roles and tasks SUCVs may take on and then weighing the pros and cons of utilizing SUCVs in these positions. The next steps will help you to develop protocols within your volunteer management plan to guide you in screening and managing volunteers in the positions you have selected for them.

5

Protocols for SUCV Management

By utilizing this guide to learn how to best utilize spontaneous unaffiliated community volunteers we will all be better prepared to address
this issue and maximize the value that these volunteers contribute to
response and recovery efforts.

Howard Butt
New Jersey State Police, State CERT Coordinator

IN THIS CHAPTER

- Internal Protocols
  - Designate Oversight and Span of Control
  - Agency Responsibilities
  - Developing Protocols for Volunteers to Follow
  - Volunteer Responsibilities
- External Protocols
  - Choosing Disqualifiers
  - Core Attributes

The unique challenges that emergency managers face in setting protocols
for filling internal capacity needs, communication, integrating the diverse
demographics of their community, and addressing liability concerns are
among the issues that this chapter will help to address. This chapter takes
you through the steps of defining and designing the essential protocols
for managing and communicating the defined roles and tasks that you
would designate for SUCVs. These protocols will put processes in place

that are easily transferable from one situation to another and used by all levels of your team, from managers to volunteers.

This chapter provides templates to document the protocols you develop, and these will facilitate consistent processes that assist you in communicating these protocols to your staff and volunteers. By utilizing and adapting these templates, you will have the first draft of the internal-procedures section for your management plan for spontaneous unaffiliated community volunteers (SUCVs).

A *volunteer packet* that contains:
- Volunteer job description
- Agency flyer of volunteer roles at your agency
- Volunteer application
- Volunteer self-assessment
- Site description
- Daily post-shift log

Internal protocols for SUCV management:
- Summary of internal protocols for all SUCV positions
- Protocols for each SUCV role/task
- Catalog of resources
- After-action report

Protocols are the organizational standards, rules, and regulations for your staff, volunteers, and new unaffiliated volunteers to follow. There are internal protocols on what is expected from your agency and staff, while external protocols will determine what you are looking for from others who are seeking to associate with you through volunteering.

Developing protocols will involve a certain amount of risk assessment, which will involve weighing the outcomes of your decisions. In this type of risk assessment, an emergency manager would have to weigh the risk versus benefit of placing a spontaneous volunteer in a position, knowing that the volunteer may make mistakes versus the option of having a client not get any service at all. Development of specific protocols for the correct placement and management of these volunteers is essential in developing an effective screening process as well as a management structure built on the decisions you make. Ultimately, these processes, when thought through and implemented, should reduce the risk and the liability associated with management of spontaneous volunteers. In this chapter, we will provide examples of the risks and benefits in relationship to placement of volunteers, oversight, shift length, and other details that should be considered in the course of managing volunteers in a disaster.

INTERNAL PROTOCOLS

Internal protocols are focused on the inner workings of your agency with regard to your staff capabilities, your mission, and the roles and tasks that SUCVs can fill. Here we will dig into the development of the protocols and procedures that will help mitigate and manage the uncertainty of engaging new individuals as just-in-time volunteers in the roles that you have chosen for them in Chapter 4.

Designate Oversight

Start with designating oversight for each of the roles and tasks performed by your agency. A good management and visual tool is the Incident Command System (ICS) chart.

Issues to consider:

1. What staff is trained to provide oversight to the management teams?
2. What level of experience is necessary for managers of volunteers, i.e., staff or affiliated volunteers?
3. How many people can one person manage? This is referred to as *span of control*, which will be detailed further below.

Review all of the roles and tasks for SUCVs and see if your decisions change for any of them.

Figure 5.1 is an example utilizing the ICS chart for the assignment of a supervisor to manage each role and the affiliated and unaffiliated volunteers conducting the tasks.

Span of Control

Span of control defines how many

- Affiliated volunteers each of your staff can effectively manage
- SUCVs each of your staff can effectively manage
- Spontaneous volunteers each of your affiliated volunteers can effectively manage

By creating a team style of management, you can further leverage the experience your affiliated volunteers have to manage the SUCVs. Another tip we mentioned in the previous chapter is to look for essential skills to fill immediate roles in your management team. As these new volunteers

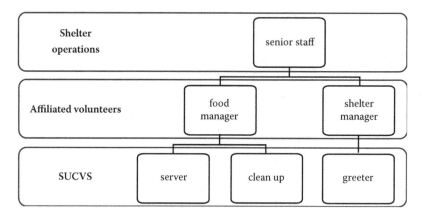

Figure 5.1 ICS for designating oversight of shelter operations.

begin to show their effectiveness, managers should mentor them through the process of taking on more responsibility, alleviating some of the burden from the original core management team and expanding its capacity. As you can see in the examples (Tables 5.1 and 5.2), your span of control will vary, depending on the task. For the task of registration, there may be one staff for five to six SUCVs working on registration. For the task of childcare, the staff may only supervise three affiliated volunteers each, not five to six SUCVs. For now, an effective span of control may vary from

Table 5.1 Example of Span of Control

Task: Registration	☐ Staff _____
	☐ Affiliated Volunteer _____
	☑ SUCV __5–6__
Supervision	☑ 1 Staff to __5–6 SUCVs__
	☑ 1 Affiliated Volunteer to __5 SUCVs__
	Teaming

Table 5.2 Example of Span of Control

Task: Childcare	☑ Staff __2__
	☑ Affiliated Volunteer __6__
	☐ SUCV _____
Supervision	☑ 1 Staff to 3 Affiliated Volunteers
	☐ Affiliated to Volunteer

100

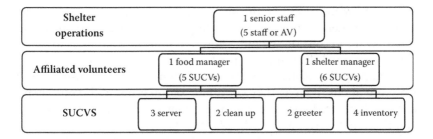

Figure 5.2 ICS showing span of control for shelter operations.

three to seven. However, a ratio of one supervisor to five reporting personnel or volunteers is recommended.

Figure 5.2 shows the span of control laid out within the ICS chart. The Food Manager can oversee five SUCVs, while the Shelter Manager oversees six SUCVs in different tasks.

Agency Responsibilities

Establish your agency's policies as they apply to your responsibilities to all SUCVs. What is your agency required to carry out as a responsibility to the volunteer, and what benefits will you be providing to them? These may depend on the role of the volunteer and whether they are affiliated with another group that is providing benefits. For instance, if you are engaging a volunteer who is given permission to volunteer with you through their workplace, the company's worker compensation policies may cover that volunteer's liability. You should consider whether you will offer

- Credentialing
- Training
- Special equipment you will provide for them, if any, and policies on returning the equipment
- Meals during shifts
- Shelter if at a remote location
- Reimbursement for travel or any expenses
- Supportive services such as mental health counseling
- Medical coverage such as workers' compensation
- Other types of access to benefits or opportunities

For some roles, you may also want to consider whether your agency is responsible for going beyond basic spot training and providing advanced

101

training opportunities to volunteers so that they can fulfill their duties to the best of their abilities and according to your needs. For other roles, you may want to consider whether you will require volunteers to be pre-certified or trained. Training is a great way to ensure that your volunteers are conducting themselves as you intend them to do, and also a way to learn more about them as they continue volunteering with your agency. The conditions on the site for volunteers may be contained within a site description that comes with each volunteer packet.

Beyond the communication and documentation of policies that takes place before an event, it is also important to keep a record of daily events, evaluate the larger response effort, and keep track of partners and resources in case of a future occurrence and to incorporate into your management and response plans.

The *after-action review* is imperative for managers to share lessons learned by documenting what went right and what could be improved and prevented in future response efforts. The after-action review is a full detailed report filled out by the manager or ICS commander that can be provided after the event to your agency as a record and analysis of efforts, which can include

- Event summary
- Response overview
- Agency's goals and objectives
- Response synopsis
- Analysis of response outcomes
- Analysis of role and task performance
  Role description
  Task description
  References
  Summary
  Consequence
  Analysis
  Recommendation
  Improvement action
- Conclusion

Catalogue Your Resources
In addition to the after-action reports, it is also good practice to note the agencies, groups, vendors, donors, and services that were helpful to you

during response and recovery. Before, during, and after an event, keep a comprehensive catalog of contacts and resources that you have been utilizing, which will come in handy during future response-and-recovery efforts. If they are public resources, post them where they are accessible to all. You may also create a database to log these resources and have them readily available to all volunteers and staff.

Follow Up with Volunteers

A good protocol to put in place within your volunteer management plan is following up with your volunteers after their time with you. Sending letters of appreciation that acknowledge their contributions, conducting a volunteer celebration that publicly honors their efforts, and sending information on any supportive services that you might offer to volunteers are all ways to do this. Conducting meetings to discuss their experiences with other volunteers or conducting exit interviews with you or their supervisors would be helpful for your after-action report and for the volunteer to express concerns or suggestions. After volunteering with you during an intense and demanding disaster-response mission, giving individuals an opportunity to reconnect with others they volunteered with gives them a chance to reflect, discuss issues with peers, and put their experiences in perspective.

Developing Protocols for Volunteers to Follow

In addition to protocols for those who will be managing SUCVs, it is critical to develop protocols for volunteers to follow. Other issues to be addressed and agreed upon between both the emergency manager and the volunteer are listed below. It will be the responsibility of the agency to create these guidelines. In each case, we give you an example that can be followed or modified for your specific agency needs.

- Length of shift
- Length of volunteer commitment
- Pre-shift and post-shift briefing
- After-action notes
- Code of conduct
- Confidentiality agreement
- Self-care
- Family-preparedness plan

Length of Shift

Establishing the length of a volunteer shift as it relates to each task should be documented in your manual and enforced for both staff and volunteer. The most common shift is an eight-hour shift with an hour break for lunch and two fifteen-minute or half-hour breaks. The U.S. Department of Labor, Occupational Safety and Health Administration (OSHA) considers anything in excess of an eight-hour shift without eight hours of rest in between and exceeding forty hours of work in a week to be "extended or unusual work shifts," which are often required during disaster response.

Extended or unusual work shifts may be more stressful physically, mentally, and emotionally. Nontraditional shifts and extended work hours may disrupt the body's regular schedule, leading to increased fatigue, stress, and lack of concentration. These effects lead to an increased risk of operator error, injuries, or accidents.*

As much as possible, a manager should maintain healthy shifts and breaks for their teams. If excessive shifts are required, adjustments should be made to reduce the continuous hours and days worked. The breaks are an important part of maintaining the well-being of your team; they give individuals time away from their task to reflect on what is happening and, if used properly, to recharge their batteries. Everyone should be encouraged to stick to the length of their shifts and to take their breaks while conducting the healthy habits we will review in Chapter 9, "Building a Resilient Team."

Length of Volunteer Commitment

The length of volunteer commitment refers to the actual number of days, weeks, or months that you are establishing to perform a role that you and a volunteer have agreed upon. When managing spontaneous volunteers or any volunteer who is new to you, a good practice is to limit the length of a commitment to a trial period (such as one or two weeks) with a "check in" at the end to see how both the volunteers feel about their role and how you as the manager think they fit. By setting this expectation up front, you have given yourself and your team the room to assess the volunteers, adjust their roles, or in extreme cases, dismiss them altogether without singling them out.

By explaining this process up front and making it a standard for all new volunteers, you will limit the negative response you may get from a volunteer. Doing so also helps the volunteers to be prepared to have their

---

* OSHA. "Frequently Asked Questions: Extended Unusual Work Shifts." http://www .osha.gov/OshDoc /data_Hurricane_Facts /faq_longhou rs.html.

roles and performances assessed as it relates to the ever-changing needs of disaster response work. You may find that, after a week, a volunteer may self-select another role that is more appropriate or decide that he or she is not cut out for disaster volunteering. By agreeing upon a short trial period, this gives the volunteer a time and opportunity to have this discussion with the manager, thereby reducing unexpected attrition or disqualifying behavior like the "lone ranger" behavior that we will discuss later in this chapter.

Briefings and Debriefings

Volunteers should be required to attend briefings and debriefings with their supervisor and their fellow team members (see Figure 5.3). Staff who manage volunteers will use this time to inform volunteers of changes in condition, updates on the status of disaster response, as well as any updates or changes to the role of the volunteer. Volunteers can utilize this time to inform their manager of daily events, tasks completed, questions, concerns, or comments, as well as issues that need to be addressed. We will continue to discuss the importance and role of briefing and debriefing in spontaneous volunteer management in the following chapters.

Post-Shift Reports

Volunteers should be asked to keep a simple log of what tasks they completed, along with what worked and what needed improvement. In the immediate aftermath of disaster, at a time when people might find it difficult to communicate on a regular or structured basis, you might want to have volunteers jot notes and comments down after each shift. But as response shifts to a structured and more regular routine, you might change this requirement to a weekly report or end-of-term briefing. Table 5.3 is a sample form that could capture this post-shift report.

In addition, volunteers may also be requested or required to give an evaluation at the end of their service with you in a modified form of the after-action report discussed previously in the Agency Responsibilities section of this chapter.

Code of Conduct

The code of conduct is an important agreement that will establish the basic expectations and boundaries for appropriate volunteer behavior and ethics. Establishing this code of conduct for volunteers and clearly communicating your expectations that they follow this code is a proactive step to minimizing the liability involved in utilizing spontaneous volunteers.

Figure 5.3 Participants, including Lisa Orloff, World Cares Center executive director, attending a briefing at Strong Angel III, an integrated disaster response demonstration in San Diego, 2006. (Source: Lisa Orloff)

Table 5.3 Post-shift Report

Date: _____ Shift: _____

Agency: _____ Location: _____

Volunteer name: _____ Contact info: _____

Supervisor: _____

Tasks	What worked	What needs improvement	Responsible team	Follow-up actions
_____	_____	_____	_____	_____
_____	_____	_____	_____	_____

You may already have a code of conduct in your agency that you will require volunteers to adhere to. If you would like to develop one that is specific to disaster response or to disaster volunteers that work with your agency, you can consider the following.

One example of a basic code of conduct can be found in a modified Hippocratic oath to share with your volunteers. Some organizations have taken this approach, such as the National Organization for Victim Assistance and the United Nations. The following list is a modified version you may want to adapt:

1. Respect the privacy of those we serve.
2. Tread carefully on matters of life and death. (This can be interpreted as being careful not to extend your personal opinion on these matters or sharing religious views that may not be appropriate to impose on others.)
3. Be responsible with your volunteer duties.
4. Remain humble and aware of your own frailty.
5. Above all, do not play God. (This can be interpreted as remaining humble, flexible, and open-minded to allow other people's opinions and contributions to make a difference.)

The code of conduct may also include behaviors that are absolutely forbidden or would require you as an agency to relieve the volunteer of his or her duties. These could pertain to inappropriate behavior, substance abuse, and use of profanity or illicit materials while volunteering. We will address more of these disqualifying features in the discussion of external protocols.

Confidentiality Agreement
A confidentiality agreement can answer some of your concerns regarding the sharing of information, whether it be through traditional means or via the new social media platforms of Web 2.0. In your agency's confidentiality agreement, you will want to include a full description of what materials are considered confidential. The agreement should specify that volunteers will only use these materials in connection with activities on behalf of your agency, and require them to hold them in strict confidence and take all necessary precautions to ensure that they remain confidential. The agreement should also stipulate the instances when the volunteers may disclose the confidential materials, such as with prior written consent by the agency or when required by law, supervisory authority, or a governmental or judicial order. The agreement should also specify that

materials should not be reproduced or copied by volunteers without prior written consent from your agency.

Self-Care

Self-care is a vital part of your volunteer management program and can be easily overlooked in disaster-response situations by volunteers and managers alike. Therefore, your internal protocols should ensure having guidelines for volunteers about self-care both on the job as a volunteer and at home. We will delve more deeply into this as a set of techniques and tools in Chapter 8.

Family Preparedness

Beyond the specific roles or tasks that volunteers are expected to complete within your organization, you can also make clear to them that their responsibilities do include ensuring that they themselves have fulfilled their responsibilities at home before volunteering, including ensuring that they themselves have individual or family preparedness plans to guarantee their own household's safety.

It has been shown that it is hard for volunteers and official responders to do the work needed in disaster response if their loved ones are not taken care of. Lack of preparation could even result in volunteers and responders walking away from the job to tend to emergencies at home. Therefore, even if you yourself or your volunteers are trained in disaster response and emergencies, it does not mean that their loved ones know what to do, even if it is the subject of conversation at home.

A basic family preparedness plan may include:*

1. *Family supply kit*: A three-day supply of items to sustain all the individuals of one's family, which may include nonperishable foods and water, flashlights, first aid kit, personal sanitation items, batteries, lights, power generators, severe weather alert device, prescription medications, cash, clothing, shoes, maps, can opener, copies of important personal documents, and "comfort items" such as books and games. It is recommended that these supplies include items required for members of the family who have special needs, such as young children or the elderly.
2. *Pet supply kit*: Pets are often forgotten in times of disaster. The kit for family pets should similarly ensure enough supplies for a three-day period, and include food and water for that period,

---

* Adapted from World Cares Center's Grassroots Readiness and Response training series.

the pet's registration and other information, pet carrier, sanitation supplies, and their favorite toys or bedding.

3. *Call tree*: Because phone lines may be down or quickly become overwhelmed, a call tree organizes the order in which you will call and notify your loved ones in the event of an emergency. It activates a chain of phone calls or notifications that each person in the call tree will be responsible for making.

4. *Home evacuation plan*: This involves marking all exits in every room of one's home, designating and visiting the location where the family will regroup outside of the residence, determining who will assist those with special needs or limited mobility, smoke escape masks, having fire escape ladders if living above the ground floor, and having at least three mapped-out routes for leaving the area and even the region if necessary, whether by public or private transportation. For those living in apartments, knowing the building's evacuation plan and the building's exits and fire alarms is crucial.

5. *Shelter-in-place plan*: Sometimes, instead of evacuating, it is best to stay where one is and create a barrier between oneself and potentially contaminated air. In creating this plan, one must designate a room with as few windows and doors as possible, and make plans for how to seal the room, including turning off all ventilation systems and ensuring that there is some means of staying connected to announcements and news, such as with a hand-cranked radio, to know when it is safe to leave.

Additional resources can be found at www.ready.gov.

Volunteer Responsibilities

By developing protocols that volunteers must follow, you and your team will be better able to communicate volunteer responsibilities and give resources on fulfilling these responsibilities with your volunteers in a consistent manner. Outlining essential volunteer responsibilities is another important internal protocol for staff who will manage SUCVs. What basic standards and tasks do you expect all volunteers to adhere to? What privileges and access are afforded to all SUCVs that they should be aware of? You might want to define the general expectations for all SUCVs, regardless of their role or task, and then go into the details for each.

Volunteer responsibilities should therefore include

- Agreement to fulfill assigned role/task
- Agreement to shift and length of commitment
- Briefing, debriefing, and post-shift report
- Respect for the chain of command
- Adherence to the code of conduct
- Confidentiality
- Self-care
- Family preparedness

The internal protocols you have developed must be translated into terms for the volunteer to follow. It is highly recommended that you share these protocols in a volunteer packet from the beginning as volunteers or even candidates seeking to volunteer with you arrive at your agency. You can include general protocols for all volunteers within their volunteer job description. The protocols such as the code of conduct and the confidentiality agreement will set the general guidelines and expectations for all volunteers to follow. Protocols should outline the role or task to be completed, the length of shift, the length of volunteer commitment, and the chain of command for the volunteer to adhere to. Self-care and family preparedness guidelines and spot trainings should be shared with the volunteer at the beginning of their time with you—not only in the volunteer packet, but preferably within an orientation or just-in-time volunteer training.

EXTERNAL PROTOCOLS

Choosing Disqualifiers

External protocols define what you are looking for in your volunteers. Without this information, it would be impossible to screen, assess, select, and manage volunteers properly. Start by identifying your disqualifiers, or the traits that would make a person unqualified to volunteer for your organization. After this, we will move on to the more positive aspect of identifying core attributes (or innate qualities) that are essential to any volunteer you would want working with your agency.

What are the disqualifying qualities that would deter you from choosing a prospective volunteer for any position within your agency? After choosing the general disqualifiers, you can then begin to narrow them down for the specific roles and tasks that you have designated for volunteers. You may also find this process helpful for affiliated volunteers and staff. The disqualifiers are as diverse as the many different organizations that are serving the community. Some of the results of our workshops have resulted in the following compilation of disqualifiers, which may help you to start your list:

- Convicted felons
- Sex offenders
- Those with extensive mental illness
- Individuals who cannot transport themselves to various locations
- Individuals with addictions
- Predators
- Opportunists
- Overt   sexist, racist, homophobic, or otherwise discriminatory tendencies that would prevent them from maintaining professionalism

Additional behaviors that would deem a dismissal (also termed "two strike" disqualifiers once those qualities are exhibited by the volunteer) are:

- No-shows
- Those who are excessively late or miss shifts
- Overzealous volunteers who take on too much or get involved where they are not needed
- The "lone ranger," i.e., someone who is assigned a task but prefers to self-assign himself or herself to a task that may be of more interest to him or her without consulting a supervisor
- Volunteers who disappear for an unreasonable length of time and cannot tell you where they were or what they have been doing

In the blank worksheet in Table 5.4, you may list the SUCV roles/tasks and the disqualifiers that pertain to each.

Core Attributes

In contrast and as a complement to defining volunteer disqualifiers, here we will look into the core attributes of a volunteer that are considered to be the basic requirements for any disaster volunteer. Core attributes differ from skills that can be taught; they transcend any role or task and focus on the essential demeanor of the volunteer. Whether perky or laid back, verbose or shy, there are three core attributes all disaster volunteers should possess. Why three? Because it is rare that you can get everything you want in one volunteer, and in a critical moment where you have limited time and resources to screen people, you want to make sure that they

Table 5.4 Worksheet: Disqualifier Chart

Role/task	Disqualifiers (please list)

have the most essential attributes. These are not quickly learned skills, but qualities that people are either born with or have acquired over time. You certainly cannot teach them these core attributes in the compressed time frame you have in the immediate aftermath of a disaster.

The first core attribute is the ability to *stay grounded*. The ability to stay calm and focused decreases stress levels and anxiety, and enforces one's ability to remain focused on the task. Staying grounded provides a calming effect, which in a disaster may be lacking. Individuals who are grounded do not get flustered easily and have the ability to address issues that come up with thoughtful consideration, often reflecting on several options before deciding on the best approach to take.

This brings us to our second core attribute. Someone who is grounded is more likely to be an *effective listener*. The traits of an effective listener are: someone who listens patiently as he or she engages with someone, does not interrupt, and has the ability to hear and understand the point that the speaker is trying to make without blurring their conclusions with their own feelings on the subject. You will often hear someone who is practicing effective listening use reflective listening techniques, repeating the speaker's story back to them using their own words. For instance you may say "I am so upset that I could punch someone," and the reflective listener would say, "I am hearing that you are angry." Other traits of an effective or reflective listener are someone who makes good eye contact while engaged in conversation with someone and retains a calm and neutral body posture, without fidgeting or making distracting movements.

Even when placing volunteers in a position that may not require them to interact with other individuals, the stronger one's ability to effectively

112

Table 5.5 Worksheet: Core Attributes of a Disaster Volunteer

Role/task	Core attributes

listen, the better chance that they will hear their instructions, thereby showing better odds to complete their tasks successfully and in the manner you intended.

The third and last core attribute is the *ability to show empathy*. Someone who is empathetic has the ability to identify with and understand other people's situations, feelings, and motives. In a disaster environment, empathy is very important, not only in relationships and interactions with victims and survivors, but also with peers and supervisors. There are a limited few who are not affected by being in a disaster situation, including even the responders and volunteers themselves, and an empathetic volunteer is more likely to understand the demands of the situation and work with you as a team member. The traits of empathetic individuals mirror those of someone who is grounded and is a good listener. Such individuals are more likely to focus on the needs of the people they are there to help or on the task they need to accomplish. In the worksheet in Table 5.5, list as many of the core attributes that you seek in a disaster volunteer as you can.

Additional Attributes: Workshop Feedback

Throughout our national workshops, emergency managers have added to the list of core attributes that they look for in their volunteers:

- Awareness of self and others
- Cultural understanding of the community they are serving
- The ability to take care of themselves emotionally
- Compassion

Table 5.6   Example of a Summary of Internal Protocols for all SUCVs

We use SUCVs for:
- Reception
- Administrative work
- Delivery
- Warehousing

Must be supervised by affiliated volunteer or staff

We do not use SUCVs for:
- Child care
- Medical care
- Security

Must be supervised by staff

- Patience
- Humility

Discussions ensued around stories of volunteers who were PhDs or CEOs in their daily lives yet who gladly took it upon themselves to clean the toilets when needed. Other less-than-encouraging stories were about those volunteers who were inflexible and demanded a different task than the one assigned and would not bend to accommodate the situation at hand.

With so little time to fulfill critical needs, you may have less time to mitigate the effects of a rigid or inflexible volunteer. Setting these core attribute as standards up front may deter the inflexible or arrogant individual from volunteering and allow you to screen for a good team. This process may then assist you in establishing a *summary of internal protocols for SUCV positions* in the manner listed in Figure 5.4.

Moreover, the complete internal and external protocols may be communicated and screened for within two forms that volunteers must complete for your agency: a volunteer application and a volunteer self-assessment, as shown in Figures 5.5 and 5.7.

Volunteer Application

You may already be familiar with volunteer applications and have one for your agency. However, it would be advisable to review the protocols you have established and update the application for a disaster-response scenario, as interested community members may converge at your agency and need to be screened quickly. In this case, the volunteer application should

TEMPLATE

SUMMARY of Internal Protocols for ALL SUCV positions

SUCVs can be utilized in the following categories in the following positions
Sub-function
Role:_____
Role: _____
Role: _____
Role: _____
Sub-function
Role:_____
Role: _____
Role: _____
Role: _____
Sub-function
Role:_____
Role::_____
Role: _____
Role: _____

We do not use SUCVs for
1.
2.
3.
General attributes and disqualifiers related to all positions:
General guideline of supervision for all SUCVs
Code of conduct:
All SUCVs must be treated equally to all others
An SUCV may be disqualified immediately for:
All SUCVs are responsible for:
SUCVs will not have the same access and responsibilities as:
All SUCVs should be allowed the opportunity to:
☐ Confidentiality agreement signed by volunteer
☐ Code of conduct signed by volunteer
☐ Self-care guidelines shared with volunteer
☐ Family preparedness training and guidelines offered to volunteer

Figure 5.4 Template: Summary of internal protocols for all SUCV positions.

Protocols for each SUCV Role/Task

FOR INTERNAL DISTRIBUTION ONLY

Sub-function:	
Emergency support function supported:	
Position:	
Position description:	
Number of SUCVs needed:	
Supervision: ___ ☐ Staff ☐ Affiliated volunteer ☐ SUCV	

Disqualifiers

Immediate:	Two Strikes
☐ Criminal record	☐ No show
☐ Mental illness	☐ Lone ranger
☐ Substance abuse record	☐ Refuses supervision
☐ No transportation	☐ Overzealous
☐ Limited physica ability	☐ Others:_____
☐ Others:_____	

Attributes

☐ Humble	☐ Compassionate
☐ Grounded	☐ Aware of self and other
☐ Effective listener	☐ Other:_____
☐ Culturally sensitive	

Specific Skills	*List here*
Qualifications:	☐ Licensed in _Expiration: ☐ Credentials_____Expiration: ☐ Other_____
Experience	
Equipment	
Debriefing	☐ Before shift ☐ End of shift
Length of shift	☐ 4 hours ☐ 6 hours ☐ 8 hours
Training provided	
Breaks	Every ☐ 2 hours ☐ 4 hours
Meals	Every ☐ 4 hours at _____ (time)

Figure 5.5 Template: Protocols for each SUCV role/task.   *Continued*

Agency Protocols Cont'd

Length of commitment	_____ Weeks
	☐ Option to renew
	☐ NO renewals

Volunteer responsibilities	☐ Responsibilities at home/work
	☐ Fulfilling delegated responsibilities
	☐ Schedule, shift, hours committed or required
	☐ Length of time commitment
	☐ Self care
	☐ Others: _____

Agency responsibilities	☐ Orientation	☐ Shift brief/debrief
	☐ Training	☐ Shelter
	☐ Reimbursement of expenses	☐ Insurance
	☐ Medical Coverage	☐ Food
	☐ Supplies	☐ Others:_____

Informational tools	☐ Volunteer role/task summary
	☐ Volunteer self-assessment
	☐ Volunteer self-care guidelines
	☐ Site description
	☐ Agency Incident Command System (ICS)

Liability	☐ Validate
	☐ Credential
	☐ Agency's insurance policy
	☐ Volunteer release form

Figure 5.5 (*Continued*)   Template: Protocols for each SUCV role/task.

be brief enough to be filled out in a reasonable amount of time, such as 10 minutes, but also detailed enough to gather the essential information you need. Beyond the applicant's contact information and emergency contact information, the application should contain questions regarding some of your immediate disqualifiers, such as a felony record. It can also contain questions about the candidate's strengths, credentials, and skills, which will help you place the volunteer in the positions that you are seeking to fill and that are most appropriate for them. This application can be posted online, or volunteers can come into your agency to fill out either predisaster or during the response phase. In addition, you can place copies of this in your disaster-response GO bag, so that wherever and whenever, you can be ready to take down essential volunteer information.

Volunteer Self-Assessment
Figure 5.6 is another initial screening tool that can ensure that interested volunteers are aware of and have taken care of their own essential responsibilities at home (as outlined in your self-care guidelines and family preparedness training), as well as understand the basic expectations and demands of volunteering at your agency as contained within your code of conduct and your confidentiality agreement. The questions may range from their time availability to their assessment of their listening skills, their time management skills, and the roles that they themselves are interested in.

In doing so, you can begin to list the skills that you would also like to see your volunteer have as well as the specific qualifications or experience with equipment or certain populations that you are seeking. If you would like to recruit volunteers in the predisaster phase, you can do so by creating various informational outreach tools, such as an agency outreach flyer or a specific job description flyer.

A site assessment template (Figure 5.7) is a tool that allows volunteers to better understand the conditions under which they will be working. This can be a template that is filled in each day as weather and circumstances change.

Agency Outreach Flyer
Figure 5.8 lists basic information about your organization and lists all the volunteer positions that you have available, along with the necessary basic requirements or qualities you seek in volunteers in your organization. This can be put on your home page or distributed via mail or e-mail to prospective volunteers.

Volunteer Self-Assessment
FOR EXTERNAL DISRTIBUTION

Please fill out in order to assess your readiness to volunteer.

1. Do my work/familial responsibilities leave time and energy to volunteer?

    ☐ Yes   ☐ No

2. Are my family responsibilities taken care of and my home secured?

    ☐ Yes   ☐ No

3. Does my family support my volunteer responsibilities?

    ☐ Yes   ☐ No

4. Do I feel confident I can manage the risks?

    ☐ Yes   ☐ No

5. Am I a good listener and a clear communicator?

    ☐ Yes   ☐ No

6. Do I have the personal discipline to practice effective self-care?

    ☐ Yes   ☐ No

7. Do I deal well when working in stressful conditions?

    ☐ Yes   ☐ No

8. Do I have the personal discipline to be punctual and to manage time well?

    ☐ Yes   ☐ No

9. Will I be comfortable and collegial working with people who are of different socio-economic backgrounds than me?

    ☐ Yes   ☐ No

10. What role(s) am I interested in and do they fit my skills?

11. What role(s) wouldn't I want and how will I feel if I'm asked to assume that role?

Figure 5.6   Template: Volunteer self-assessment.

TEMPLATE
Site Description
FOR EXTERNAL DISTRIBUTION

Location:
Date/time:
Site supervisor:
Contact info:
Site description:
☐ **Area map: (Attach)**　☐ **Directions**

Hazardous conditions:	Weather conditions:	Environmental conditions:
☐ Falling debris		
☐ Fire	☐ Sunny	☐ Mountainous
☐ Flooding	☐ Cloudy	☐ Forest
☐ Infected waters	☐ Slight rain	☐ Urban
☐ Other	☐ Heavy rains	☐ Suburban
	☐ Heavy winds	☐ City
	☐ Snow	☐ Country
		☐ Other:
	Daytime temp _____	
	Evening temp _____	_____

Location Requirements & Limitations
- ☐ Limited cell phone coverage
- ☐ No internet connectivity
- ☐ Food Provided
- ☐ Food not provided, bring your own
- ☐ Shelter provided, bring your onw sleeping bag, etc....
- ☐ Shelter (not provided) make own arrangements
- ☐ Safety gear provided: _____
- ☐ Safety gear: bring your own: _____
- ☐ Recommended clothing: _____

Figure 5.7　Template: Site description.

TEMPLATE

Agency Outreach Flyer
FOR EXTERNAL DISTRIBUTION

Organization name: _____

Address: _____

Contact person: _____

Phone number: _____

E-mail address: _____

Website: _____

Twitter: _____

Background
information: _____
Mission: _____

Open volunteer opportunities:

    Sub-function: _____
    Volunteer Position 1. _____
                  2. _____
                  3. _____

    Sub-function: _____
    Volunteer Position 1. _____
                  2. _____
                  3. _____

    Sub-function: _____
    Volunteer position: 1. _____
                  2. _____
                  3. _____

    Sub-function: _____
    Volunteer position: 1. _____
                  2. _____
                  3. _____

Figure 5.8 Template: Agency outreach flyer.   *Continued*

TEMPLATE
Job Description an SUVC Position
FOR PUBLIC OUTREACH

World Cares Center

Collaborate, Prepare, Recover

World Cares Center works within communities to foster sustainable, locally-led disaster preparedness, response and recovery initiatives.

Name:
Contact info:

Position: Community Trainer
Qualifications (possesses one or more of the following): comfortable in public speaking*, interpersonal skills training or teaching experience, able to travel in the greater New York City Metropolitan Area, detail-oriented, bi-lingual a plus.
*These may be considered attributes rather than skills!

Job summary: As a community trainer, you will be facilitating World Cares Center's Grassroots Readiness and Response training program,which includes Disaster Volunteering I, II, and III. This program addresses comprehensive disaster and emergency preparedness as it pertains to the specific needs of the community. As a representative of World Cares Center, it is important that you are culturally sensitive to th needs of the community as we work with all different constituencies. As the trainer you may also help witt the community outreach and follow-up as well as the distribution of flyers.

Roles/responsibilities:
- Facilitate Grassroots Readiness and Response – Disaster Volunteer I, II, and III
- Research information about community population and possible disasters affecting them
- Guide participants through activities and discussion
- Distribute surveys to participants
- Assist participants with any questions regarding their preparedness plan

Reports to: DPTM Training Associate

Steps to become facilitator:
- Complete World Cares Center Train the Trainer Program
- Co-facilitate with Grassroots Readiness and Response

Figure 5.8 (*Continued*) Template: Agency outreach flyer.

With the specific job description flyer (Figure 5.6), your agency can recruit for specific open positions that you have designated for volunteers. In this flyer, you can specify these skills and core attributes, along with any relevant disqualifiers, so that volunteers can self-select whether or not they will apply.

END-OF-CHAPTER QUESTIONS

- What are the internal protocols that are needed to manage SUCVs?
- Has your agency designated oversight over SUCV roles?
- Has your agency designated how many staff and volunteers will be managed by each supervisor or manager?
- Has your agency determined what your agency responsibilities are to all volunteers?
- Has your agency determined what the volunteer is responsible for?
- What are the disqualifiers?
- What are the core attributes?
- Has your agency determined the disqualifiers and core attributes you seek in volunteers?

CONCLUSION

By the end of this chapter, you should have determined the internal and external protocols that would ultimately result in a volunteer packet and the internal management protocols for all SUCV positions. This set of standards and the templates that communicate these standards will streamline the process of selecting, training, and managing SUCVs. They will also (a) reduce the liability of using spontaneous volunteers and (b) ensure that your internal capacity in disaster response will be enhanced by volunteers who know what is expected of them.

6

A Volunteer Reception Center and Point-of-Distribution Model

IN THIS CHAPTER

- Planning Your Volunteer Reception Center (VRC) Model
  - Networking and Communication
  - Logistics
  - Preparing an Efficient Floor Plan
  - Staffing Policies and Procedures
- VRC Roles and Positions
- VRC Model Applied to the Public-Health Sector's Points of Distribution (PODs) Model

Now that we have addressed the challenges of disaster response and the internal and external protocols for managing volunteers, we are ready to look at these processes, along with spot screening and good management protocols, that can be implemented in a coordinated and central location in disaster response. The VRC model outlines the steps for the setup of a room or building that will put a roof, both literally and functionally, over the Spontaneous Volunteer management process outlined in subsequent chapters, including spot screening, selection, and placement of spontaneous volunteers. This model can help to address the internal capacity challenges that emergency managers face, especially by drawing volunteers as additional capacity and resources to one central and coordinated location to implement much of your volunteer management protocols and processes. In addition, the VRC model can also address the more public challenges, first of providing disaster relief and recovery services to diverse populations, as well as the communication challenge of getting information out to the public by housing this function within the center. We will also touch upon how VRC functions can apply to POD models developed by the public health section to help alleviate the burden from hospitals in dispensing vaccinations.

VOLUNTEER RECEPTION CENTERS

Also referred to as a *walk-in center* and a *volunteer center response plan*, the VRC is one of the planned and structured approaches to incorporate all types of volunteers into disaster response initiatives. The purpose of the VRC is to coordinate, track, orient, deploy, or refer spontaneous volunteers out of one central location situated at a safe distance from the impacted area or areas. The assumption behind developing and establishing a VRC is that in a major disaster, traditional coordinators may be incapacitated, overwhelmed, or otherwise unavailable to manage the outpouring of volunteers. Therefore, a separate physical and organizational structure to conduct these tasks will alleviate the burden away from them.

All types of volunteers can be referred to a VRC, including spontaneous unaffiliated community volunteers (SUCVs), out-of-town volunteer groups, and affiliated volunteers who may not have an assignment with their agency. Skilled and pretrained staff or volunteers manage the influx of volunteers, and in some cases the VRC may offer additional training and support for volunteers.

In many states, the VRC has been modeled in various forms. I have worked on several such VRC plans and researched the various adaptations. Most notably, I have worked through World Cares Center (WCC) on the NYC Voluntary Organizations Active in Disaster (VOAD) Spontaneous Volunteer Management Committee that developed a volunteer reception plan included in the city's spontaneous volunteer management plan.

Adapting to Your Size and Needs

A VRC, like the Incident Command System (ICS), has the ability to expand and contract based on your needs. In the case of NYC's VRC, it requires the collaborative commitment of many agencies and their staff to manage such a facility. A citywide VRC may take years in the planning and require Memorandums of Understanding (MOUs) between multiple agencies as well as considerable equipment and funding. The New York City Office of Emergency Management (NYC OEM), in conjunction with the members of NYC VOAD, prepared the volunteer reception center plan, and all have a role in managing it. Protocol follows the NYC OEM initiating the activation of the VRC, with the designated coordinating agency setting up and managing the VRC with the assistance of many partner agencies. This is the type and size of VRC that I will refer to as a *mega-VRC*. In a mega-VRC, there is a structure to register volunteers, orient them, and refer them to the volunteer opportunities that are posted by other agencies. There may also be housing assistance and other resources available for out-of-town groups.

As we look at utilizing the VRC model for single agencies to manage their community volunteers, we refer to this model as a *Volunteer Reception Area* (VRA), in which the same system is used but in a scaled-down version to fulfill the needs of community-based agencies. For community-based agencies, a VRA is an invaluable tool to organize your constituency and neighbors that has the benefit of local knowledge and resources. Agencies should consider creating a VRA plan rather than depending on the creation and implementation of a larger, multiagency, or municipal VRC. If you are an organization that is known to offer volunteer opportunities, people who are familiar with your organization and who trust you will emerge at your door with the expectation that you will know where help is needed and how to guide them to volunteer. You are an agency that would benefit from a VRA plan.

In nondisaster times, many community- or faith-based organizations that regularly provide services to their community every day, such as soup kitchens or shelters for the homeless, struggle to make ends meet. But in times of disaster, local needs will significantly increase, furthering the burden by adding new individuals who need help in addition to current clients. The scale of impact from a disaster or the influx of national responders needing housing and food are some examples where additional community support may be called upon. New volunteers will be needed to help local groups fulfill this surge-capacity need, all while still maintaining services to regular constituents. Preparing a VRA model to properly screen, place, and manage individuals to meet the increased need will reduce the burden to these local groups, compared to trying to figure it out during a response situation. Planning and exercising to run a

VRC is an opportunity to train staff and collaborate with the other groups you will come in contact with during disasters.

The VRC and VRA plan is one of the many resources and structures that make up a comprehensive Spontaneous Volunteer Management Plan and tool kit. Taking into consideration that every community-based organization and faith-based group should have a VRC or VRA plan, the following pages outline the preparation recommended to establish one in the predisaster phase.

PLANNING YOUR VOLUNTEER RECEPTION CENTER

There are many steps that you can take predisaster to set up a VRC or VRA. As we review the guidelines for setting up a VRC and VRA, make sure to adapt the model that best suits your capacity as well as the number of people you expect to process.

Networking and Communication

Rather than immediately taking on all the tasks associated with establishing a VRC or VRA, you may want to collaborate amongst agencies in the same locality to share VRC-VRA management responsibilities and staff, to refer volunteers, or to request volunteers. Take the time to find out who your neighboring agencies and partners are and what they are doing to prepare for and respond to disasters and emergencies. There may be an existing volunteer center in your area that you may want to affiliate with or even refer your volunteers to. Another source is VOAD, which is a networking group for organizations that have a mission in disaster management. Start with a simple list of the agencies in your area, contact names and numbers, and what services they provide. Once you have become familiar with neighboring agencies in the area, you may want to enter into agreements and MOUs to further define your respective roles and responsibilities during disaster response. This may be facilitated by partner agency agreement forms, such as the one below. Once you have set up these agreements and determined your role in disaster response, make sure that your neighbors and all partner agencies are informed of the services that you will be providing.

Logistics

Location, location, location: There are a number of things to consider when deciding the location of your VRC or your VRA.

- Take into consideration the number of individuals that you may be receiving. Will it be hundreds or thousands of visitors a day?
- Assess whether the building or room you are using has the capacity to handle the VRC setup and tasks you are planning to perform without crippling the daily responsibilities of your organization.
- Whether you are implementing a VRA or VRC model, either one will require adequate room, with
  Main entrance
  Secondary exit
  Public toilet facilities
  Phone lines
  Computers
  Desks, chairs
  Waiting area
  Copy machine

In addition, depending on the size of your VRC or VRA and the extent to which you will be conducting interviews or providing social support services, you may want to consider spaces that may be set up to allow for privacy and confidential discussions.

Preparing an Efficient Floor Plan

The physical set up of your volunteer reception area is crucial in maintaining flow and reducing confusion. Think through the steps that your VRA plan will follow and how you would like traffic to flow so that people are not crossing paths to get from one area to another. Set up only as many stations as your staff can handle, and utilize the first appropriate volunteers who come to help to fill empty roles in the reception center.

While potential volunteers are standing in line waiting to sign up, you may want to have greeters inform them of the processes they will be following once inside the center. If the line is not long, a step-by-step overview of the volunteer interview process can be given at the reception area. Either option is fine, as long as applicants are informed of the steps to follow before they start the process, thus eliminating confusion.

A floor plan and easily readable signs on each table or area will help guide people through the steps and identify where their next stop is as they go from station to station. If you are able to put tape on the floor, an effective way to guide people is to place large yellow lines and arrows in the direction they should follow.

The illustrations presented here are examples of VRC and VRA layouts that may guide you in setting up your own. Figure 6.1 is a layout example for setting up a mega-VRC or a multiagency VRC. Figure 6.2 is a layout for a mid-size VRC or VRA. Figure 6.3 shows the setup for a single-agency VRC. However, this is still a large undertaking and will require many staff and affiliated volunteers to run.

Some Considerations in Laying Out Your Floor Plan

Running a VRC/VRA while Continuing to Serve Those in Need

Special consideration should be made if you are implementing a VRC while serving those in need and affected by disaster. There are very distinct differences between the needs and emotional states of persons wanting to volunteer and of persons in immediate need of help. It is important to keep the VRC operations and the disaster victim operation areas separate, with separate entrances, exits, and service areas.

Public Information

Aside from printed material that you may have prepared predisaster, keep in mind that many people may be calling in for information or to help after a disaster has occurred. *Create a flyer or post information on your Website or your online newsletter about your new VRC program.* This will inform those who may want to help now or later as to the roles, location, and procedures of the VRC. You may want to define who you are looking to engage as volunteers. For instance, the Agency Outreach form that you created in Chapter 5 may be modified for the VRC to indicate the types of volunteers sought by an agency.

Staffing Policies and Procedures

Ensure that your staff is ready to take on the additional responsibilities of running a VRC or a VRA. Staffing policies and procedures should be

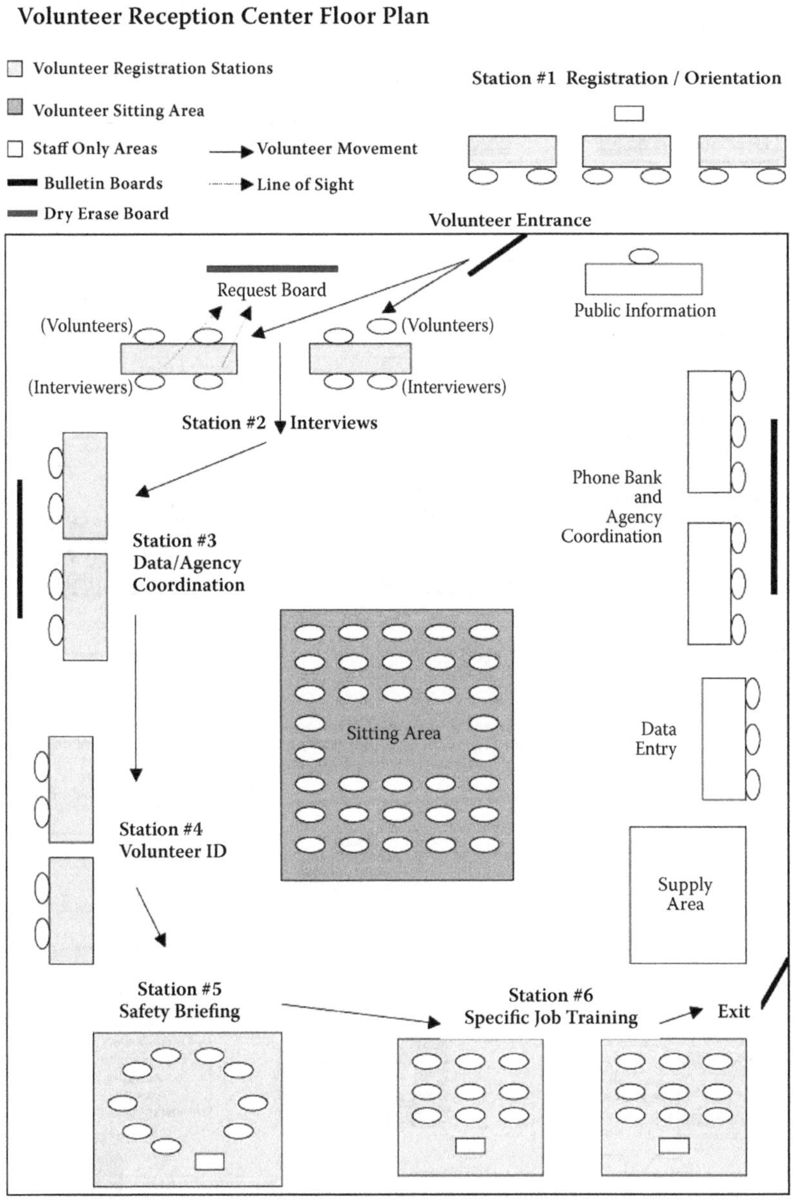

Volunteer Reception Center Floor Plan

☐ Volunteer Registration Stations

▨ Volunteer Sitting Area

☐ Staff Only Areas   ⟶ Volunteer Movement

▬ Bulletin Boards   ┄┄▸ Line of Sight

▬ Dry Erase Board

Station #1 Registration / Orientation

Volunteer Entrance

Request Board

(Volunteers)

(Volunteers)

(Interviewers)

(Interviewers)

Station #2 ▾ Interviews

Public Information

Phone Bank
and
Agency
Coordination

**Station #3
Data/Agency
Coordination**

Sitting Area

Data
Entry

**Station #4
Volunteer ID**

Supply
Area

**Station #5
Safety Briefing**

**Station #6
Specific Job Training**   ▸ Exit

Figure 6.1   Mid-size VRC or VRA. (Source: World Cares Center)

131

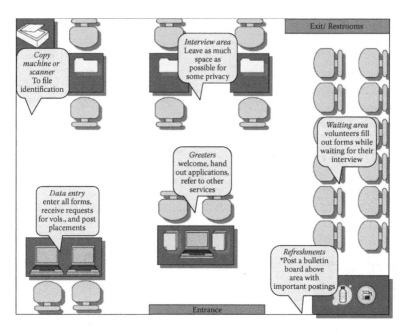

Figure 6.2 Setup for a single-agency VRC.

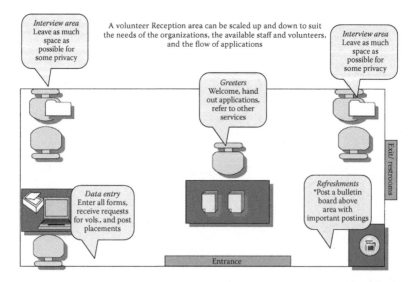

Figure 6.3 VRA floor plan.

established and communicated before launching your program. The following paragraphs outline many of these policies and procedures.

> *Training and orientation*: Employees should go through the appropriate training for their roles and responsibilities, and understand what role each will have as a disaster-response worker when a disaster or emergency occurs within your community.
>
> An *orientation* for all staff with disaster-response roles should be provided to review expectations and policies, and to ensure that steps are taken to guarantee the welfare of their families. The same list that we have used for spontaneous volunteer spot screening can be modified for employees.

Outside Normal Business Hours

Policies for when a disaster occurs outside normal business hours should be put into place. Establish who the decision maker or incident commander is who then determines what steps are to be taken. Predisaster, all employees and volunteers should be provided with a specific number to call in for updates and information, or a call tree can be implemented to relay information when disaster does strike.

> *Healthy shifts and breaks*: For staff who will be working in your VRC, setting staff shifts and breaks to maintain a healthy work environment should take into consideration that a healthy shift for any employee or volunteer is eight hours and at least one ten-minute break every two hours. Procedures such as a preshift briefing and postshift briefing should be included as a policy, along with setting shifts to overlap with each other so that departing staff can share important information.
>
> *Documentation of time*: All staff and volunteers should sign in and out for each shift.
>
> *Safety*: No person should work alone. The buddy system should be implemented, and a minimum of two staff must be on site at all times. This also applies to opening and closing the VRC in the evening.

VRC ROLES AND POSITIONS

Roles and positions that need to be filled in order to run a VRC or VRA include:

- Volunteer reception center director (i.e., incident commander)
- Executive officers (depending on resources):
    Operations
    Planning
    Logistics
    Finance
    Public Information
    Safety
- Greeters
- Runners
- Interviewers
- Resource coordinator and data entry
- Volunteer orientation and training coordinator
- Social support services
- Food/water/first-aid services
- Security

The following pages provide an outline of what these roles and tasks entail, and can also be used as templates for VRC job descriptions.

Executive Responsibilities

The position of VRC director should be filled with a staff person or a seasoned affiliated volunteer if a staff person is not available. If you are following an ICS for your VRC or VRA, the director is the incident commander and is responsible for overseeing the entire operation of the VRC or VRA. The director will also be the individual responsible for initializing the VRC and activating the call list for all the staff and affiliated volunteers who are signed up to help. The director is responsible for managing all aspects of the VRC; if this is a small operation or a VRA, he or she may be directly responsible for executive-level duties, including operations, planning, logistics, finance, public information, and safety functions. If this is a large VRC, the incident command chart will expand to accommodate additional members of the executive-level team, which will then include section chiefs or officers in charge of operations, planning, logistics, finance, public information, and safety. The director will coordinate all the staff and volunteer roles, adding both human and physical resources as needed.

Operation responsibilities include the management and coordination of all staff and volunteers, including assigning them

134

to appropriate tasks as outlined in your plan. Conducting VRC operations also involves keeping track of all the resources that are needed and monitoring the progress of operations.

Planning responsibilities include establishing reporting guidelines for all staff and collecting data to assess and evaluate the current operations. As data is collected, the VRC plan as well as plans of action must be updated, disseminated, and implemented.

Logistics responsibilities include ensuring that you have a facility and all the needed materials and equipment so that your VRC can operate safely and effectively. This includes setting up your facility in keeping with your plan and layout; ensuring that all the needed equipment is provided, set up, and working; coordinating safety and feeding operations; and establishing sleeping facilities for your team if necessary. It is also crucial to oversee proper sanitation, maintenance, and cleaning of the VRC. Coordinating the logistics with the operations officer or the person in charge of operations will ensure that the VRC is well-maintained and equipped with all that it needs to run smoothly.

Finance responsibilities include tracking all expenses, handling all contracts, and logging all injuries and compensation claims. The person in charge of finance may also be tasked with tracking and logging all volunteer hours.

Public information responsibilities include providing accurate and relevant information to the general public and to the media. The person in charge of public information should brief all staff and volunteers within the VRC about information-sharing policies and who is authorized to speak with the press. In this role, a useful tool that should be developed is an frequently asked questions (FAQ) handout that greeters may pass out to press at the door without being put on the spot to answer questions they may not have the most updated information on.

Safety responsibilities include monitoring the daily operations of the VRC to assess that the environment is safe and that it is being run in a safe manner. If there is damage, a damage assessment will need to be conducted, as it may impact the safety of all those in the VRC. Developing staff and volunteer safety measures is an important part of the role as well as conducting safety briefings, and being alert and available to help with any distressed visitors.

Whether the executive team consists of one person or several, all of the executive-level officers and personnel should always meet to coordinate and brief each other, as well as remember to thank all volunteers who help in the VRC.

In review, if you have a large VRC and enough staff or affiliated volunteers, each of the executive-level duties can be managed by a separate person. However, in the case of a VRA or smaller operation, one person may handle all of the executive functions.

The following executive officer descriptions can be used to select for these positions, if you have enough human resources to staff them as separate positions. Following the executive officer descriptions are the roles that volunteers may fill.

Executive Positions

VRC Director/ICS Commander

Description: Oversee and manage all aspects of the VRC.

Responsibilities:

- Activate call list for all staff and affiliated volunteers who are signed up to help
- Create initial incident action plan
- Brief and assign tasks to staff and volunteers at the center
- Appoint executive-level officers and captains of VRC stations as needed
- Monitor operations and make staffing changes/add human resources if necessary
- Conduct debriefings of staff at end of shift
- Meet and thank volunteers
- Authorize release of information by public information officer
- Review and approve requests for procurement and release of resources
- Approve plan for demobilization

If the VRC operations are large-scale, then the director will additionally

- Oversee executive-level team, including operations, planning, logistics, finance, public information, and safety officers
- Ensure that the executive-level team meets to debrief and update

If the VRC operations are small-scale, then the director will directly be responsible for

- Coordinating operations, planning, logistics, finance, public information, and safety responsibilities, based on staff resources

Qualification/requirements:

- Staff or affiliated volunteer only
- Extensive managerial experience
- Trained in disaster response
- Has experience managing volunteers
- Organized
- Friendly

Supplies/equipment needed:

- ID badge
- VRC plan: operations, safety policies
- Phone
- Computer and printer
- Desk
- Display board, markers

Manages: All executive-level staff, other staff, and volunteers

Operations Officer
Description: Manage and coordinate all staff and volunteers, assigning them to appropriate tasks to maintain VRC operations.

Responsibilities:

- Manage all operations applicable to VRC mission
- Brief staff and volunteers as outlined in your plan
- Develop operations section of the plan
- Notify director if additional resources are needed
- Coordinate all operations staff and volunteer functions
- Monitor work progress and maintain time records of staff and volunteers

Qualifications/requirements:

- Staff or affiliated volunteer only
- Trained in managing volunteers in disaster response
- Detail-oriented and organized

- Responsible
- Good communication skills

Supplies/equipment needed:

- ID badge
- Operations plan
- Time sheets
- Record storage/file storage
- Phone
- Tables, chairs
- Display board, markers

Manages: All staff and volunteers

Planning Officer
Description: Responsible for collection, evaluation, and use of information about the VRC

Responsibilities:

- Collect all data to assess current operations, including records of safety and job training provided to volunteers and hours worked in the VRC by employees and volunteers
- Establish reporting guidelines for all stations
- Prepare action plans based on information collected
- Identify needs for use of specialized resources
- Submit plans for approval
- Disseminate plans
- Implement plans

Qualifications/requirements:

- Staff or affiliated volunteers only
- Experience in evaluation and action planning
- Detail-oriented
- Database and data assessment experience

Supplies/equipment needed:

- ID badge
- Tables and chairs
- Orientation and safety training records
- Reporting guidelines for each station

- Clipboards, pens
- Phone
- Computer and printer

Manages: Data entry staff

Logistics Officer
Description: Ensure that the VRC facility and its operations are running effectively.

Responsibilities:

- Provide the facility and all materials needed to run the VRC
- Set up and assign work locations and preliminary tasks
- Identify service and support requirements for operations
- Ensure that all needed equipment is in place and that it is in working condition
- Advise on communications capabilities or limitations
- Coordinate safety and feeding needs
- Coordinate medical emergency needs
- Establish sleeping facilities if needed
- Oversee sanitation, maintenance, and cleanup

Qualifications/requirements:

- Staff or affiliated volunteers only
- Detail-oriented
- Reliable
- Ability to multitask
- Experience with inventory/maintenance/multifunction institutions
- Good communication skills

Supplies/equipment needed:

- ID badge
- Agreements pertaining to facility
- Agreements pertaining to supplies, materials, equipment
- Supply inventory list
- Equipment list
- Storage space/secure area for supplies and equipment
- Phone
- Log of donations
- Sanitation/maintenance policy and schedule

Manages: Food/water/first-aid services

Finance Officer
Description: Manages and oversees all financial matters for the VRC.

Responsibilities:

- Track all expenses and maintain all receipts for expenses
- Handle all contracts for goods and services
- Log all injuries and claims
- Handle all compensation claims

Qualifications/requirements:

- Staff or affiliated volunteers only
- Responsible
- Detail-oriented
- Experienced at handling financial contracts, tasks, accounts receivables

Supplies/equipment needed:

- ID badge
- Table, chair
- Computer and printer
- Secure storage for receipts and financial records
- Injury claim forms
- Compensation and reimbursement forms

Public Information Officer
Description: Responds to external requests for information, including from the general public and the media

Responsibilities:

- Provide accurate and relevant information to the general public
- Brief staff and volunteers about who is authorized to speak to the press
- Establish and maintain single contact point with media
- Develop public information tools for staff and volunteers, including a FAQ form
- Coordinate release of information
- Update information on Website or through other medium

Qualifications/requirements:

- Staff or affiliated volunteers only
- Experience handling media and communications
- Excellent communication skills, both oral and written

Safety Officer
Description: Ensures safety of VRC location and all staff, personnel, and volunteers

Responsibilities:

- Monitor daily operations of the VRC to assess that the environment is safe and that the VRC is being run in a safe manner
- Develop staff and volunteer safety policies
- Conduct safety briefings for staff and volunteers
- If there is damage, conduct damage assessment and determine impact and risks of damage for staff and volunteers
- Manage security team

Qualifications/requirements:

- Staff or affiliated volunteers only
- Experience with security and safety trainings in disaster response

Supplies/equipment needed:

- ID badge
- Other apparel marking security/safety role
- Walkie-talkie system to communicate with security team
- Phone
- Safety briefing log
- Facility blueprint/layout
- Safety policy and handouts

Manages: Security team

Position Descriptions for Roles That May Be Fulfilled by SUCVs

Moving onto the staff and volunteers, we will review the roles that need to be filled in order to operate the VRC. Remember that you may want to fill some of these roles with your newly arrived, screened, and approved spontaneous volunteers.

Greeters or Receptionists

Role: The person or persons in this role will be the first person to meet and greet those entering the VRC and direct them to the correct location. Greeters should have a friendly demeanor and the ability to quickly determine the purpose of those wishing to access or provide services in the VRC and direct them accordingly. It will be important for greeters to know where the services for survivors and victims are located and direct anyone looking for these services to this area. Greeters may also be the first persons to come into contact with the media; therefore, they should be briefed on proper protocols for dealing with the press and media and given an FAQ document to hand out to them. The greeter should give each volunteer an application to fill out along with any other information flyers available and guide them to the waiting area. A simple numbering system can be implemented to track who is next for the interview.

Greeters may be affiliated or unaffiliated volunteers.

Reports to: Operations officer

Tasks may include:

- Answering the phone
- Passing out flyers or volunteer applications
- Providing a brief orientation to those interested in volunteering
- Passing out the FAQ flyer to the media and press
- Answering questions about the application
- Assisting applicants with their application
- Referring applicants to the waiting area or information tables
- Referring those who need victims services to the appropriate location
- Accepting donated goods if this is appropriate, or refer to an agency or location that is accepting donations

Depending on the size of the VRC or VRA and the number of people wanting to volunteer, the greeter can be stationed outside the VRC greeting people who are waiting in line. If clipboards are available, volunteer applications can be filled out by those waiting in line and distributed and collected by the greeters.

Greeters, as the first person that volunteers encounter, may also have to fill in the ad hoc role of screening for those who may possibly need support services immediately rather than undergo the volunteer screening process. If a greeter feels that a prospective volunteer is emotionally disturbed and they are outside, they may want to ask for someone from the safety or mental health services, if available, to come out and speak to the individual. If they are already inside, they may walk them over to the safety or mental health services and ensure that they make contact with a professional who can further evaluate them.

Supplies/equipment needed:

- ID badge
- A table sign
- A table and chair
- Job descriptions
- Agency outreach flyer
- Volunteer applications
- Pens
- Clipboards
- Referral agency listings
- FAQ flyers for media or general public

Interviewers

Role: Interviewers will conduct the spot screening and assessment procedures outlined in this field guide. Interviewers will use the five-minute spot screening interview and the checklists to guide them through the process. After the interview and selection process, interviewers will set realistic expectations for the volunteer and assign a role appropriate to his or her abilities and interests. The templates and processes included in this field guide will facilitate this process. Interviewers will work in conjunction with the resource coordinator/data entry staff and volunteers.

Interviewers may be staff or affiliated volunteers.

Reports to: Resource Coordinator

Tasks may include:

- Welcoming potential volunteers
- Collecting and reviewing the application
- Conducting five-minute interviews of potential volunteers and documenting responses
- Conducting an orientation
- Assigning a role to interviewees and directing them to next steps
- Reviewing policies and procedures with applicant

Supplies/equipment needed:

- Desk
- Two chairs
- Paper and pen
- Spot-screening checklist
- Volunteer self-assessment forms
- List and handouts of job descriptions
- Flags to summon runners
- Alphabetical file storage for applications

Resource Coordinator and Data Entry

Role: Resource coordinator and data entry duties involve coordination with the volunteer coordinator at your agency or other agencies and groups to understand and fulfill their volunteer needs. When planning a VRC, you can establish relationships with each partner organization's volunteer manager or the person in your organization who will know what the volunteer needs are before a disaster occurs. These may be multiple persons, and you will need to ensure that you are not duplicating efforts. The resource coordinator will have volunteer request forms readily available on the Internet ready to fax over for an agency or department to fill out. In the case of a VRA, it may be as simple as having the form at your desk for someone to fill out or a few questions to be answered via e-mail.

If you do not have the volunteers to split the responsibilities, this person will also work with the interviewer to match and track volunteers to positions that are most appropriate for them.

Resource coordinators/data entry staff and volunteers should keep a running list of volunteers who are available and those who are assigned, or two files that contain open and closed requests for volunteers. This can be done in a database or on a bulletin board with note cards representing each volunteer opportunity.

Resource coordinator should be staff or affiliated volunteers. Data entry can be handled by spontaneous volunteers.

Reports to: Operations officer

Tasks may include:

- Keeping a running list of volunteers who are available and those who are assigned
- Having volunteer request forms readily available
- Coordinating volunteer requests of partner agencies

Supplies/equipment needed:

- ID badge
- Desk and two chairs
- Computer and printer, or large display board and markers
- Paper, pens
- Volunteer request forms
- Open-request file folder and closed-request file folder
- Volunteer-management database
- Secure storage area/file cabinet for records
- Phone
- Flag to summon runners
- Volunteer ID tags/wristbands

Volunteer Orientation and Training Coordinator

Role: Volunteer orientation coordinator duties include orienting new volunteers to agency protocols, policies, general expectations, safety, and other necessary information. In our model, the interviewer conducts both the interview and the orientation. Orientations or briefings also take place at the beginning of each shift by the volunteer manager in charge of the team. In a larger VRC operation, the volunteer orientation function can be given to multiple volunteers at a time in a separate area and regularly conducted on a schedule.

This role must be undertaken by staff or affiliated volunteers.

Reports to: Operations officer

Tasks may include:

- Create and review all training materials
- Schedule and conduct orientations
- Keep records of volunteers who participated in orientation
- Explain seriousness of volunteer commitment
- Describe safety and liability issues to volunteers
- Respond to volunteer questions and concerns

Supplies/equipment needed:

- ID badge
- Facilitator's orientation guide
- Orientation handouts for volunteers
- Safety policy handouts for volunteers
- Clipboards, pens
- Table sign

- Chairs for the volunteers
- Forms to record volunteers who have taken orientation

Social Support Services

In any disaster, those whom we consider victims and those who volunteer may need social support or an encouraging word to work through a particularly difficult volunteer experience. There are many situations in which those entrusted with social support services in the VRC can offer assistance to the disaster community victim, volunteer, and staff person.

Volunteers who come to help may often be the very individuals whose lives have been changed by the disaster. Rather than viewing themselves as victims, they prefer to respond proactively by coming out to help. This is acceptable and part of the healing process. Other individuals may not be ready to volunteer and become overwhelmed by what they are seeing or hearing. Someone who needs help may have found the VRC before they have found a source of support, or they may just not be emotionally stable enough to help. In any of these situations, individuals trained in disaster mental health can provide a valuable service, including professional social workers, clinicians, or faith-based leaders with experience in disaster mental health.

Role: Oversee and assess the well-being of all staff and volunteers and tend to individuals who are showing signs of stress.

The role of social support services must be undertaken by professionally trained medical personnel, mental health professionals, or social workers, whether they are staff in your agency or in a partner agency.

Reports to: Operations officer

Tasks may include:

- Meet with individuals who have entered the VRC seeking social support as well as those individuals who are interested in volunteering but do not appear to be fit to do so, with such individuals being referred to additional care if needed
- Follow-up on their referral
- Notify supervisors and data entry staff of volunteers and staff who are not ready to work at this time

Supplies/equipment needed:

- ID badge
- Chairs placed in a quiet yet public area
- Space where confidentiality and privacy are ensured
- Tissues
- Forms for relevant mental or social services or claims
- List of agencies and contacts that can provide support for referral
- Table sign

Food, Water, and First-Aid Services

Keep in mind that you, your staff, your volunteers, and the people who are coming to help may be at the VRC for a while. Therefore food, water, and first-aid services are necessary to ensure that snacks, water, basic medical supplies, and coffee will be available and readily replenished. Food plays a large part in comforting and bringing people together.

Role: Provide food, water, and first-aid services to the VRC staff and volunteers. The person or team in charge of this role should make sure to have a first-aid kit that is well-stocked and available, and should be trained in basic first-aid techniques.

The role of food and water services may be undertaken by unaffiliated or affiliated volunteers. First-aid services require proper precertification and may be handled by affiliated volunteers.

Reports to: Operations officer

Supplies needed:

- ID badge
- Storage area for food/water
- First-aid kit and supplies
- Inventory forms
- Table sign

Runners

Role: Runners can contribute greatly to keeping the flow of traffic moving. This person or persons will run information, requests, and forms between stations, restock each station's supplies, assist volunteers, and offer general assistance. They may also summon security or medical resources when necessary.

This role may be undertaken by unaffiliated or affiliated volunteers.

Reports to: Operations officer

Tasks may include:

- Restock each station's supplies on an as-needed basis
- Assist each station with needs and requests
- Summon security or medical resources when necessary

Supplies/equipment needed:

- ID badge
- Clear marking that they are a runner
- Pens or markers
- Notepads

Security

Role: Security personnel will ensure that the VRC is a secure and safe working environment for all personnel, staff, volunteers, and those who come to help. The person or team in charge of security will ensure the safety of the location, oversee the safety of staff and volunteers, and manage crowd control. They may conduct periodic inspections or be responsible for a specific posted area. In case a problem or damage occurs at the site of the VRC, they will intervene with appropriate measures and communicate potential safety concerns to a supervisor and the director, if needed.

This role must be undertaken by staff or affiliated volunteers.

Reports to: Security officer

Tasks may include:

- Ensure the safety of the location
- Oversee the safety of staff and volunteers
- Crowd control
- Conduct periodic inspections or be responsible for a specific posted area
- Communicate potential safety concerns to safety officer

Supplies/equipment needed:

- ID badge
- Apparel that marks the role of security clearly
- Safety policy
- Walkie-talkie
- Incident report forms

THE VOLUNTEER RECEPTION CENTER MODEL
APPLIED TO THE PUBLIC-HEALTH SECTOR'S
POINTS OF DISTRIBUTION MODEL

There are many definitions for PODs, including the following from FEMA and the US Army Corps of Engineers, as "a centralized location where the public can pick up life-sustaining commodities following a disaster or emergency, such as shelf-stable food and water."* However, we will focus on the public-health sector's POD model as a location that dispenses vaccinations in the event of a pandemic to relieve the burden from hospitals.

The process of setting up a point of distribution is similar to setting up a large-scale VRC, with a focus on equipping the POD with medical expertise, equipment, and trained and credentialed staff to dispense medications and vaccinations. While most of the roles must be fulfilled by a licensed, trained, and vetted volunteer or staff member, there are several supportive roles that SUCVs can be assigned to reduce the burden on medical personnel, who can then focus more on providing medical services. Applying spontaneous volunteer management strategy and leveraging nonmedical spontaneous volunteers has the potential to fill administrative and supportive roles in the POD.

As per the Nassau County POD training manual, this section outlines the essential roles in the POD, followed by a short list of roles that may be designated for SUCVs.

Essential roles within a POD:
- POD manager
- Safety specialist
- Medical consultant
- Medical team leader
- Triage specialist
- Screener coordinator
- Screener
- Dispenser/vaccinator
- Educator
- Staff coordinator
- Clerk
- Supply specialist
- Medication officer

---

* FEMA and U.S. Army Corps of Engineers, "IS-26 Guide to Points of Distribution (PODs)," 2008. http://training.fema.gov/EMIWeb/IS/IS26.asp.

- Food officer
- Situation status specialist
- Volunteer coordinator
- Runner coordinator
- Runners
- Mental health counselor

Possible roles that a volunteer may have in a POD:

- Clerk assistant (data entry)
- Screener
- Educator
- Food service
- Supply (nonmedical)
- Runner

Position Descriptions for Roles That May Be Fulfilled by POD Volunteers

POD volunteer job descriptions are presented in the following pages.

Clerk Assistant (Data Entry)
Role: Perform clerical duties as assigned by the clerk tasks.

Reports to: Clerk

Tasks may include:

- Distribute POD registration forms to clients
- Ensure that there are enough POD registration forms
- File and record registration forms, ensuring proper storage and filing
- Organize medical and other forms
- Enter data in computer or paper database
- Report any medical records that cannot be entered in database
- Count medical records and enter them in the medical records transmittal form
- Complete the medical record transmittal form for each batch of records
- Follow directions from the supervisor regarding disposition of forms and records

Supplies/equipment needed:

- Vest or ID badge
- Watch or clock
- Clipboards
- Supply of forms
- Pens
- Chairs
- Secure file storage, whether paper or computer

Greeter

Role: Meet and greet those who enter the POD seeking services and direct them to the correct location.

Greeters may be affiliated or unaffiliated volunteers.

Reports to: Runner coordinator

Tasks may include:

- Answering the phone
- Passing out flyers
- Passing out the FAQ flyer to the media and press
- Referring applicants to the waiting area or information tables
- Referring those who need services to the appropriate location
- Accepting donated goods if this is appropriate or refer to an agency or location that is accepting donations

Supplies/equipment needed:

- ID badge
- A table sign
- A table and chair
- Map or information about the POD
- Agency flyer
- Pens
- Clipboards
- Referral agency listings
- FAQ flyers for media or general public

Screener

Role: Assess clients for eligibility to receive vaccination or medication.

Reports to: Screening coordinator

Tasks may include:

- Review and understand screening process for approving clients to receive medication/vaccination
- Receive and review screening form from clients
- Determine if client is eligible for medication based on responses on medical screening form and by following supplied dispensing algorithm:

    If client answers screening with no contraindication to medication/vaccination, place *green check* at the top of the form. Direct client to medication dispenser.

    If client answers screening showing a contraindication to medication/vaccination, place a *red check* at the top of the form. Direct client to the medical consultant for review.
- Assure that information on registration form is complete with signature in appropriate location

Supplies/equipment needed:

- Vest or ID badge
- Green and red markers
- Chairs
- Pen

Educator

Role: To provide education as instructed and according to the event.

Reports to: Medical team leader

Tasks may include:

- Provide basic information about medications and disease through distribution of preprinted information sheets, ensuring that all clients receive a copy of these sheets
- Answer questions about the POD process or flow that were not answered by the triage specialist
- Direct clients to medical registration
- Order additional medication and disease information sheets as needed

Supplies/equipment needed:

- Vest

- Supply of disease information sheets and medical information sheets

Food Service
Role: Distribute food and beverages for POD staff and volunteers.

Reports to: Supply specialist

Tasks may include:

- Arrange food and beverages for delivery
- Notify supply specialist when supplies are running low
- Set up food area and distribute food and beverages
- Arrange and ensure for proper clean-up and removal of discarded food and waste

Supplies/equipment needed:

- Vest or ID badge
- List of POD staff and volunteers for food/beverage needs
- Tables and chairs

Supply (nonmedical)
Role: Ensure that all necessary forms, signs, communication, nonmedical equipment, and nonmedical supplies are on-site and available in sufficient quantities.

Reports to: Supply specialist

Tasks may include:

- Dispatch nonmedical supplies to POD stations as directed
- Communicate frequently with supply specialist leader regarding the supply status
- Establish and maintain log and monitor supplies
- If there is no food officer, order and supply food and beverages as necessary to POD staff and volunteers

Supplies/equipment needed:

- Vest or ID badge
- Watch or clock
- Clipboard, pens, markers, paper
- Other stationery items as required

- List of nonmedical POD supplies and supply of requisition/communication sheets

Runner

Role: Facilitate the needs of the POD staff by relaying communications throughout the POD.

Reports to: Flow control team leader

Tasks may include:

- Receive POD assignments from flow control team leader
- Participate in POD set up as directed
- Maintain communication with flow control team leader and obtain materials/items as requested

Supplies/equipment needed:

- Vest or ID badge
- Pens and markers

END-OF-CHAPTER QUESTIONS

- In times of disaster, will your agency (or an agency or agencies you partner with) operate a VRC or VRA?
- If partner agencies are involved, have agreements or MOUs been set in place?
- Will you also be receiving disaster survivors in need or continue serving your regular clients? If so, what steps will you take to separate the VRC from this receiving area for disaster survivors?
- Where will your VRC or VRA be located? Does it fulfill all the requirements of your VRC and the functions you will serve?
- What stations will you have in your VRC or VRA? Have these been laid out in a floor plan?
- What roles will you have your staff fulfill?
- Have staffing procedures and policies regarding the VRC operations been set into place?
- Have you prepared an orientation or training for staff regarding their VRC roles?
- What roles will you have SUCVs or affiliated volunteers fill?

CONCLUSION

In this chapter, we have reviewed the VRC model as a structure, both physical and functional, that can house all of the volunteer management processes and procedures outlined in this manual. These include: identifying your partners, preparing your staff policies and procedures, creating and training staff and volunteers on their VRC roles, determining an adequate location, and setting up an efficient floor plan to make sure the center runs smoothly.

7

Spot Screening, Assessment, and Selection

In the aftermath of September 11, the American public has demonstrated an encouraging willingness to assist the professional emergency responder community in disaster situations. These spontaneous and unaffiliated volunteers possess vital skills and experience that can provide essential support to first responders who are faced with a disaster of potentially overwhelming magnitude. One key to success is the ability to quickly and effectively identify these skills and direct them to where they can do the most good.

Howard Butts
New Jersey Citizen Corps Coordinator

IN THIS CHAPTER

- Interview Fundamentals
  - Spot-Screening Logistics
  - Spot-Screening Safety
  - Spot-Screening Checklist
  - Keep an Objective View
  - Share Relevant Data
  - Use Spot-Screening Time Wisely
  - Modeling Values: Actions Speak Louder than Words

157

- The Process
  - Volunteer Application and Self-Assessment
  - Interviewer Templates
  - Five Types of Interview Questions
  - Cultural Sensitivity
  - Assessment
- Outcome of Interview: Steps to Take upon Selection
  - Offer a Role
  - Agree on a Communication Strategy
  - Validate or Check Credentials
  - Decline with Gratitude

Now that you have decided in what roles you will place staff, affiliated volunteers, and spontaneous or just-in-time volunteers in disaster response; have developed the protocols for who you are looking for; and have reviewed how the volunteer reception center (VRC) can house these functions, you can move on to the fundamentals of spot screening and selecting spontaneous volunteers. Establishing spot-screening and selection procedures helps to address the internal-capacity and communication procedures of recruiting and building your disaster response force with volunteer capacity.

This chapter identifies preferred methods for spot screening and selection of spontaneous volunteers. The techniques and methods for just-in-time interviews, assessments, and selection of spontaneous unaffiliated community volunteers (SUCVs) must incorporate your agency's needs in order to be effective, based on the work you have completed in previous chapters. Each interview should take into consideration what roles and tasks spontaneous volunteers would fill, the core attributes they will need to posses to volunteer, and the disqualifiers that would eliminate them as a volunteer.

This section will be important for anyone on your team who will be conducting interviews and should be taught to all individuals who will be on the front lines, screening and managing citizens as they emerge to help. Experienced staff will benefit from a uniform process with templates that help to manage information. Less experienced interviewers will benefit from the guidance your templates and procedures give them. For everyone, a standardized set of interview steps that are based on the needs and standards of the organization will ensure that your agency's principles are complied with.

INTERVIEW FUNDAMENTALS

Spot-Screening Logistics

Citizens will go to places they know and trust to both seek and offer help. If you are a well-known community agency, faith-based institution, club, or voluntary agency, individuals may come to you. One example given by Scott Graham of the American Red Cross (ARC) of Greater New York in a person-to-person interview was that, after the events of 9/11, citizens were wrapped around the ARC headquarters for five city blocks, standing in line to offer their help. It is estimated that over 22,000 volunteers offered their services through the ARC during the 9/11 relief effort. In this case, potential volunteers came to the organization because they had a sense of what the ARC does and how they might help. Many other examples such as this reflect that all trusted community agencies with a local branch or affiliate where people may emerge to volunteer should be encouraged to develop a plan.

Therefore, spot screening spontaneous volunteers can occur in a multitude of places, and training your community leaders and potential deployable managers in spot screening will assist in this process. As noted earlier, the limitations and challenges to faith-based and nongovernmental groups performing valuable functions within the Gulf Coast Hurricane recovery effort were stated as inadequate coordination and a lack of integration with official responders as well as inadequate training and experience. There are two ways to address this issue, perhaps more. The first is to ensure that every community leader will have the same training; the second is to develop teams of deployable managers to assist at convergent locations. Another way to manage this process and interface between official and community-based groups and volunteers is to establish a centralized location to conduct spot screening and coordinate other response functions, as in a VRC, a model of which was outlined in Chapter 6 of this field guide. If you do decide to set up a VRC or a scaled-down version, the Volunteer Reception Area (VRA), interviews and spot screening would be established as one of the stations in this center or area.

The VRC model can be developed as a multiagency center with many groups assigned to undertake certain roles, or it can be a small-scale effort within your organization. In the case of a multiagency VRC, citizens are informed through the media that there is a location for them to sign up for volunteer assignments, and the success of the VRC will depend on the willingness of citizens to report to that location.

Regardless of whether or not you rely on a VRC model or other process to spot screen and select volunteers, it is highly recommended that you give volunteers all informative documents and tools related to volunteer roles and agency protocols before the actual interview. In a best-case scenario, you will be able to hand candidates a complete volunteer packet, which will contain the summary of open positions, your external agency protocols, and a volunteer application that they can fill out while they wait for their turn to interview or for a call back.

Spot-Screening Safety

There are a few basic safety rules to follow to ensure that your team and the people around you remain safe in the spot-screening process. First, there are some important space setup considerations. As with most activities, interviews should never be conducted in a closed room, alone with a candidate. The ideal setup is to have interview stations in an open area that are far enough apart so that the interviewer and interviewee are able to hear each other properly, yet close enough for the interviewer to keep eye contact with associates. Setting up an interview area in this manner ensures that both the interviewer and the interviewee have other people around them, which reduces the opportunity for impropriety and ensures that assistance is readily available should the need arise. In addition, should the interviewer need to leave the area due to a security risk from the interviewee, he or she should never have to step around the interviewee: The means of egress should be behind or near the interviewer.

Along with an open environment, all staff and volunteers should always know where the exits to the area and building are. Interviewers should never block their egress with furniture, chairs, or where the interviewee will be sitting.

Despite these precautions, there is always a chance that you will come across a person who is either mentally disturbed or just plain difficult. It is best not to get into any kind of confrontation with them. If they become difficult and you feel that you are not capable of handling the situation, there are a few steps you can take, starting with implementing a buddy system.

Establishing a buddy system among interviewers or with nearby stations is ideal. Set some ground rules with your buddy, such as when you will check in on each other, and establish a signal for when there is an emergency and agree ahead of time on what to do when either one of you receives that signal. Thus, if an interviewee becomes difficult or threatening and you feel that you are not capable of handling the situation, signal to your buddy that you may want to get up from the interview and step away. As mentioned previously, in leaving the area, interviewers should not have to step around the person they are interviewing to do so. If there is an emergency, security should also be immediately made aware of the event, and you should also discuss your emergency signals with them, along with whether 911 should be called. If you have a safety manager or officer, this signal-and-response system is something they can implement and review with all staff and volunteers.

Spot-Screening Checklist

Any interview is only as good as the person conducting the process. Every person who is conducting interviews will need to have interpersonal skills. While it is only human nature to have predispositions from life experience and from what we are taught, the interviewer should strive to balance good judgment and intuition while remaining consistent and objective with each interviewee, treating all prospective volunteers equally. To help keep an interview on track, the interviewer should follow all the interview steps and procedures as they are laid out in this chapter, not skipping ahead or asking questions in a different order.

The interview "cheat sheet," called a spot-screening checklist (Figure 7.1), that is provided in this guide can be modified to meet the needs of the organization. The interviewers' job is to follow the steps you have laid out for them in this guide or in your adapted guide.

Keep an Objective View

If you are new to disaster interviewing, remember that you may be in the middle of a chaotic environment where individuals will be coming to you at the spur of the moment from any number of circumstances. They may not be wearing what you would expect; they may be new to volunteering in a disaster or may not know exactly the processes that are in place; but they may very well be a valuable resource. I remember one of the comments a FEMA voluntary agency liaison made about one of the first meetings she had with 9/11 volunteers who wanted to know how they could continue to help FEMA after the immediate response. She said that never before had she gone to a volunteer meeting in the middle of a disaster and walked in feeling like she was in a board meeting. Everyone had been dressed in suits! However, that was the work culture that many volunteers had come from, as office workers, executives, and professionals who lived and worked near the World Trade Center. It by no means meant that they could not roll up their sleeves and get their hands dirty if required.

The interview process should not be modified based on the interviewer's perception of the interviewee's level of experience. It will take more than a quick glance at someone's outfit or demeanor to find out what skills the individual possesses.

In addition, people seeking to volunteer may be survivors of the same disaster that you are responding to or have past experiences with trauma and disaster. Again, an objective assessment of their ability to help is necessary before determining whether or not they are ready to help. Individuals who emerge resilient and able to objectively help are immensely important, as they have firsthand experience and the ability to connect like no other. One account of such support is recounted by someone who lost her 35-year-old son in the 9/11 attacks who was comforted by a survivor of the Oklahoma City bombing.

"There is one thing that I do remember distinctly, and that was an Oklahoma City bombing victim's mother called me. How she got my name and number I do not know. She sent me notes, books and poems, and she called me and called me. Though there is so much that I just can't seem to remember, I do still remember her name and her calm, patient and reassuring voice. She had lost her daughter in the Oklahoma City bombing, and she understood. In one of our early conversations, she told me a story that I will never forget. In my moments of deepest pain, it has brought me comfort and given me strength. She said, 'If God came to you and said, "I'll make you a deal. I'll give you a beautiful, happy, and healthy son for 35 years and then I'll have to take him back." Would you have taken the deal?' That's the story, and the answer, of course, is, yes—in a heartbeat."*

Therefore, a history of living through a specific trauma can give volunteers an intimate perspective that can be a great comfort and resource to other survivors. The challenge will be to distinguish if these individuals have had enough time and experience to process their own losses in a way that they can now help others with impartiality. This means that they can separate their own personal experiences from the lessons they

---

* World Cares Center, "We Are Still Walking: Stories of Resilience." From Forums of Communities for a Resilient Future, April 18–20, 2006, Oklahoma City/New York City.

have learned, which can be shared to help others who are going through a similar experience. Another important factor is to look out for individuals who begin to recount or relive their own grief and who interject their own stories, making it about their own experiences instead of listening to those of the recent survivors.

Share Relevant Data

In all cases, as you greet each new potential volunteer, share relevant data on your organization's mission and how volunteer roles fit into the big picture, all of which will be contained in your volunteer packet. Along with this preprinted information that you will be providing, review all the positions that need filling. It is natural for individuals to arrive on scene with expectations of what their volunteer role may be. It is your job to clarify their expectations along with your own.

Use Spot-Screening Time Wisely

During the interview, use the Pareto principle or the 80–20 rule that states that roughly 80 percent of the effects come from 20 percent of the causes. Applying this rule to interviewing, you will gain most of the information you need if your questions take no longer than 20 percent of the time in the interview. Do not be afraid to allow a pause in the conversation. Most people are uncomfortable with silence and will fill the empty space with chatter. Resist the temptation to do this and encourage interviewees to share further by telling them this interview is a way to get to know them a little better so they can be placed in the most appropriate role for them.

Modeling Values: Actions Speak Louder than Words

Adults learn from observation. Modeling the culture and value of your organization is the first step in teaching your potential volunteers what is appropriate or not. How you dress, speak to the interviewee, and communicate via body language all signal the interviewee what you or your organization considers to be acceptable behavior. If you interrupt the interview to take a call or eat lunch, they will see that as acceptable behavior and will most likely emulate it in their activities. Keep in mind that modeling the behavior that we see is the way we have been raised, so if you do not want a certain behavior copied, do not engage in it yourself. To put it simply, the key thing is to be professional and attentive to the interviewees while hearing what they have to offer.

THE PROCESS

Volunteer Application and Self-Assessment

The tools and templates that you have created for your organization in Chapter 5 should be on hand to pass out to the volunteers that are waiting to be interviewed. Volunteer applications should be filled out by the potential volunteers and, if possible, as much informational material should be provided beforehand so that the interview process starts with a common understanding of what disaster volunteers can contribute and the structure within which their services can be carried out.

Materials for volunteers to review before the interview:

- Agency outreach flyer
- Site description
- Volunteer self-assessment
- Volunteer application

Once volunteers have read through the materials provided, decided there is an appropriate role for them, and completed the volunteer application and self-assessment, they should come to you and give you their application for review. It may be ideal to collect all applications and review them before asking a volunteer to sit down for an interview. However, you may not have the manpower to do so.

Review the application and ensure that all areas are filled out and that all the information is in order. Throughout the interview process, your interviewees will be supplementing your guidance through the material you provide them, such as the spot-screening checklist (included in this chapter), with good old common sense and their own experiences. It may be useful for interviewers to have the volunteer roles that need to be filled laid out before them, to take notes and jot down questions or comments during the interview, and to use all the templates provided.

Interviewer Templates

- The spot-screening checklist will walk you through all the questions to ask and serve as a place to keep your interview notes.

- The protocols for each SUCV role/task will remind you of what attributes and disqualifiers you will look for in the candidate and remind you to double check that all the necessary steps have been taken.

Five Types of Interview Questions

The following step-by-step interview process can be applied to all types of situations. If you have interviewing experience, you will find some familiar practices. When I implemented this process with my own potential staff members, I found that I was making wiser choices for every empty position. There are five types of questions in the just-in-time interview process that we call spot screening:

- A lifetime question
- A preference question
- A strength question
- A specific question
- A proof question

When practiced and done well, this interview can take five minutes per person. Remember, of those five minutes you should be speaking for one minute and listening for four minutes. The questions build upon each other and depend on the answers the candidate gives, as explained in the following pages.

The *lifetime question* sets a foundation of facts you will verify by asking each subsequent question in the interview process. This is an open-ended question for which there is no right or wrong answer. Ask one simple question that brings the candidate to a common point in time to reflect on his or her life experiences up until now as it pertains to volunteering. Perhaps you may start with, "Tell me about your first volunteering experience." No matter what, avoid questions that can be answered with one or two words, and allow interviewees to tell you their story. Listen, and be careful not to lead the applicant in one direction or the other, simply nodding your head in understanding. Saying, "I see," or, "That is interesting," are appropriate in encouraging interviewees to share their life experiences without interrupting the conversation. Look for relevant information, like what type of volunteering experience they have, their skills, their weaknesses, and the things that they learned in the process. Keep careful mental notes or even jot down key points and dates on a notepad. This could be the longest of the five answers.

The *preference question* will help you discover what your volunteers prefer among a list of options. Rather than stating the openings you have and asking the candidates if they would like to fill that role, here you are asking them to choose between the types of activities, environments, and other features of the volunteer positions that you have open. The question should be posed with no more than two options to answer. You can be as specific as you need to be, or the question can be geared to the core competencies or attributes you identified in Chapter 5.

Comparing their preference response with the information you received in their response to the lifetime question and ensuring the answers make sense is fundamental to the process. If candidates answer with one word or too briefly, you can follow up by asking them why they have that preference. For example, a question such as, "Do you work better in an organized or a chaotic environment?" would give you insight as to whether or not this person is appropriate to volunteer in a disaster setting where the situation is often hectic. A question such as, "Do you enjoy working alone or talking with people?" might offer you a perspective on whether or not this volunteer would be better in a team environment or in a data-entry or warehouse position.

Make certain that the candidates' answers align with the information they provided you through their lifetime answer. If the answers do not correlate, ask for clarification.

Example: The candidate answers the *lifetime question* with a story about how the candidate got involved with a youth group in high school that volunteered to teach English to people with limited English proficiency. This work included working as a team to develop a curriculum and spending time with students, both adults and children. This positive experience leads the candidate to pursue a career in teaching. This lifetime experience would lead you to believe that the person would want to volunteer in an interactive setting with people.

During the *preference question,* you might ask: "Do you prefer to work with people or doing office work such as filing?" If the candidate answers that she prefers to work with people, this response aligns with her lifetime response and makes logical sense. However if the candidate replies, "I much prefer doing office work alone over working with people," then you must ask for clarification. An acceptable clarifying answer could be that she is a teacher and would prefer a change of venue doing something that differs from her work life. However, if the answer is that after that experience of working with children, she really got burnt out on people, you should take note of this, as this could be a red flag for a position where this person has to interact with others.

The *strength question* determines what the candidates' greatest strengths are and when they are at their best. This information will add to your assessment to help you place the volunteer in the most appropriate role. Ask the candidate to describe his or her strengths with regard to the different positions they have held and environments they have been in. One example of a strength question is to ask the candidates what their greatest strength is in their current job, in the school they are attending, at home, or where they have volunteered, based on the information they have given in previous responses.

The *specific question* asks interviewees for concrete examples on how they have applied their experience (lifetime question), where they would rather volunteer (preference question), and their strengths as it relates to working in the areas they prefer to be in (strength question). Candidates should be asked to describe specific instances where they have exhibited the skills that relate to the areas of strength they have identified. This question will allow you to gauge whether or not the candidate has actually done the things he or she has claimed to have accomplished. It can also serve as another verifying factor in a process where all the answers should make sense together.

An example of a specific question is: "Can you give me an example of some of the routine tasks you had to accomplish during your time as a teacher?" The interviewee should be able to answer this question with ease and recite several examples that come to mind, such as curriculum development, coordinating school trips, and facilitating group activities.

The *proof question* is the final and perhaps the most direct question in the interview that should provide you with the outcomes and results, or the "proof," of the candidate's work and experiences. The interviewee's response should further enable you to verify everything that he or she has shared with you and help you to assess their level of experience in order to finalize or clarify your decision on what roles and tasks they will be designated for. With this question, ask the candidate to list the accomplishments and provide evidence of what he or she has specifically provided as a benefit or positive outcome to a situation, population, or organization. An example of a question for the person who had been a teacher would be, "You mentioned that the adults you taught loved the way you brought a physical prop to your class to provide a visual for their lesson. How do you know that your teaching practices were effective?"

Questions not to ask: Even though you are in a disaster environment and may feel you should be more candid about your requirements, there are still questions that should never be asked. You should not ask questions that would discriminate based on a candidate's race, gender, age, religion, marital status, sexual preference, military record, or national origin. In addition, you cannot ask about their personal health, credit history, child-care needs, length of community residency, their English language skills, or birthplace. For example, questions such as, "What religious holidays do you observe?" "Are you married?" or, "What country are you from?" should never be asked in an interview.

Cultural Sensitivity

If you are going into a community other than your own or not one that you are very familiar with, keep in mind that the individuals you are interviewing are most likely from within the community; it is you who is the outsider. There are considerable benefits to engaging their services despite the obstacles you may need to overcome.

For example, communication styles normal to a particular community may differ from your own or what you are used to. Short or terse sentences may be a speech pattern, even though they may seem rude or terse to you. Language barriers may lead to awkward word choices that may act as a barrier to truly understanding the capabilities of the volunteer. You may find that talking about one's strengths may be perceived as boasting and might require some extra effort on the interviewer's part to ask for an interviewee's strengths. It may also be the case that self-promoting is the cultural norm, and you need to sort through the boasting to find the true capabilities of the applicant. If you know the community that you will be assisting and it is not your own, try to become familiar with it before arriving to manage the disaster response. Ask around, seek local leaders to assist you, and follow the interview process to loop back on the issues that concern you to make a distinction between a cultural difference and behavior that is not acceptable.

The task of spot screening volunteers in your own environment can be stressful. When this is combined with the additional factors discussed previously, you may find yourself forgetting the steps you need to take. To assist you and your staff, Figure 7.1 presents a snapshot of a spot-screening checklist. A full template is located in the appendix at the end of this book. You should make enough copies of this template as part of an emer-

Spot Screening Checklist

FOR INTERNAL DISTRIBUTION ONLY

Date:_____ / _____ /_____

Name: _____

Identification: _____

Address: _____

Phone/cell: _____

Place of employment/school: _____

Emergency contact name: _____

Emergency contact phone/cell: _____

Interviewer: _____

Location: _____

Disqualifiers	Attributes
Immediate Disqualifiers: ☐ Criminal record ☐ Mental illness ☐ Substance abuse ☐ No transportation ☐ Cannot lift heavy items ☐ Other _____ **Two-Strike Disqualifiers** ☐ No Show ☐ Overzealous ☐ Lone Ranger ☐ Refuses Supervision ☐ Other:	☐ Humility ☐ Grounded ☐ Effective listener ☐ Compassion ☐ Awareness ☐ Cultural sensitivity ☐ Others _____

Interview Questions

☐ **Lifetime** – What has happened in your life that has made you interested or prepared to volunteer with us? Share a story about yourself.

Notes:_____

_____

_____

_____

_____

☐ **Preference**—Do you have a preference as to what type of work you take on? *(Name two different choices among the roles or tasks—For example: prefers working with people or quiet office work).*

Figure 7.1 Worksheet: Spot-screening checklist. *Continued*

Notes:_____

☐ Preference response aligned with lifetime response
☐ If not, explanation:

    ☐ **Strength** – What are your strengths, based on your current or past work or volunteering experiences, that would also apply to volunteering with us?

Notes:_____

☐ Strength response aligned with lifetime and preference response
☐ If not, explanation:

    ☐ **Specific** – Do you have specific details that show evidence of the strengths you just mentioned?

Notes:_____

☐ Specific response aligned with previous responses
☐ If not, explanation:

    ☐ **Proof** – Please tell me a few accomplishments that demonstrate evidence of your competence.

Notes:_____

☐ Proof response aligned with previous responses
☐ If not, explanation:

Other questions: _____
_____
_____

Additional notes: _____
_____

Recommendation:		
☐ Selected for: _____	☐ Decline	☐ Refer to:
☐ Other: _____		

Figure 7.1 (*Continued*) Worksheet: Spot-screening checklist.

gency response kit or "GO bag" so that you can use one for each interview and thereby use your notes to conduct your post-screening assessments.

Assessment

In Chapter 6, you identified and documented attributes and disqualifiers for each role, and you will want to interview using these as a guide. There may be technical skills specific to a career that a volunteer may have expertise in; however, these skills are not generally the information that you will be making the final decisions on. What you should be looking for is consistency from the biography through to current history, which is to say from lifetime question through to the proof question (see Figure 7.2). Candidates should answer the questions readily and with ease, and not be thrown off when you bring them back to something that they have to clarify.

Review the spot-screening outcomes in comparison with the roles and tasks that spontaneous volunteers would fill, their core attributes, and the disqualifiers that would eliminate them as a candidate.

OUTCOME OF INTERVIEW: STEPS TO TAKE UPON SELECTION

Offer a Role

If a candidate meets your criteria for a particular task, the obvious course of action would be to *offer a role*. If the candidate is interested, the next step is to *review the responsibilities* associated with the role or task you have offered. Responsibilities are not one-sided, and include the agency's responsibilities along with the volunteer responsibilities that we outlined in Chapter 5, "Protocols for SUCV Management." It is best to clarify expectations up front in accordance with your policies.

Agency responsibilities
- Credentialing
- Access that volunteers will have
- Equipment
- Meals
- Training
- Shelter
- Reimbursement

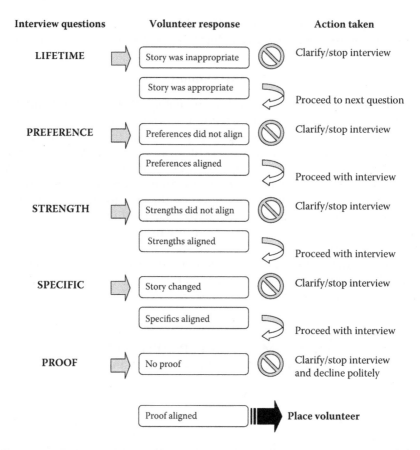

Figure 7.2 Interview questions as an assessment tool.

- Supportive services
- Insurance/liability
- Site description
- Briefing/debriefing

Volunteer responsibilities

- Length of shift
- Length of volunteer commitment
- Preshift and postshift briefing
- After-action notes
- Code of conduct
- Confidentiality agreement

- Self-care
- Family preparedness plan

Agree on a Communication Strategy

Once you have offered the position and the candidate has accepted, it is time to agree upon your communication strategy. This is not as simple as outlining whether or not you will use the phone or e-mail and what number to reach each other at, but involves outlining a comprehensive set of tools that are used in the Incident Command System (ICS) to avoid confusion as disaster and emergency management evolves and changes.

The steps within your communication strategy should include:

- Reviewing all the materials provided before and after the interview to answer any questions and clarify any details.
- Using the incident command chart to show volunteers where they fit into the structure and who their direct supervisor will be. Tell them where this information is posted and updated so that they may refer to it if supervisors change during their volunteer time.
- Reinforcing the importance of check-ins, pre- and postshift briefings as a tool to update volunteers on the changes that take place, as well as an opportunity to share any experiences, ask questions, and get to know your team. It should be reinforced that all briefings are mandatory and considered to be part of a volunteer shift.

Always end by thanking the volunteer for their willingness to help and the contribution they are making.

Validate or Check Credentials

Whether you choose to validate or credential your volunteer will depend on a variety of issues. It is best to review all of the issues involved with verifying the identity and credentials of volunteers with the worst-case scenario in mind: a facility with no electricity or no immediate Internet access with a definite need to fill positions with SUCVs. Considerations include:

- What positions are you assigning someone to?
- How many supervisors will be present at all times?
- What crisis are you responding to?

The policies that you make should take multiple situations into consideration. Once your policies are in place, review them with the proper authorities within your agency. The individual who handles your insurance policies would be a good start. Where such regulations exist, it is necessary that your policies comply.

Validate

The term *validate* in this manual refers to the confirmation of an individual's identity as provided in the application and in the interview with you. This does not require any technology and can simply be performed by checking a valid piece of identification such as a driver's license or passport. You may keep a copy of the applicant's ID on file if you have access to a copy machine or mark down identification codes and numbers for your records.

Credential

Credentialing has two levels:

1. Confirming evidence of the individual's authority, training, and status. This can be conducted through a background check and by calling or e-mailing their references.
2. Training individuals in your own agency's training procedures and then credentialing them with your agency's authority to perform certain functions with the knowledge that they have completed your training in a satisfactory manner.

In some cases, credentialing implies that you will then supply the volunteer with some form of agency ID to prove the individual's status with the agency. It is also widely assumed that with such a credentialed ID, the volunteer would be assured access to certain areas and perhaps restricted areas to assist in disaster.

Your "worst-case scenario" policy (in which you do not have access to the Internet or a computer) might include steps to collect as much data as possible in the initial screening with the individual's identification information and getting their signed permission to run a background check as soon as you are able.

Decline with Gratitude

If the candidate is not suitable for the roles that you currently need fulfilling, *decline with gratitude*. There are additional steps, depending on the reasons for not choosing the candidate.

- If they are suitable for volunteering but you do not need them now, you may either ask them if you may contact them at a later date, explaining that the recovery effort has several phases in which different skills are needed, or refer them to another agency that would be a good match for this candidate.
- If the candidate is not suitable for volunteering, it is best to simply thank them for offering their services, and explain that you do not have a position for them. Do not refer them to another agency. In this case, you should mark on the candidate's application the reasons why they have been declined in order to avoid someone else reassigning them at a later date or referring them to another agency.

END-OF-CHAPTER QUESTIONS

- What are some key interviewing fundamentals that you have learned about in this chapter?
- How should you set up the interview area, considering safety concerns for your staff?
- How will the five types of interview questions help to assess the interviewee?
- What are the steps to take in the interviewing process after you have selected the roles your interviewee will fill?
- What are the steps you may take if you cannot utilize the interviewee's services?

CONCLUSION

In this chapter, you have reviewed

- Spot-screening fundamentals, from staying objective to informing potential volunteers of all relevant information and setting up the interview area for safe screening.
- Five essential spot-screening questions that allow you to assess the consistency, accuracy, and range of your interviewee's interests and skills: the lifetime question, the preference question, the strength question, the specific question, and the proof question.

- The key steps for following up on an interview, from selecting volunteers for a role, reviewing responsibilities, agreeing on a communication strategy, validating or credentialing volunteers, or declining with gratitude.

Now that you have reviewed and understood the essentials of spot screening, assessing, and selecting volunteers, you are ready to review the essential elements of good management and building resilience in volunteers.

8

Reducing Attrition and Unwanted Behavior through Proactive Management
A Competency Model for Leaders and Managers

IN THIS CHAPTER

- Why Good Management of Volunteers Is Essential
- Find Existing Resources to Manage Volunteers
- Understand the Needs of Your Managers and Your Volunteers
- Proactive Management Protocols
  - Team Orientation
    - Provide Just-In-Time Training
    - Share Your Agency's Mission, Vision, and Values
    - Clarify Expectations
    - Promote Self-Care
    - Prepare for Sunsetting
    - Long-Term Recovery Roles
  - Build Your Team
  - Leverage Command Presence

WHY GOOD MANAGEMENT OF
VOLUNTEERS IS ESSENTIAL

The spontaneous volunteerism of citizens and communities is a fact in every disaster. However, the management of these good citizens must never be spontaneous. One of the most common complaints that I hear from volunteer managers around the country is that they spend all their time training volunteers and then these volunteers leave, never to be heard from again. The first question I ask is, "What did you do to keep them?" I am sometimes met with a confused look, followed by the response, "They're volunteers! What do you mean, 'What did *I* do to keep them?' I don't have time to entertain our volunteers; they are here because they want to be." As harsh as these statements sound, they are true; most emergency managers do not have the time to focus on volunteers, and the majority of volunteers are present because they want to be there.

As recognized by emergency managers who face the challenge of internal capacity and changes in traditional volunteerism, volunteering habits have changed as our society has evolved from a single-income household to a double-income household and beyond. People have less time to volunteer within the traditional frameworks that agencies have established. This does not mean that people are any less caring. However, it does mean that they have less time to devote to training and are more inclined to help where they can be put to use immediately.

What happens during their volunteer experience will be a factor as to whether or not these individuals becomes permanent members of your organization's volunteer efforts, become donors, or walk away discontented with their experience.

Just as we have taken the time to develop spot-screening and assessment protocols to place spontaneous volunteers in the correct roles, we need to develop management techniques to guide them in those roles. After all, you may be spending days, perhaps weeks, with these individuals, and after that time spent working together, you have an experienced disaster volunteer who would add value to your team beyond the immediate disaster response period. By managing spontaneous volunteers with the same level of care as you would your affiliated volunteers, you are increasing your chances to increase your affiliated volunteer pool with people who now have disaster volunteering experience under your management. In speaking with Scott Graham, chief response officer at the American Red Cross (ARC) chapter of Greater New York, it turns out that approximately 1,000 of the 7,442 volunteers in his New York chapter were spontaneous volunteers who emerged to help during events such as 9/11 and Hurricane Katrina.

Good management not only retains and protects the volunteer, but it protects the agency and the constituents whom the agency is serving. By providing good management, you will ensure that volunteers complete their tasks without harming themselves or putting your constituents, the disaster survivors, in harm's way. It prevents a host of problems from occurring down the line, as volunteers are clear about your expectations of their conduct, about the specific task before them, and the ways they must function within your team and with the disaster survivors they are helping.

What follows are some considerations and steps to take as you develop your agency's management protocols.

FIND EXISTING RESOURCES TO MANAGE VOLUNTEERS

The first issue often mentioned by emergency managers around the country is the lack of available resources within an agency's current staff pool to manage spontaneous volunteers. Preplanning and predesignation of additional resources to be recruited and trained to help should begin to take place as soon as your spontaneous volunteer management plan is completed and approved. If you are an emergency manager, there are many existing groups that can be leveraged to assist in the screening, training, and management of spontaneous volunteers. As mentioned in Chapter 1, organizations such as community emergency response teams (CERT), local clubs, community-based groups, and faith-based organizations are all resources that can and should be trained to assist within their communities and to support local authorities. This approach is proving to be effective in New Jersey, where World Cares Center (WCC) is working in partnership with the New Jersey Office of Emergency Management to train their CERT members to act as spontaneous-volunteer managers in the event of a disaster, thereby force multiplying their ability to manage new resources and alleviating this responsibility for emergency managers themselves. Both community-based organizations and emergency managers can establish memorandums of agreement (MOAs) with local clubs and groups who might be interested in providing volunteer management in times of disaster.

UNDERSTAND THE NEEDS OF YOUR
MANAGERS AND YOUR VOLUNTEERS

In Chapter 5, you flushed out your protocols and assigned who would manage what and how many staff and volunteers. Review those leadership positions. As the director of this initiative, it is important to understand both what your volunteer managers want and what they *may* want. It is also important that you ensure that the individuals you assign in management functions have the proper training predisaster.

Finding the common goals of both your managers and your volunteers and focusing efforts around these goals are key steps to ensuring a cohesive volunteer management effort. Examples of some common goals include:

- We all want a safe and effective volunteer effort that helps as many people as possible.
- We all want to be appreciated and respected in our roles.
- We all want to be able to sustain our efforts, in a healthy manner, for as long as we're needed.

In order to achieve these and other common goals, certain requirements must be met.

Managers want:
- Volunteers who have been properly screened and selected for the roles they will undertake.
- Volunteers who understand not only their tasks, but how they fit into the larger picture.
- Volunteers who understand the role of the managers they will report to and accept their guidance and authority.

In a disaster response situation, there is a large and diverse pool of people with a high level of professional skills and knowledge, experts in their fields who will come out to help. Everyone will have different experiences managing or being managed; therefore, establishing a comprehensible line of authority and having the volunteers accept that authority will make the manager's job easier and provide a clear chain of command for the volunteers and everyone involved. This will be facilitated by communicating with tools such as the Incident Command System (ICS) chart (Figure 8.1).

Managers also want volunteers who have the ability to stay grounded and make self-care part of their daily ritual. Managers often

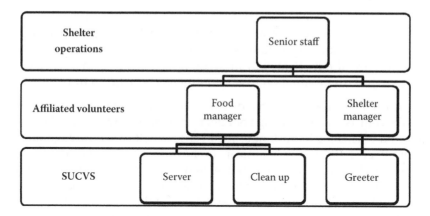

Figure 8.1 ICS chart for shelter operations.

discuss the issue of inexperienced volunteers unprepared to work in the emotionally and physically stressful environment of disaster volunteering who then turn into people that the managers and the agency need to take care of rather than performing as the helpers those volunteers intended to be. When this occurs, it detracts from the entire team effort and takes time and focus away from delivering services to the community directly impacted by the disaster at hand. In this regard, much of the groundwork of screening for people who cannot stay grounded or emphasizing the importance of self-care will be done in the interview and orientation process, but it is the job of the managers to implement effective management protocols that ensure the physical and emotional health of their volunteers.

> We found from the interviews that the primary motivation for volunteering was a compelling need to help in some way, particularly a need to assist victims, a desire—even obsession—to "do something" in order to contribute something positive and find something meaningful in the midst of a disaster characterized by cruelty and terror.
>
> Seana Lowe and Alice Fothergill
> *A Need to Help: Emergent Volunteer Behavior after 9/11*

Exemplified above are some motivating factors that drive individuals to provide service without any monetary compensation. Listed below are additional reasons individuals seek to volunteer. When developing a volunteer management program, it is prudent to keep these in mind and to address them in the programs you develop.

- Volunteers want to be engaged and utilized effectively.
- Being part of a team is an important part of why people volunteer.
- Many community volunteers who emerge to help during disasters are also motivated by an underlying need to gain a sense of control over a situation where control has been taken from them.

Everyone understands that disasters are unpredictable and that there will be confusion. But placing volunteers in a role where they can be effective and efficient is important to their sense of self-worth throughout the effort. Repeatedly asking volunteers to show up at a certain time and then having nothing for them to do but sit and wait several hours before they can begin to help will wear thin on them, as it would on anyone. They will leave and find an organization or effort where they feel they are needed and their time is valued, or they might even be discouraged from volunteering altogether.

As for being on a team, there will be volunteers who will prefer to spend the bulk of their time working alone, but being part of a large team effort will still be important to them. In most cases, we have found that people who are coming to volunteer are looking to interact in a team setting, which allows them to seek and gain support among their fellow volunteers, form bonds and friendships, and foster opportunities for volunteers of all levels of experience to learn from each other.

Finally, for volunteers who seek to regain a sense of control over their lives through their service with your agency, this is a natural and healthy reaction that may not be an obvious goal even to the volunteer. Volunteering can contribute to the resiliency and recovery of these individuals, as it invests them with a sense of purpose and accomplishment in a situation where such feelings are otherwise difficult to realize.

Now that we have discussed the needs and motivating factors for both the manager and the volunteer, we will discuss how to achieve these goals through proactive management protocols. In this way, you can create an atmosphere that inspires your team to return time and time again.

PROACTIVE MANAGEMENT PROTOCOLS

Provide a Team Orientation

A team orientation includes a review of expectations, agency responsibilities, volunteer protocols and responsibilities, and tools for volunteer self-care and training. Some of this information may have been shared with the volunteers individually after the interview process, but it is critical to review these policies and answer questions in the team setting to build and reinforce the structure needed to work well together.

The orientation should include information such as:

- Your agency's mission, values, and vision
- Clarification of volunteer roles and tasks
- Credentialing
- What kind of access your new volunteers will have
- What special equipment you will provide for them, if any, and policies on returning the equipment
- Whether you will provide meals during their shifts
- Whether you will provide training, such as a just-in-time training
- Whether you will provide shelter if they are at a remote location
- Whether you will provide reimbursement for travel or any expenses
- What supportive services are available, such as mental health counseling
- The extent of medical coverage, such as workers' compensation
- What conditions and requirements are at the site where they will be volunteering
- Preparing for sunsetting
- Possible long-term recovery roles

Agency responsibilities will also be supplemented with protocols for volunteers, including:

- Length of shift
- Length of volunteer commitment
- Pre-shift and post-shift briefing
- After-action notes
- Code of conduct
- Confidentiality agreement
- Self-care
- Family-preparedness plan

Just-In-Time Training

A just-in-time training can be delivered within the orientation or while volunteers are waiting to be placed. This training is a brief, generalized training for all volunteers—regardless of their role—that imparts the core competencies and qualities that you seek in all volunteers, thereby ensuring their safety and self-care.

The training would consist of

- Evaluating a volunteer's readiness to volunteer
- Assessing which volunteer roles would match the volunteer
- Appraising the conduct and behavior of an effective volunteer
- Reviewing self-care in disaster response
- Engaging the support of friends and family in dealing with the experience of volunteering

The volunteer self-assessment would include questions such as a volunteer's limitations, schedule, need to ensure that family members are safe, and the types of situations he or she is most comfortable in as well as whether or not the volunteer would be comfortable in a disaster-response situation. In posing the qualities of effective volunteers, the training would include those attributes they need to be a responsive and caring volunteer, no matter what task they are undertaking (e.g., showing empathy, staying grounded, ability to listen reflexively). In discussing conduct and self-care, the training would include the possible negative impacts of volunteering, such as sources of stress and indirect trauma from working with disaster victims, along with steps and suggestions that volunteers can take to mitigate these effects.

Share Your Agency's Mission, Vision, and Values
With so many needs that have to be tended to in disasters, setting a focal point and parameters around what your organization and team will do in disaster response will help to keep everyone on track. That focal point is your organization's mission and how each team's function and each volunteer's tasks relate to that mission. It is also important to relate how each volunteer fits into the big picture and how what he or she is doing is a valuable and important part of accomplishing a larger task. Associating what each volunteer is doing with the larger disaster relief effort instills a sense of ownership, pride, and responsibility. This will also help keep everyone mission-focused and effectively working together.

Example: In the wake of a storm, if your organization is responsible for clearing debris and you find a volunteer questioning why your team cannot rebuild a storm victim's home, it will be important to put your organization's work and its task in perspective. What may be obvious to you may not be to a new disaster volunteer. Taking the time to explain the ecosystem of disaster response may put the various roles into perspective, so that volunteers understand how and why their role is important and who else is making a difference along with them. Thus, an explanation such as the

Figure 8.2 Participants at the World Cares Center's leading and managing training for the New Jersey State Police, going through a tabletop exercise in 2009 (Source: World Cares Center).

following can help to do this: "We are clearing the debris so that essential services like electric and water can be restored. Next, our fellow volunteer agency will have access to assess all of the damaged homes. This agency will then send in engineers who will assess the safety of those homes and plan what needs to be done to rebuild. Without our efforts, none of those other teams can get in to help. So the faster we clear the street, the sooner they can get to those homes and fulfill their mission."

Clarify Expectations

As a manager, presenting volunteer roles and tasks clearly in terms of what they are and what they do not include is essential to your mission because it helps you to organize your teams effectively as well as build up the volunteers' sense of accomplishment and even their sense of recovery from disaster. You can clarify expectations by:

- Setting realistic goals and expectations for each day's assignment in order to keep everyone on track. Rather than having the sense of being overwhelmed by an unachievable list of needs, volunteers will feel a sense of accomplishment when you set realistic goals and responsibilities for the day and when those tasks are completed.
- Educating volunteers or team members who ask questions about their role or the function of your organization, taking it as an opportunity to educate not only the individual asking questions, but also others who may not have understood their roles completely. First commend the individual for stepping forward with a question by saying, "That is a great question, thank you." By doing this, you are creating an environment where clarification is acceptable and expected. Emergency managers have stated that they much prefer volunteers who seek to clarify their roles and duties than those who process their responsibilities incorrectly because they are too embarrassed to ask questions. You can help to foster this behavior with management techniques that positively reinforce those who ask questions.
- Clarifying expectations such as time commitment also prevents volunteers from burning out and trying to take on too much work. As we discussed in Chapter 5, setting a specific time period for a volunteer commitment to last will not only clarify the expectations for the volunteer, but also for you as a manager, because it will be easier to rotate volunteers and relieve them of exposure to a specific stressor.

Promote Self-Care

Inexperienced volunteers can easily be consumed by the enormity of the workload that needs to be accomplished. In most cases, except for immediate lifesaving efforts, volunteers will be helping for many days, weeks, months, and in some cases, years. I like to tell everyone that volunteering is a marathon, not a sprint. Therefore, it is not only acceptable but expected for them to take care of themselves, and as a good manager, you should make this clear. You can structure some of these aspects of promoting self-care into everyday routines for volunteers; other aspects require you to lead by example.

Some key reminders to promote self-care include:

- Stress the importance of a good balance between a volunteer's home life and the duties as a volunteer.
- Set healthy shifts with breaks.
- Set and maintain mandatory pre-shift briefings and post-shift debriefings.
- Remember to monitor your volunteers for signs of fatigue.
- Keep in mind that if you do not take care of yourself, you will not be able to take care of anyone else.
- Encourage staff and volunteers to have individual and family preparedness plans in place for themselves.

Because self-care is such a vital part of your volunteer management program, and yet can be so easily overlooked in disaster-response situations, Chapter 9 provides a comprehensive set of guidelines for healthy self-care practices that you can share with your volunteers. In addition, Chapter 9 also includes a condensed version of an individual family preparedness plan that you can share with your staff and volunteers.

Prepare Volunteers for Sunsetting

The role of the disaster volunteer in a particular community during a particular disaster response will inevitably change, evolve, or come to an end. This fact may not be the first thing on a volunteer's mind, nor will it be evident to some as they become more engrossed in their newfound roles as disaster volunteers. With the surge of need and the experience of helping comes a rush of adrenaline that can make volunteering addictive. Some individuals forge important relationships and go through experiences they have not shared with others before. Knowing these things ahead of time may help to understand the emotions and feelings that a volunteer may go through and why it may be difficult to look ahead and accept that the need for volunteers, and therefore for their services, will end.

A good manager should help to keep things in perspective and prepare for long-term recovery by making sure to:

- Share with the volunteer that it is the nature of disaster response to have an immediate, urgent need for help that eventually ends, and that efforts in the first phase of disaster relief will eventually "sunset."
- Set a limited time frame for volunteers to foresee how long they are expected to volunteer, such as an initial two-week period that may be renewed.
- Encourage individuals to fully integrate activities and routines from their pre-disaster life—e.g., gym, dinner with family members—alongside their volunteering duties, which will help them to transition from their role as disaster volunteers back into a full and healthy life postdisaster.

These steps will reinforce the fact that disaster volunteering is not a permanent situation and assist volunteers in transitioning into the phase where their services may no longer be needed.

Long-Term Recovery Roles
As you monitor your volunteers during the initial stages of disaster relief, keep an eye out for the volunteers who may be effective in the long-term recovery effort. Then, as you plan for this next phase of disaster response, begin to discuss possible opportunities to refocus volunteers' efforts with those you feel are most capable or whose skills are most relevant to your agency's planned efforts. This is also the time when you may call upon those volunteers whom you screened and could not use during immediate-response phases but recognized as potential volunteers in long-term recovery efforts.

Roles for volunteers in long-term recovery initiatives include:

- Helping in family-assistance centers
- Joining a community board
- Organizing a peer-to-peer support group
- Setting up a one-stop recovery center where all services are concentrated, such as a community resiliency center

For an example of a community resiliency center, see the Appendix, which contains a description of the WCC's September Space Program.

Build Your Team

Team building is not only making sure that everyone knows their roles or works together well. It is also leveraging the knowledge and leadership of each of the individuals on your team to maximum effect. Everyone, from the volunteers who are new to your organization to your affiliated volunteers, should be considered your most powerful assets.

Team building consists of the following proactive steps:

- Assessing your volunteers and recognizing the ones who have previous disaster response experience
- Trying your best to diversify the team, matching those with experience to those with little or none
- Encouraging a buddy system where you ask each volunteer to choose a partner on whom they will depend for support during their volunteer experience
- Recognizing not only when individuals do great work, but also taking the time to recognize good teamwork
- Spotting conflicts and misunderstandings between team members early on and cooling them down before they become bigger problems
- Finding ways for volunteers to have input, even as they stay on mission and on task

These steps and others will encourage your volunteers to share their skills and knowledge with each other and your organization, further building your team and improving its ability to respond effectively.

Leverage Command Presence

As you train and build your team, supervise them in an encouraging manner while leading through influence and manner as well as through direct action and words. Leveraging a command presence will reassure those who are looking to you as a leader during challenging times.

- Always maintain a calm demeanor and speak assertively, but not harshly.
- Show respect for your volunteers and their abilities by being a visible and accessible presence, but without interfering with their work or micromanaging them.
- Whenever possible, lead with praise before correcting errors.

Disaster volunteering is serious work, but it does not have to be a sad or harrowing experience. Remember to keep spirits high by recognizing your team members' accomplishments, their positive attitude, their willingness to help others, and their contribution to the greater effort.

As a leader, bring an appropriate amount of humor to the situation. Encourage your team to do the same when they are amongst themselves and during breaks and briefings. However, remind them that it may not be appropriate to use humor in the presence of survivors and family members. Always be professional as a manager. There is no room for horseplay where the lives and well-being of others are concerned.

END-OF-CHAPTER QUESTIONS

- What are the benefits of developing good management protocols for your agency and your volunteers?
- Will you use existing resources in your locality to manage volunteers? If so, which resources?
- Have you identified the common goals of managers and volunteers within your agency?
- Have you prepared a team orientation or just-in-time training for your spontaneous volunteers?
- Does your orientation or your training include your agency's mission and values?
- What are the methods you will use for clarifying the expectations you have of volunteers?
- What are some team-building techniques that you apply to volunteer management in your agency?
- How will you leverage a command presence with your team members?
- Does your volunteer management plan include self-care guidelines or training? (Chapter 9 contains further information and guidance on this topic.)
- Does your volunteer management plan include plans for sunsetting?
- Have you considered what roles volunteers might take on in your agency's long-term recovery work?

CONCLUSION

In this chapter, you have reviewed the tools and techniques necessary for proactive management of volunteers and the competency model for managers. From finding existing resources for managing volunteers to understanding the needs of both managers and volunteers, you can begin to develop a comprehensive management program and set of guidelines for those on your staff who will manage volunteers.

9

Building a Resilient Team

It has become increasingly evident that anyone responding to both acute and chronic disasters suffers many of the same symptoms of trauma as the people they are there to help. Failure to address this issue on the part of agencies results in burnout, dysfunctional behavior, difficulty in readjusting to "normal" life, administrative disconnect from realities on the ground, high staff turnover, and increased training costs.

Dr. Juliet Bruce

Director of Institute for Transformation through the Arts,
Larson Fellowship in Spirituality and Health at the Library of Congress

IN THIS CHAPTER

- The Impact of Mental Health Issues in Volunteers
- Potential Negative Side Effects of Volunteer work
  - Risk Factors for Trauma and Stress Disorders
  - Secondary or Vicarious Trauma
  - Compassion Fatigue
  - Posttraumatic Stress Disorder
- Signs that Stress Is Taking a Toll
- Managing with Self-Care in Mind
  - Creating a Safe Space
  - Matching Skills and Roles
  - Orientation
  - Briefings

- Training
- Free and Confidential Resources
- Bonding with Your Team
- Communicating Self-Care Concerns
- Self-Care Training for Your Volunteers
  - Family Preparedness and Care
  - The Buddy System
  - MEDS: Move, Eat, Drink, Sleep
  - Relaxation Techniques
  - Self-Care outside of Volunteering

THE IMPACT OF MENTAL HEALTH ISSUES IN VOLUNTEERS

Now that we have reviewed a competency model for the proactive management of volunteers, we will turn to one vital aspect of management: building resilience in your volunteers to handle the stress of disaster volunteering. Incorporating this as an essential part of your spontaneous-volunteer management program will help to address the challenge of the lack of staff and affiliated volunteers, because resilient spontaneous volunteers may well become affiliated or long-term volunteers that significantly increase your ability to respond to disaster. This proactive approach also helps to minimize the risk of utilizing spontaneous volunteers and reduces liability by creating an environment in which volunteers feel supported and in turn can continue to support disaster survivors and your agency.

It is well documented that being involved in disaster-response activities can cause emotional stress. This stress is not limited by the proximity to the location of the event or to those who have directly experienced it. The impact of disaster-response-induced stress may occur during volunteering or well after an individual's involvement in helping has ended and the person has the time to process what he or she has experienced. Stress factors can affect the individuals who are helping in a multitude of ways, from those who are providing phone bank services for survivors to those who are cataloging the details of the survivors' experiences, as so many volunteer lawyers did in filling out death certificates in the aftermath of the 9/11 attacks. For example, a study undertaken one year after the attacks found symptoms of

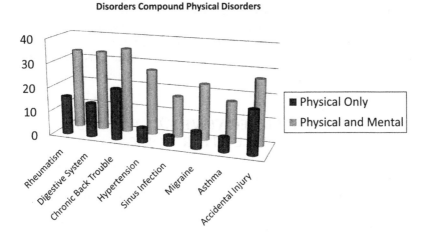

Average Days Per Year of Work Lost When Mental Disorders Compound Physical Disorders

FIGURE 9.1 Average days per year of work lost when mental disorders compound physical disorders. (Original illustration, statistics from M. A. Buist-Bouwman, R. de Graaf, W. A. Vollebergh, et al. *Acta Psychiatrica Scand.* 111 [2005]: 436–443)

posttraumatic stress disorder (PTSD) among 13 percent of the rescue and recovery workers.*

Emotional stress and other psychosocial conditions and disorders have a significant impact on overall health. Leaving such issues unaddressed will affect the health and capacity of your volunteer force. For example, data collected on work productivity shows that mental health issues aggravate or intensify physical health issues and contribute to further days lost on the job. The graph in Figure 9.1 displays the evidence gathered on the individuals with physical illnesses compared to those with physical illnesses compounded by mental health issues. As you can see, the days out of work are significantly increased when a mental-health-related issue is involved. Maintaining a healthy volunteer workforce will depend on keeping your volunteers safe both physically and emotionally.

---

* R. P. Smith, C. L. Katz, A. Homes, R. Herbert, S. Levin, J. Moline, P. Landsbergis, L. Stevenson, C. S. North, G. L. Larkin, S. Baron, and J. J. Hurrell, "Mental Health Status of World Trade Center Rescue and Recovery Workers and Volunteers," New York City, July 2002–August 2004, MMWR 53 (2004): 812–815.

The first step toward mitigating the harm that disaster work can cause is to become familiar with what the symptoms of stress can be and what causes them, and then training yourself and your volunteers in self-care techniques that will mitigate their effects. Self-care translates to any situation and can help in everyday life as well as during the most trying times, such as disaster response.

POTENTIAL NEGATIVE SIDE EFFECTS OF VOLUNTEER WORK

On May 30, 2002, the clean-up was complete. Ten stories of cement and iron, silica and gypsum, asbestos and rock salt, mica and quartz, glass and fiberglass were removed from Ground Zero. But the garbage is still there, not only in the dust that blows over lower Manhattan, but in the minds of the people permanently affected. How do I know when an injury will ever heal and when it is permanent? How can I tell who will recall that day like a scene in a movie and who will remember it as a day they will never recover from?

9/11 Mental Health Worker*

The term *posttraumatic stress disorder* (PTSD) has frequently been used in relation to war experiences and after the attacks of 9/11. However, the impact of traumatic stress does not develop only into PTSD, but it can manifest in the lesser known yet more commonly acquired disorders that, when not attended to, can lead to the more well-known PTSD. The knowledge of those disorders and recognizing the risk factors and the symptoms related to these disorders can prevent them from manifesting into the more serious and long-term disorder of PTSD. These other stress- and trauma-related conditions include secondary or vicarious trauma and compassion fatigue.

Risk Factors for Trauma and Stress Disorders

Some of the risk factors include:

- A previous history of trauma
- Age, as it relates to years of experience and the ability to be resilient
- Length of time and experience in the field

---

* From World Cares Center's "Forums of Communities for a Resilient Future," Oklahoma City/New York City, April 18–20, 2006.

196

- High caseload with repeated contact with survivors
- Current life situation, as it relates to increased stress

As we have discussed in Chapter 6, experience dealing with and over-coming personal trauma in a volunteer can be an asset or a risk based on the readiness and willingness of the volunteer to both learn from his or her own experience and be open to the experiences of others. People come forward, believing that their personal experience in overcoming similar losses gives them an enhanced capacity to help others in their healing process. From experience, it has been found that a history of overcom-ing trauma in a volunteer can be a great comfort and resource to other survivors. You must be able to distinguish whether or not the history of overcoming personal trauma in your volunteers is causing them to reex-perience the trauma or is a source of strength that is helping themselves and others in a healing and recovery process.

Additional risk factors for stress disorders may include:

- Poor interpersonal relationships
- Lack of a support network
- The caregiver's level of empathy and emotional tolerance.*

Now we will review the lesser-known stress disorders that disaster volunteers may be at risk for.

Secondary or Vicarious Trauma

Secondary trauma or *vicarious trauma* is a condition caused by indirect exposure to trauma through firsthand accounts or narratives, for instance, by repeatedly listening to the accounts of survivors who have suffered directly from trauma. In this case, the individual who is listening begins to experience the same emotional trauma as the survivors themselves. Secondary trauma can be found in individuals who care for those who have been directly traumatized, whether they are family members or complete strangers. Thus, it is not uncommon for caregivers, therapists, advocates, and, by extension, volunteers providing such services, to feel the symptoms of secondary trauma.

Symptoms of secondary trauma include a feeling of incompetence and hopelessness when dealing with victims and survivors of disaster.† These

---

* B. Hudnall Stamm, Secondary Traumatic Stress: Self Care Issues for Clinicians, Researchers, and Educators (Baltimore: Sidran Press, 1999).
† Barbara Whitmer, "Trauma: Post-Traumatic Stress Disorder and Secondary Trauma."

feelings cannot be underestimated, for they can increase the volunteer's sense of vulnerability and can lead to distrust or hopelessness, which may then manifest in the reactions that result from such feelings, such as displays of anger or frustration.* Trauma symptoms may also include withdrawal, feelings of numbness, and other intense reactions.

Compassion Fatigue

Compassion fatigue is a related condition that causes a lack of sympathy or empathy for clients by caregivers. This is usually caused by the demands placed on volunteers in stressful situations.

Symptoms for compassion fatigue, as for secondary and vicarious trauma, include:

- Excessive blaming
- Isolation from others
- Compulsive behaviors
- Dreading listening to or meeting with survivors
- Refusing to rest or take necessary breaks, believing they should be working
- Difficulty concentrating

Those with compassion fatigue may be bothered by thoughts and images associated with survivors' traumatic experiences or may avoid or dread hearing about these experiences. On the other hand, those with compassion fatigue may also have a compulsive or obsessive desire to help certain clients, as they see constituents as fragile and in need of their services as "saviors."† They may be unable to let go of their volunteer work and let it encroach on their personal time, trying to work even harder to resolve their anxieties and stress, further compounding the risk of developing stress and trauma disorders. For others, they may be filled with feelings of inadequacy, or begin to view the world in terms of victims and perpetrators. Manifested broadly across a work environment, compassion fatigue can lead to organizational symptoms, such as the inability of teams to work together, the inability of staff or volunteers to complete tasks, a lack of flexibility among volunteers or staff, and negative feelings toward each other.

---

* Judith Herman, Trauma and Recovery: The Aftermath of Violence, from Domestic Abuse to Political Terror (New York: Basic Books, 1992), p. 70.
† J. Eric Gantry, "Compassion Fatigue: A Crucible of Transformation," Journal of Trauma 1, no. 3/4 (2002): 37–61.

Posttraumatic Stress Disorder

PTSD is a psychological condition brought on by a traumatic event and lasting longer than 30 days.* This event can be direct exposure to trauma such as a life-threatening event or a situation that causes intense fear. Such events can include either experiencing or witnessing a severe accident or physical injury; receiving a life-threatening medical diagnosis; being the victim of kidnapping or torture; being exposed to war combat or to a civil conflict; being exposed to a natural disaster or other disaster (for example, plane crash or terrorist attack); being the victim of rape, mugging, robbery, or assault; or enduring physical, sexual, emotional, or other forms of abuse. Although the diagnosis of PTSD requires that the sufferer has a history of experiencing a traumatic event as defined here, people may develop PTSD in reaction to events that may not qualify as traumatic but can be devastating life events such as divorce or unemployment. In addition to these triggers, the exposure to secondary trauma and vicarious trauma, when unaddressed, can lead to PTSD.†

Symptoms of PTSD

PTSD is characterized by flashbacks or nightmares that cause someone to feel like he or she is reexperiencing the traumatic event. PSTD may also manifest in the ways in which people will try to avoid the conditions or things that might cause them to experience flashbacks. Finally, PSTD can also show up as a feeling of hypervigilance, or an increased tendency to be startled by events and a high intensity in their reaction to being startled.

Symptoms usually develop shortly after an event, but may also take years to emerge, and can be triggered by an experience related to the event. Not only does PSTD significantly impact the emotional well-being of those who suffer from it, but it also contributes to their inability to engage in family activities, go to work, sustain their marriages, and continue their lives as they normally would.

Research‡ shows that:

---

* According to the DSM-IV(TR) (Diagnostic Statistical Manual of Mental Disorders, 4th Version, text revision), PTSD can only be diagnosed if the individual is experiencing the symptoms after 30 days.
† Medicine Net, "Post Traumatic Stress Disorder." http://www.medicinenet.com/posttraumatic_stress_disorder/page3.htm.
‡ Everly, G. S., Jr., & Mitchell, J. T. (1999). Critical Incident Stress Management (CISM): A new era and standard of care in crisis intervention (2nd ed.). Ellicott City, MD: Chevron.

- As many as 45 percent of those exposed to mass disaster may be at risk for PTSD or depression.
- Generally, about 9 percent of those exposed to trauma may develop PTSD.
- Emergency managers and first responders are at high risk: 10 percent–15 percent occurrence of PTSD in law enforcement, 10 percent– 30 percent in fire suppression.
- Following 9/11, 1.5 million persons in New York City sought counseling.

It is clearly critical to intervene before these symptoms develop, as anyone impacted by PTSD affects the response community as well as their loved ones and the communities they reside in.

SIGNS THAT STRESS IS TAKING A TOLL

When stressors have not been mitigated and the stress of disaster volunteering begins to take its toll, there are several signs that you, as an objective manager, can identify in your team. It is important that early signs of stress not be ignored by both the individuals experiencing symptoms and by supervisors who are in a position to observe from a safe distance emotionally. If these signs are caught early enough, healthy self-care techniques or the support of a professional may mitigate the increased stress and prevent it from ballooning into one of the trauma conditions we have just discussed.

Volunteers and official responders alike may display the following visible signs that stress is taking a toll:

- Having trouble sleeping
- Slurred speech
- Forgetfulness
- Lacking coordination, whereas before they were fine
- Loss of appetite
- Appearing to be more vulnerable to becoming ill and having various physical aches and pains

More severe signs of stress include:

- Substance abuse
- Frequent crying
- Nightmares
- Withdrawal from others

For instance, a volunteer who is normally patient and detail-oriented who begins to constantly fidget with others and becomes forgetful, making simple mistakes, may be someone to monitor closely or talk to in a one-on-one briefing.

Compounded with the possible lack of awareness on what can happen to an individual's emotional well-being during disaster volunteering, for volunteers there is also a stigma attached to being susceptible to emotional setbacks. This is especially true among firefighters, police, and caregiver groups, including volunteers. This population of helpers feels that these symptoms are those of the people they help, and that they themselves should be impervious to having such issues. Most volunteers picture themselves as the ones who are there to provide assistance rather than receive it and, therefore, might believe that showing these feelings or symptoms are a weakness that they are ashamed of admitting to.

Thus, among volunteers, there may be a resistance to seek help or even acknowledge that they might need help. Historically, any of these psychological disorders was looked at as a weakness in character and fortitude. Questions for dealing with these trauma symptoms may be posed as if we as human beings can endure such trauma unchanged or unaffected, such as: "What went wrong with me? Why couldn't I cope?"

After living through the aftermath of a traumatic event, with so many people affected all around us, we understand that such reactions are normal and that it is the situation that is abnormal. As managers and supervisors, it is important to indicate to volunteers that we acknowledge our susceptibility to trauma as a normal condition and that we encourage volunteers to seek support early enough to mitigate trauma's effects. As a manager, you can create this healthy environment and attitude toward the stress of disaster volunteering with the following techniques.

MANAGING WITH SELF-CARE IN MIND

Preventing the onset of secondary trauma and supporting volunteers who deal regularly with direct trauma survivors is vital, and this can be accomplished with healthy patterns of behavior and appropriate volunteer management.

The practice of consistent self-care techniques can minimize the potential of developing one of the psychological disorders associated with trauma by restoring and refueling volunteers in healthy ways. It may seem that, in a disaster response situation, habitual self-care activities or

201

the time to commit to them may not be as accessible. However, a manager in charge of volunteers can make the best use of available resources to ensure that basic self-care is practiced and that a healthy work environment is secured.

Structuring a healthy volunteer environment is the first step that you can take in keeping your team safe. Good management techniques set the foundation for self-care and give you, as a manager, ample time to catch signs of stress early on.

Creating a Safe Space

One way to help mitigate the stressors of disaster volunteering is to provide your team with a safe and comfortable place away from their responsibilities to decompress, such as a quiet room or place away from people in need. This is a place where reflection can take place and individuals can practice any number of the self-care techniques you will teach them. In longer-term recovery, some groups set up a room with a separate computer area where people can check in, with a couch to rest on, where soothing music can be played and chat groups can be organized to share challenging experiences and seek guidance. In the aftermath of 9/11, spontaneous volunteers and emergency responders helped to establish one such space, called September Space, where volunteers could gather and find the support they needed. As one volunteer counselor shared:

> Every day the stories and their voices haunt me, hurt me and weigh me down. The grief and misery hovers over me and follows me, gets in my clothes, in my skin. This place is my Sanctuary; it is the Place where I must go when my work is drowning me. This is the place that takes the pain away. September Space is my Space.

Matching Skills and Roles

> Effective and meaningful volunteer service begins by matching the right people with the right task. Recruiting appropriate volunteers and placing them in volunteer roles that match their skills and interests can lead to greater retention.
>
> The Corporation for National and Community Service

In a study that compared PTSD rates among different occupations involved in the 9/11 disaster response efforts, the rates of PTSD were lowest among police officers (6.2 percent) and highest among unaffiliated volunteers (21.2

percent), which was attributed to performing tasks that were not common to one's everyday occupation.* I would delve further into the cause of stressors that lead to PTSD as 9/11 volunteers described the frustrations of long lines, uncoordinated leadership, disorganized lists, and unclear information about what to do. Yet where there is proactive coordination, we see the direct positive outcome when skills are effectively matched with the roles that volunteers performed.

In relation to this, Sandy, a local disaster volunteer officer, discussed how the activities of over 15,000 volunteers enhanced the effectiveness of meeting emergency response and recovery needs. "They are feeding people, they are cooking food, they are moving food, and they are moving products in and out of warehouses.... They come in, they work their time, and they go home."

In Chapter 4, you defined all the roles your agency serves in disaster response, followed by defining proper protocols for spontaneous volunteers in Chapter 5, how to screen and select for those roles in Chapter 7 and finally how to manage volunteers in those roles in Chapter 8. All the work you have done so far ensures that you have the knowledge and ability to delegate assignments that suit the capabilities of each of your volunteers to serve your agency's mission while staying healthy.

Orientation

Previously, we discussed the team orientation as a way of informing volunteers of their roles and expectations. A team orientation also gives everyone a chance to get to know one another to start building a support network and the relationships that are vital to sustaining oneself on the job. The orientation also gives you a second chance to assess whether your volunteers are able to handle their assignments based on their interaction with their team members and with you, as well as their responses to the tasks at hand. Even though the volunteer has reached the point of participating in an orientation, do not accept someone whom you think is not ready or able to volunteer.

Part of your orientation should also include a primer on self-care not only when volunteering, but also to ensure that self-care and family care are addressed at home. Walk through the keys to both family care and

---

* M. A. Perrin, L. DiGrande, K. Wheeler, et al., "Differences in PTSD Prevalence and Associated Risk Factors among World Trade Center Rescue and Recovery Workers," American Journal of Psychiatry 9 (2007): 1385–1394.

self-care with your volunteers while suggesting several options for them to choose from, providing handouts for your volunteers to refer to.

Briefings

Conducting briefings allows you, as a manager, to regularly observe your team and gauge how they are handling their volunteer duties and taking care of themselves outside of those duties. Talking to volunteers before and after shifts is when, as a manager, you can observe and monitor the behavior of your team and also ensure that people are not overworking or otherwise on unhealthy shifts. For the volunteers, the briefings are a perfect time for them to share their experiences of the day. It is important that you, as a manager, ensure that volunteers understand that the briefing is very much their own time, a crucial opportunity in the day where they can share their questions, experiences, and concerns with you. If they are not comfortable sharing within a group or need more specialized attention, arrange to speak with them individually or refer them to a support staff person who is experienced at counseling and social support services. As you become familiar with your team, be aware of and note any changes in general attitude or any extreme personality changes.

Training

As a reminder, another resource to provide for your volunteers is training that can provide them with the skills and tools to cope with the effects of disaster work. For those volunteers who will regularly interact with survivors, it may also help both your volunteers and your constituents to ensure that the spot training includes simple but effective techniques to interact with disaster survivors. In the aftermath of the devastating Kobe earthquake in 1995, for example, local mental health workers taught volunteers how to listen, encourage, and keep confidentiality.* These were the services most appreciated by the disaster victims, as they tended not to go to professional psychiatric services but, rather, shared their concerns and experiences with the volunteers who came to help them with other services.

---

* Naotaka Shinfuku, "Disaster Mental Health: Lessons Learned from the Hanshin Awaji Earthquake," World Psychiatry 1, no. 3 (2002): 158–159.

Free and Confidential Resources

Set up an environment where seeking outside or additional resources is accessible and encouraged, such as by setting up a resource table or bulletin board for your volunteers where, along with schedules and notifications, there is contact information for free and confidential support services for those who may want to seek help on their own where they do not have to ask for it. Because confidentiality is often a concern for those who are thinking of seeking mental health support, this discreet but clear avenue of support offers individuals some privacy while they consider the options available.

Bonding with Your Team

Research shows that most volunteers are motivated by altruistic and humanitarian values, desire to increase understanding, need to enhance self esteem, and interest in fitting in socially (Clary 1996; Omoto and Snyder 2002).

As an emergency or volunteer manager, forming bonds with your volunteers is healthy and can contribute to the development of a healthy team. When a trusted relationship is developed, it facilitates a manager's ability to gauge the resiliency of a volunteer and ensure he or she is practicing healthy self-care habits. However, because disaster response can be emotionally challenging, there can be times that unhealthy behaviors develop in forming these bonds—issues of unclear boundaries, emotional dependence, and so on can be tricky to handle. This is where a well developed agency policy on appropriate interaction between staff members, staff, and volunteers, volunteers and clients will be an essential tool.

Always encourage your team, thank them for their efforts, and remind them that what they are doing is making a difference and that it is enough.

Communicating Self-Care Concerns

In the instance where you will need to ask a volunteer to take active steps for self-care or seek professional help, keep in mind that volunteers may not always be ready or willing to hear your concerns about their self-care or mental health. Therefore, communicating self-care concerns should be handled with care, tact, and compassion. Such consultations should be made with respect for the volunteer's confidentiality.

SELF-CARE TRAINING FOR YOUR VOLUNTEERS

Some of the basics to self-care seem obvious but are nevertheless forgotten or disregarded in times of disaster. Additionally, new volunteers may not know what is acceptable and expected of them. Explain to your team that by mitigating and managing stress through good self-care, they can strengthen their physical and mental well-being, and ensure their ability to continue to serve effectively. You may want to hand out a journal or go through one or two of the exercises with the team.

Family Preparedness and Care

As outlined in Chapter 5, volunteer responsibilities include ensuring that their own families and other responsibilities at home are taken care of. As emergency managers and community leaders, this step, as a reminder for volunteers, cannot be omitted.

The Buddy System

Implementing a buddy system will allow volunteers to develop a peer-to-peer support system, which can be a vital source of support and build their resilience in the midst of disaster response work.

One of the most moving stories was told by an Oklahoma City police chaplain who responded to the Oklahoma City bombing in 1995. He and a fellow officer were standing next to each other as they were being briefed on their response tasks, when they both realized that this would be the most challenging experience in their careers. They agreed at that moment that they would depend upon each other for support, to share stories they could not share with family members, and to be a fail-safe support for each other. They made an agreement that if one was showing signs of stress and the other mentioned it, the person showing stress must take a break. This supportive relationship, this "buddy" system, continues to serve them both through difficult times.

In relation to this, remind your volunteers to keep in touch with their friends and family and seek them out as a source of support.

MEDS: Move, Eat, Drink, and Sleep

In the beginning we were doing 12 hour shifts and you just go and go, and when you go home you are just totally exhausted.

S. S. Lowe and A. Fothergill
"A Need to Help: Emergent Volunteer Behavior after 9/11," 2003

The basics of healthy living are often thrown out the door when our workload gets overwhelming. This is also true in the midst of disaster response. If you and your volunteers plan on helping for any extended period of time, for example, for more than 36 hours, and healthy habits are not practiced, fatigue and burnout can be a common occurrence. Remind your volunteers of the basics. If you have control over what food is being served to your volunteers, try to create a healthy menu of choices.

- Engage in moderate-intensity physical activity and movement daily.
- Limit your intake of saturated and trans fats, cholesterol, salt, alcohol, and added sugars.
- Minimize your intake of caffeine.
- Remember to eat healthy, well-balanced meals that include two cups of fruit and 2½ cups of vegetables daily; at least half of your grains should be whole grains (brown rice, whole wheat products, oatmeal, popcorn).
- Stay hydrated with water and fluids with electrolytes, like sports drinks.
- Get seven to eight hours minimum of sleep per night (more if you wake up tired).

Avoid meals that consist of coffee and an energy bar. I must admit that this was my favorite during my 9/11 volunteering before a fellow volunteer insisted on bringing me healthier meals. When the short-term energy boost from sugar wears off, it can leave you even sleepier and slower to react than before, according to a study from England's Loughborough University. While caffeine can give you a boost of energy within fifteen minutes of drinking a cup, the caffeine can stay in your system for twelve hours, affecting your ability to fall asleep. Try to eat a meal that includes proteins and complex carbohydrates that are burned more steadily, giving your body a more sustainable supply of energy.

207

Relaxation Techniques

The following are relaxation techniques that you can share with your volunteers as handouts or in exercises during orientation or periodically throughout disaster response.

Meditation
- Sit or lie in a comfortable position.
- Close your eyes and breathe deeply (three seconds in, three seconds out)
- Focus all your attention on your breathing; notice the movement of your chest and abdomen in and out.
- When you feel your attention wandering, briefly focus your attention on wherever it goes. Then, gently return your attention to your breathing.
- Continue for five to ten minutes.

Journals
- Keep a notebook that details your experiences with a beginning and an end.
- Spend fifteen to twenty minutes writing in your journal at the end of each day or when you take a break.
- Review what you have written.
- Pay attention to
  - How much you've done and experienced
  - Signs of stress

Other Relaxation Techniques
- Pleasure reading
- Taking a quiet stroll
- Running
- Singing
- Massage
- Yoga
- Stretching
- Kickboxing
- Prayer or other spiritual activity
- Listening to calming music

Beyond family care, there are other recommendations you can provide on self-care outside of volunteering. These can also be included in a handout to volunteers at orientation or at the start of their service with you.

Self-Care outside of Volunteering

- Manage time away from volunteering to recharge yourself.
- If needed, get support from friends and family. Remember that the people around you (family, friends, spiritual advisors, or coworkers) are a wonderful source of support. Give them permission to tell you when they notice signs of stress in your behavior.
- Find your local volunteer support center and register for support groups or programs.

For more information on traumatic stress, please see:
United States Department of Veterans Affairs, National Center for PTSD. "Effects of Traumatic Stress after Mass Violence, Terror, or Disaster." http://www.ptsd.va.gov/professional/pages/stress-mv-t-dhtml.asp

END-OF-CHAPTER QUESTIONS

- What types of trauma may affect your volunteers?
- How will you know when your volunteers are experiencing disorders or mental health issues related to the stress of volunteering?
- What can you do to mitigate these effects of stress for your volunteers?
- Does your volunteer orientation or spot training include individual and family preparedness planning and practical self-care techniques?

CONCLUSION

In this chapter, you have learned about the stress factors and potential negative side effects of disaster volunteering and the types of trauma and psychological disorders that may result if left unaddressed. To combat the signs of stress and the development of trauma symptoms, you have also reviewed the essential steps that managers can take to structure self-care into the volunteering experience, as well as reviewed the resources and guidelines that you can give to volunteers to incorporate into their lives outside of volunteering. This chapter concludes the work that needs to be done to set up spontaneous volunteer protocols and procedures that make up your spontaneous volunteer management plan.

VOLUNTEER SELF-CARE GUIDELINES

For External Distribution

Self-Care while Volunteering
- **Briefing and De-briefing Time is Your Time:**
  - Do you understand your responsibilities? If you have any uncertainty, ask your supervisor in your briefing.
  - Talk about your questions, your experiences and your concerns.
  - If you feel overwhelmed or exhausted, please tell your supervisor.
- **Having a "buddy" is helpful**
  - Find a buddy who is also a volunteer or responder. Meet on a regular basis to discuss your experiences, what you achieved, and what is bothering you.
- Wear the required safety equipment.
- Drink plenty of fluids and eat healthily.
- Take regular breaks and rest when you need to.
- Practice relaxation techniques (see note on Relaxation Techniques below).

Self-Care outside of Volunteering
- Manage time away from volunteering to recharge yourself.
- If needed, get support from friends and family. Remember that the people around you (family, friends, spiritual advisors, or coworkers) are a wonderful source of support. Give them permission to tell you when they notice signs of stress in your behavior.
- Find your local volunteer support center and register for support groups or programs.
- Engage in sixty minutes of moderate-intensity physical activity and movement daily.
- Eat a balanced and nutritious diet.
- Stay hydrated with water and fluids with electrolytes, like sports drinks.
- Get seven to eight hours minimum of sleep per night (more if you wake up tired).

Additional Self-Care Notes

Relaxation Techniques: Deep Breathing
1. Sit or lie in a comfortable position.
2. Close your eyes and breathe deeply (3 seconds in, 3 seconds out)
3. Focus all your attention on your breathing; notice the movement of your chest and abdomen in and out.
4. When you feel your attention wandering, briefly focus your attention on wherever it goes. Then, gently return your attention to your breathing.
5. Continue for five to ten minutes.

Keeping a Journal
1. Keep a notebook that details your experiences with a beginning and an end.
2. Spend fifteen to twenty minutes writing in your journal at the end of each day or when you take a break.
3. Pay attention to
   - How much you've done and experienced
   - Signs of stress

Other Relaxation Techniques
- Running
- Massage
- Yoga
- Acupressure
- Singing
- Stretching
- Kickboxing
- Acupuncture
- Prayer
- Your Own Preference: _____

Be Aware: Some Signs of Stress
- Exhaustion
- Difficulty sleeping
- Inability to focus
- Making simple mistakes
- Short-tempered or easily agitated
- Decrease in quality of work
- Change in general attitude or in health
- Forgetfulness

- Shortness of breath or tight chest
- Change in appetite

Remember: What you are doing is enough.

Experiencing stress is normal, given the circumstances.

If, however, any sign of stress lasts more than a few days, please seek professional support.

Resources to call:

Here, agency may list local resources in your area for professional support.

10

Social Media and Emergent Technologies in Spontaneous-Volunteer Management

More and more, individual people first on the scene of natural disasters, political crises, and war share their experiences and information via the Internet. Anyone involved in disaster response and humanitarian assistance needs to adopt better standards and governance for the inclusion of both the raw internet AS WELL AS the early, ad hoc responders with this organic capability at their fingertips.

William Barlow
Chief Information Officer, Deputy Director for Integrated ICT Support,
Department of Defense

IN THIS CHAPTER

- New Web 2.0 Technologies in Disaster Response
  - Federal Measures
  - Social Technologies in Action
    - Wikis

- Twitter
- SMS Texting
- Flickr
- Information-sharing portals
- International Applications
  - The Case of World Cares Center's Response in Haiti
  - The Case of Bangladesh: Citizen Response to Floods
  - The Case of Burma: Citizen Response to Cyclone Nargis
  - The Case of India: Women's Organizations Response to Gujarat Earthquake
  - The Need to Engage Social Media and Web Technologies

In this chapter, it is my goal to offer insight into the ways new information-sharing technologies can be used to improve communication, an essential element of disaster preparedness and response, thereby saving lives and property and ensuring that resources are shared and there is no duplication or waste in response efforts. These new technologies, which we noted as posing unique challenges for emergency managers in communicating with the public in Chapter 2 of this book, can be harnessed for their potential to improve communications for both official response agencies and the general public alike.

The second section of this chapter highlights international examples of spontaneous-volunteer efforts where coordination has been successful and shows how these social technologies and the implementation of protocols and procedures outlined in this manual can further improve these local efforts.

NEW WEB 2.0 TECHNOLOGIES IN DISASTER RESPONSE

As briefly described in Chapter 2, Web 2.0 technologies are creating new space for the exchange and sharing of resources and ideas across communities that consist of multidirectional communication and information sharing, in essence allowing conversations to begin between people who would not normally be communicating. Social networking Web sites offer tools to work on common issues and problems, and pose almost unlimited opportunities for citizens to share information, training, skills, and solutions. Examples of this type of information sharing can be found on social networking platforms like LinkedIn, MySpace, and Facebook.

Federal Measures

World Cares Center (WCC) has been called upon as a subject matter expert advising the U.S. Department of Defense, the largest response agency the United States has, on several information-sharing projects that aim to improve communication between all parties involved in disaster response and humanitarian assistance, with a focus on communicating with communities.

The Department of Defense (DoD) has been pursuing the application of Web 2.0 technologies as a way to build trust amongst organizations and enable an unclassified, open collaboration tool to interact with organizations and individuals responding to humanitarian assistance or disaster-response crisis. The idea behind this development is to identify the means to account for the growing external and online response community and to more efficiently incorporate information sharing between the DoD and the ecosystem of humanitarian aid organizations, including but not limited to federal agencies, international partners, private industry, nongovernmental organizations (NGOs), and community responders. As William Barlow, chief information officer and deputy director for Integrated ICT Support at the DoD, states, "It is envisioned that the use of these new methods and technologies will foster the building of trust, a key ingredient to effective collaboration and communication between organizations and individuals. Building effective, trusted networks of people and organizations involved in the humanitarian assistance and disaster response prior to an actual crisis could lead to more effective collaboration between those involved and ultimately to a much more efficient response on the part of all participants."

Taking on improved information sharing using today's new technologies should be championed by all partners in disaster response. The success of this endeavor requires an information enterprise that fosters operations, collaboration, and trust that is utilized before, during, and after a crisis situation. The significance of open and collaborative communication with impacted communities and responders was never so clear as in the aftermath of Hurricane Katrina, when FEMA director Michael Brown admitted almost a week after the storm had hit that the agency had not known that evacuees had been stranded without adequate food and water supplies in the New Orleans Convention Center until he saw news reports.* Transcripts of the response on CNN revealed numerous conflict-

---

* CNN, "The Big Disconnect on New Orleans." http://www.cnn.com/2005/US/09/02/katrina.response/index.html.

ing reports between official response agencies, local officials, and disaster survivors on the ground, sometimes within minutes of each other. The isolation of thousands of evacuees in the New Orleans Convention Center and the Louisiana Superdome made it evident that accurately communicating needs and resources after a disaster strikes is only enabled with responsive and effective communication networks.

Consideration must be given to ways we can connect to the individuals and groups on the ground who are affected by disaster yet are outside of official circles and not privy to closed networks of information sharing. Dr. Linton Wells of the National Defense University states, "Situational awareness and the communication networks to share it are not the technical adjuncts to major deliverables such as food, shelter, water and security; they are the critical enablers of everything else that happens."

Based on lessons learned from Katrina, Brian Humphrey, a veteran firefighter and Los Angeles Fire Department spokesman, also cautions organizations and agencies from simply thinking of the Web as providing a larger audience—as a one-way channel for spreading information. For example, even though the Los Angeles Fire Department serves more than 4 million people, its Twitter feed only has about 6,000 followers.[*] Rather, he and other experts who specialize in information technologies emphasize that the main benefit of many of these networking tools is "to listen more accurately, to be able to gather information more clearly,"[†] and that government should "help facilitate communities and individuals at the heart of crisis and listen to them as they talk and trade information. What it should not do is attempt to be their go-to place immediately after a disaster occurs."[‡]

The advantage of the Web and Web-based technologies can also be seen in its resilience to disasters compared to more traditional communication infrastructures. Examples of this can be seen during the California earthquake of 1989 and the Kobe earthquake in 1995, when the Internet stayed intact.[§]

---

[*] As of October 15, 2009.

[†] Amy Harper, "Smarter Disaster Relief May Begin Online," *National Journal Online.* http://www.nationaljournal.com/njonline/in_20090113_9416.php.

[‡] Amy Harder, "Smarter Disaster Relief May Begin Online," *National Journal Online.* http://www.nationaljournal.com/njonline/in_20090113_9416.php.

[§] G. Ivefors, "Emergency Information Management and Disaster Preparation on the Internet," IDA Fifth Annual Conference on Computer and Information Science, Linkoping University, Sweden. November 22, 1995. http://www.ida.liu.se/~guniv.

In addition, Web technologies offer the immediacy of on-the-ground citizens and volunteers posting information, which not only allows for local sharing, but also sends information to the global online community, thus fostering a sense of shared tragedy or need, as well as tapping into specialized skills and resources elsewhere.* For example, the quickest source of news after both the Indian Ocean tsunami and Hurricane Katrina was on blogs.† Postdisaster, affected citizens on the ground and those who come to help will often turn to use existing technology online, posting to blogs (personal online diaries), message boards, and Web portals.

Social Technologies in Action

This brings us to what can be called the online disaster-response community, or the networked and tech-savvy citizens and community-based organizations that emerge when disaster strikes. The level of information-sharing opportunity and the reach of Web 2.0 is becoming more and more apparent in the humanitarian assistance and disaster-response fields. By allowing nonprofessional emergency responders to interact directly with their peers as well as with professional emergency responders, these online tools not only support an integrated response, but also foster the growth of a self-sufficient network of citizen responders.

The extent to which the Internet, Facebook, and other methods of social networking and communication over the Web improved our ability to connect with those in need became apparent during WCC's response to the Haiti earthquake that occurred on January 12, 2010. Messages for help and postings on Facebook by orphanage directors who were cut off from aid streamed in. Messages were passed from group to group and person to person. Information gathering traditionally done only by on-the-ground "reconnaissance" or assessment began in New York City at our desks and laid a solid framework for the steps we would take when we arrived in Haiti, through our utilization of WCC's online networking

---

* Melina Laituri and Kris Kodrich, "The Online Disaster Response Community: Multiple High Magnitude Disasters and Geospatial Technologies," paper presented at the annual meeting of the International Communication Association, Dresden International Congress Centre, Dresden, Germany, June 16, 2006. http://www.allacademic.com/meta/p91385_index.html.

† K. Kodrich and M. Laituri, "The Tsunami and the Internet: The Role of New Media Technologies in Disaster Awareness and Relief," Technology, Science and Communication 1, no. 3 (2005): 53–62.

portal, the ReadyResponders Network. I will describe the features and benefits of Web portals in greater detail later in this chapter.

The following are several common types of Web 2.0 technologies used in disaster response.

Wikis

Wikis are Web sites that allow the simple creation and editing of inter-linked Web pages by volunteers. Wikis involve all users in collaboration and creation of a Web site, whether for information-sharing or data-storage purposes. Wikipedia, one of the best-known examples of wikis, is a collaborative encyclopedia that, in disaster response, can be used by all parties to clarify what terms mean and to identify a common lexicon of terminology to aid in efforts. In the wake of disasters such as Hurricane Katrina, savvy volunteers used wiki software as an organizational tool and created Web pages to identify immediate shelter needs, such as ShelterFinder, and to find missing family members, such as PeopleFinder.* Wikis can also be added and combined for new purposes, and these are called mashups.

Twitter

Twitter is a form of communication that allows users to broadcast messages limited to 140 keystrokes that can be sent directly to an individual's phone or e-mail address. Unlike other forms of technology that may rely primarily on computers, Twitter is impressively accessible, as users may receive and send Twitter updates through their cell phones alone. Compared to the rate of computer usage, many places around the world are increasingly able to afford cell phones. In the 2009 uprising in Iran over allegations of election fraud, the use of Twitter accounts allowed for information sharing when all other communications were shut down by the government† or overwhelmed by the surge of users.‡ FEMA also launched

---

* Melinda Laituri and Kris Kodrich, "The Online Disaster Response Community: Multiple High Magnitude Disasters and Geospatial Technologies," paper presented at the annual meeting of the International Communication Association, Dresden International Congress Centre, Dresden, Germany, June 16, 2006. http://www.allacademic.com/meta/p91385_index.html.

† Nazila Fathi, "Protesters Defy Iranian Efforts to Cloak Unrest," New York Times, A1, June 18, 2009.

‡ Evgeny Morozov, "Iran Elections: A Twitter Revolution?" The Washington Post, June 17, 2009. http://www.washingtonpost.com/wp-dyn/content/discussion/2009/06/17/DI2009061702232.html.

a Twitter account in January 2009* and a YouTube page in October 2008.†
In a blackout or a period of turmoil when traditional networks and channels are overwhelmed, the use of this technology may be one of the few
ways to share information immediately.

SMS Texting

SMS texting is a communication service that also allows for short text
messages to be sent to mobile users, and is the most widely used data communication service in the world. In the wake of Typhoon Ondoy's (also
known as Ketsana) devastation in the Philippines in late 2009, citizens
enlisted their cell phones and relied on Web 2.0 platforms to post requests
for rescue, food, and medicine to specific locations (see Figure 10.1).‡ At
the other end, those who were not directly affected but were receiving the
alerts and monitoring the situation through these social networking sites
were able to garner tens of thousands of dollars in donations as well as
locate their missing relatives and pinpoint areas of dire need.§ Text messages were the most reliable form of communication between the WCC
team and the local community leaders that WCC was communicating
with. In addition, texts were used to tremendous effect in the American
Red Cross's (ARC's) fundraising efforts in the wake of Haiti's earthquake.
By nighttime on January 12, ARC tweeted that those who texted "HAITI"
to 90999 would donate $10 to the ARC relief efforts, effective across all
wireless networks. This tapped into a generation of donors who were traditionally hard to reach, and raised $7 million in the space of a few days.
This amount alone exceeded the $4 million total raised in fundraising
efforts in 2009 and donated to charities.

Flickr

Flickr is an online photo-management and -sharing application that allows
people to label photos with information, such as location, and self-organize
the information into interest groups. For example, when documenting a

---

* http://twitter.com/FemainFocus
† http://www.youtube.com/user/FEMA.
‡ For an example of a map made by citizens requesting assistance: see this customized
Google map: <http://maps.google.com/maps/ms?ie=UTF8&hl=en&msa=0&msid=11086
8206150348750692.00047479b6400ee29bd89&ll=14.645791,121.107874&spn=0.107954,0.15432
4&source=embed.
§ Benny Evangelista, "Social Media Keep Flood Victims Connected," San Francisco
Chronicle, September 29, 2009. http://www.sfgate.com/cgi-bin/article.cgi?f=/
c/a/2009/09/29/BU3819U0E8.DTL.

Figure 10.1 In the Philippines, Typhoon Ondoy (also known as Ketsana) left many stranded and without supplies. Many used SMS text and Internet-based information platforms to call for assistance. (U.S. Navy photo by Mass Communication Specialist 2nd Class William Ramsey)

disaster, community members can post to a common pool of photos on Flickr, which serves as an up-to-date resource on the spread and impact of a disaster. When a wildfire threatened 800 acres of Los Angeles' Griffith Park in 2007, firefighters made sure to monitor the news that locals posted online to Twitter and the pictures that they were uploading to Flickr, and in this way they were able to "crowdsource" their assessment of public needs to direct their resources where they were most needed.*

Information-Sharing Portals
Information-sharing Web portals, your agency's own or a shared platform, can link you to many parties involved in disaster response and be customized to provide information, training, and resources as well as gather vital data and generate reports. One example of this is WCC's ReadyResponders Network (www.readyresponders.org), which is a free, multiplatform portal designed to function both as a central resource in

---

* Amy Harder, "Smarter Disaster Relief May Begin Online," National Journal. http://www.nationaljournal.com/njonline/in_20090113_9416.php.

disaster preparedness and response that can engage any person or organization, and also serve as a bridge between nongovernmental organizations, governmental organizations, and individual community members. The ReadyResponders Network houses tools and templates designed specifically for the community to file information on disasters, and that can be shared with like-minded organizations for similar purposes. Additional tools like the Volunteer Application database allow volunteers to register, and a robust search engine allows managers and leaders to search for volunteers by skill, location, availability, and more, as well as import their data into their proprietary software/databases. It also contains numerous types of communication tools, such as a blog, a chat room, a forum, and a calendar (see Figure 10.2). In the aftermath of the January 12 earthquake that devastated Haiti, WCC saw a spike in the use of ReadyResponders Network, which served to engage, educate, and organize doctors and

Figure 10.2 A sample of the options available at World Cares Center's ReadyResponder Network. (Source: World Cares Center, www.readyresponders. org)

nurses deploying to Haiti to work with three clinics that the organization partnered with.

Likewise, RISEPAK (Relief Information System for Earthquakes-Pakistan), is a Web 2.0 tool created in the aftermath of the devastating 2005 earthquake in Pakistan to rapidly disseminate information about all 4,000 affected villages and to ensure real-time coordination between traditional relief agencies and communities and responders trying to help.* It offers a searchable database containing information compiled from statistics, satellites, geographic databases, relief agencies, workers, and local officials. Anyone can post to the site with their needs via phone, SMS text, fax, e-mail, and online submission. Information about each village, its current accessibility, the level of supplies, the damage, and so on, can be collated and placed on the site within hours.† Within two months, there were 1,800 posts, 2,000 messages, information on 1,000 affected villages, and 38,000 visitors to the site. Playing a role in long-term recovery efforts, RISEPAK also began to give monthly bulletins on underserved and excluded villages or populations, which are picked up by relief agencies and the press to ensure that the most needy are being served.

A similar tool developed to effectively channel donations and connect the world of humanitarian relief providers to each other is Aidmatrix Network. Its technology connects NGOs, governments, and businesses to deliver aid quickly and efficiently where it is needed by using the best supply chain management technologies.‡ This project is supported in part by FEMA and private funders.

While it is noted that not all communities have access to or an understanding of all the technologies available, we would be remiss to discount the way that new generations are communicating. Diversification of communication by combining Web 2.0 technologies with standard communication formats like radio, telephone, paper mailings, and face-to-face community group work is the only way to outreach to all populations, including the range of special-needs communities.

To connect to communities and volunteers on a regular basis, organizations can:

---

* Harvard University, Center for International Development, "Coordinating Disaster Relief Efforts: A New Tool for Relief Operations in Pakistan." http://www.cid.harvard.edu/cidresources/risepak_pr_051020.html.
† Stockholm Challenge, "RISEPAK: Relief Information System for Earthquakes: Pakistan." http://www.stockholmchallenge.org/project/data/risepak-relief-information-system-earthquakes-pakistan.
‡ Aidmatrix Foundation. http://www.aidmatrix.org/aboutus/index.htm.

- Start Facebook and Flickr pages of their own
- Open a Twitter account to post regular updates and track local conditions
- Add functions to their Web sites that connect to these online portals
- Develop their own information-sharing networks designed specifically to meet the needs of the community and organization
- Participate in community-based or hazard-specific information-sharing Web portals
- Use text and e-mail in disaster response

INTERNATIONAL APPLICATIONS

In developing countries ... the most vulnerable people tend to live in areas which are the most dangerous. People in Bangladesh don't live in low-lying areas because they're stupid, it's because they're extremely poor. People in Iran who live in these mountainous areas know the risk of earthquakes, but again they have no other options because this is the only land you have access to. They know their huts made of bricks can crush them, but they don't have access to earthquake resistant structures which would cost far more to erect. So people make suboptimal choices, taking high risks, knowing it, because this is the only way they can scramble out a livelihood. But these are also the ones whom you would want to most engage in helping themselves when things go wrong.

Dirk Salomons
Director of Program for Humanitarian Affairs, Columbia University

The lessons encapsulated in this book are designed to enhance the planning and management of community resources and spontaneous volunteers by emergency managers and community leaders based not only in the United States, but also globally. The prevalence of and response to disasters in the international context provide important lessons learned on community engagement that WCC, along with scholars and practitioners, have studied and put into practice. While the context of developing countries differs greatly from that of countries such as the United States, the need to engage and empower communities right down to their individual citizens and grassroots leadership is a clear need globally as well. We have never seen this as clearly as in the process of helping in Haiti's recovery.

The high population density, the settlement of communities in disaster-prone areas, and the higher prevalence of various natural hazards in some of these developing countries frequently make the headlines. In addition, much is made of the lack of material resources, technical training, or other such perceived requirement of proper disaster management efforts. Through the more widespread use of technology, appeals for aid and assistance postdisaster in the case of developing countries can make it appear as if affected communities are passively waiting for outside assistance, as they broadcast images of victims seeking refuge, standing in the ruins of their homes, or waiting in line for food aid.

But the communities who settle in disaster-prone areas, the ones who are the most vulnerable, are often the ones who are making the biggest difference, especially those equipped with the education, tools, and infrastructure in an integrated disaster-response program. Deep in communities, leaders are working with whatever resources are at hand to rebuild together, but their efforts are often overlooked. Moreover, NGOs, faith-based organizations, and community-based organizations in other parts of the world also play a spectrum of essential roles and often provide vital services those governments and businesses may not be able to fulfill.

The Case of World Cares Center's Response in Haiti

WCC saw this firsthand in Haiti, where local orphanage directors, managers who ran small clinics, and social groups all came together to help each other and connect with resources that would ensure that they could continue to serve their communities. In contrast to and as a complement to the work of the larger NGOs in feeding the masses of individuals, as well as establishing refugee camps for internally displaced persons, empowerment of grassroots local leaders must be a priority. These citizens, leaders, and organizations can make contact with communities that are hard to reach or have special needs in times of disaster. Such organizations and communities may especially benefit from creating plans along the guidelines posed in this book to engage local community members and select and spot-train spontaneous volunteers in responding to the particular hazards that their locales face. Of course, the circumstances and environment change. However, the need for safe shelter, food, and water are a constant in any country.

In the case of Haiti, WCC reviewed what role each organization would fulfill in disaster and how volunteers could help. In the effort to connect to larger humanitarian NGOs, WCC brought local leaders to a UN meeting specifically set to engage community leaders to be responsible for food distribution for their community. However, it became clear that the standards and expectations of local leaders by the international humanitarian sector did not take their needs and constraints into consideration. The agency in charge of the meeting only said a few words of warning about security and informed the group of community leaders that they would have to devise logistics plans to distribute food in a safe and fair manner. Most local leaders left the meeting very discouraged, as little to no training was given, nor was there a blueprint for how to proceed, and they had no prior experience with mass food distribution before the earthquake.

A few cases of disaster response in developing countries demonstrate how preparation by local leaders and partners was effective in saving lives.

The Case of Bangladesh: Citizen Response to Floods, from Cell Phone Early-Warning Systems to Hand-Cranked Radios

In the case of Bangladesh, its location and geography make it one of the most flood-prone countries in the world, and the communities settled in low-lying areas in the river delta are especially vulnerable to their impact.* However, with help from the Red Cross, Bangladeshi authorities and communities got organized and developed relevant tools and methods to involve citizens. They developed a culturally relevant early-warning system that reached all civilians. Steps such as broadcasting warnings to cell phone networks in local languages improved the effectiveness of these warnings greatly by reaching all the way down to the villager,† as well as the distribution of hand-cranked radios, which fishermen and others in low-lying areas could listen to for regular weather bulletins. In terms of basic prevention and preparedness, Bangladesh also created large mounds so that people could reach higher areas above sea level in a short amount of time as refuge from rising waters. Third, knowing that supplies would be hard to distribute in the midst of flooding, the disaster plan pre-positioned food and water and established a system in which citizens would be organized to distribute these supplies.‡ In sum, citizens were empowered as well-equipped disaster-response forces with four levels of integration:

---

* A. N. H. Akhtar Hossain, "Integrated Flood Management Case Study: Bangladesh: Flood Management," World Meteorological Organization and Global Water Partnership, September 2003.
† A. N. H. Akhtar Hossain, "Integrated Flood Management Case Study: Bangladesh: Flood Management," World Meteorological Organization and Global Water Partnership, September 2003.
‡ International Federation of Red Cross and Red Crescent Societies, Final Report: Bangladesh, May 29, 2009.

communication through early-warning systems, data training, access to supplies, and life-saving infrastructure in the form of the mounds. As a result, flood casualties were reduced by tens of thousands.

To get a sense of how effective the early-warning system was, in 1971, a tropical cyclone took the lives of more than 300,000 people due to the storm surge. In 1991, 100,000 lives were lost in a similar storm. However, in 2007, when a storm of similar magnitude struck, about 10,000 lives were lost—a 97 percent reduction in the loss of lives.* This great difference in lives saved was made possible through the effective engagement of citizens and communities when the forecast was given eight days in advance and reached all the way down to the level of the villager. The difference was 290,000 lives saved.

The Case of Burma: Citizen Response to Cyclone Nargis

Looking at the response efforts that took place in the aftermath of Cyclone Nargis in Burma in 2008, the cyclone devastated many villages in the Irrawaddy Delta, causing 140,000 deaths and directly impacting 3.4 million persons. While this would be a challenge to any government, the military regime in power complicated aid efforts by refusing to give access to external aid groups and workers for twenty-four days after the impact. But survivors, spontaneous volunteers, nonprofit organizations, and ordinary Burmese citizens from all walks of life worked mightily to save lives and reach those who were isolated.

Citizens in the former capital of Rangoon filled up their cars and trucks with supplies and drove them down to the delta. Spontaneous volunteers organized themselves, including health workers from the Thai-Burma border along with community-based organizations in cyclone-affected areas, composing teams that received training in emergency response, food and water distribution, and first aid provision. They worked "under the radar" to go deep into the affected areas. Such teams ended up providing assistance to some 180,000 survivors in eighty-seven villages. As one relief worker shared, "If you aren't local, it is difficult to go; you won't know the areas." Others had monks go with them to legitimize the relief workers to the local authorities, once again showing the important role that local,

---

* Andrew Freedman, in an interview with Dr. Peter Webster, Georgia Institute of Technology, "Bangladesh's Example for a Post-Nargis World," Washington Post blog, Capital Weather Gang, May 14, 2008. http://voices.washingtonpost.com/capitalweather-gang/2008/05/tropical_cyclone_nargis_which.html#.

culturally oriented, faith-based leaders play in disaster response. In addition, international organizations that already had staff on the ground as well as large NGOs became the first responders who were able to leverage their agencies' international capacity by handling shipments, as they were the only organizations allowed to receive shipments initially.

These national staff were not specifically trained in disaster response, but because there was no one else, they found themselves essential first responders and frontline staff. In the independent after-disaster report written by the Johns Hopkins Bloomberg School of Public Health, survivors shared that local organizations were able to begin relief in the initial forty-eight hours after the cyclone, but it was several days, anywhere from six days to weeks later, when the government began to give assistance.*

Within two weeks of the disaster, 40 percent of villages surveyed had received assistance despite difficult terrain and circumstances. Within a month, 80 percent of the villages had received support. In the end, all villages—even the most remote ones—had been reached," stated a World Bank social monitoring report.†

The Case of India: Women's Organizations Response to Gujarat Earthquake

In Gujarat, India, the experience of spontaneous volunteers and nongovernmental organizations was seen in the wake of the 2001 earthquake, which struck with a force greater than the ninety earthquakes that had hit the area in the past 185 years.‡ The quake caused the death of more than 20,000 and left hundreds of thousands injured and homeless. However, there was an outpouring of individuals, organizations, and aid, with more than 150 local NGOs and 300 international NGOs on the scene to assist in the epicenter of the quake, the Kutch district.

---

* Department for International Development (DFID), UK Aid, "Cyclone Nargis: One Year On." http://www.dfid.gov.uk/Media-Room/News-Stories/2009/Cyclone-Nargis-One-Year-On.
† Department for International Development (DFID), UK AID, "Cyclone Nargis: One Year On." http://www.dfid.gov.uk/Media-Room/News-Stories/2009/Cyclone-Nargis-One-year-on.
‡ The quake measured 6.5 on the Richter scale, according to the United Nations Volunteer site. "The Gujarat Earthquake: National volunteers rekindle hopes in communities to build lives." http://www.unv.org/en/news-resources/news/doc/the-gujarat-earthquake-national.html.

In the relief efforts, the nongovernmental organizations involved in the relief efforts included 300 grassroots women's groups who had experience in disaster response from working as directly affected citizens on community-level reconstruction after the devastating Latur earthquake that had occurred nearly ten years earlier in 1993.* This network of women's groups, called SSP, or Swayam Shikshan Prayog, a Self-Learning Network of Women, included women who had already experienced the trauma of the loss of lives and property. They were organized into teams that conducted village assessments of shelter needs after the Gujarat earthquake. As the organizations stated, "We believe it will help if they speak to others from Latur, who have gone through this trauma, and maybe begin to see how they can work together."

In addition, they saw their mission as an offer to the affected communities "to do what we know best: to use the reconstruction process of houses and public buildings as a means to empower people. Right now, with the enormous destruction, the trauma is very high. To cope with this, combat this, and turn a crisis on its head, the involvement of people, both men and women, is needed." Disaster response by citizens also created opportunities for marginalized social groups to be recognized as they responded. An independent collective of rural women called Kutch Mahila Vikas Sangathan relied on women to carry out relief distribution efforts in the impacted areas.† Their visibility in distributing relief gained them the appreciation and respect of local officials and of men, and they were empowered in their participation in the relief efforts. These women's organizations were also active in creating projects to restore women's livelihoods, even as they were still living in relief tents. These accomplishments must be seen as all the more exemplary, given that women were traditionally excluded from the public sphere in all aspects and the fact that there were efforts to exclude women from repairing, planning, and designing their homes and communities.‡

---

* In their case, the Latur earthquake had claimed over 10,000 lives and damaged hundreds of thousands of homes across 1,300 villages.
† TVE Asia Pacific, "From Victims to Managers: South Asian Communities Coping with Disaster," Children of Tsunami January 1, 2005. http://www.childrenoftsunami.info/arts/view.php?id=25; http://www.tveap.org/?q=node/314.
‡ Elaine Enarson, "SWS Fact Sheet: Women and Disaster," Sociologists for Women in Society, 2006. http://www.socwomen.org/socactivism/factdisaster.pdf.

THE NEED TO ENGAGE SOCIAL MEDIA
AND WEB TECHNOLOGIES

The overwhelming level of spontaneous volunteer response in which survivors and civilians persevere, despite the severe obstacles in these contexts, shows what can happen if more people and organizations are prepared for a potential role in disaster response. The previous experience of community members in addressing disaster and trauma, and the effectiveness of citizen preparedness to enable spontaneous volunteers to respond effectively, were also illustrated in these examples. It shows that even when official government or institutions are not working, community institutions and civilians can leverage their own advantages to match the situation at hand: local and cultural knowledge, a sense of mission, and their networks with the broader global community.

Hard-to-access communities, difficult terrain, rural unpaved roads, and other such conditions found in various international contexts are not always obstacles; they are the reason why communities and local citizens should be trained and warned. The examples of Haiti, Bangladesh, Burma, and India demonstrate the power of the local community and the need to engage them and empower them with training. Lives are saved, livelihoods recovered, and skills imparted to ordinary people, which become lessons learned for the next time disaster strikes.

Although there are vast cultural differences that exist between the United States, European nations, and less developed or Third World countries, some challenges remain constant. In all of the above, there are communities that cannot afford proper preparedness, whether this includes the time to prepare or because of the prohibitive cost associated with collecting supplies and saving them for when they are needed. Planning for everyday living supersedes planning for the "what if."

One characteristic that is seen repeatedly is the amazing resiliency of people who struggle with the daily challenges of life and their capability to adapt and take on additional responsibilities for their community. They represent the most common scenario, but the media and politicians typically present the picture of individuals desperately waiting to be fed. Behind the scenes of the masses struggling to collect their daily rations of food, there are pockets of communities with leaders struggling valiantly to help those who depend on them. Most often, those invisible leaders are not the politicians who can make their way to the spotlight. Rather, they are everyday managers who are cut off from their supplies and support. A shift in approach, implementing the methodologies outlined in this book, would go a long way to empower these leaders by preparing them to serve as distribution points for their communities or as community liaisons reporting directly to the UN or USAID cluster groups that are responsible for aid distribution.

In Third World countries, since people's everyday needs significantly outweigh the need to prepare for disasters, considerations should be made by larger entities that come in to support response on how they can mentor local leaders immediately. An example of this would involve having a logistician work through distribution plans with these leaders to determine how implementation would best take place in their specific community.

END-OF-CHAPTER QUESTIONS

- What are the advantages of using Web 2.0 technologies over traditional formats like mailings and phone calls?
- Does your agency or organization have plans to consider social networking tools for spontaneous volunteer management?
- Can you think of a recent disaster where Web 2.0 technology was utilized by a victim or in response? In what way was the technology used, and how did it help efforts on the ground, or otherwise?

CONCLUSION

Technology is a part of everyday life and can make the difference between life and death, between getting resources to a community or having to go without in disaster response. Technology, the Internet, and social networking can make information sharing, situational awareness, and just staying connected much more efficient than without. The ability to connect to, and communicate with, people from around the world—and organize the sharing of resources and knowledge through the use of the Internet and handheld devices—should not be overlooked. As we have seen through case studies and experienced personally through direct response, both technology and the methods espoused in this book apply to all communities near and far. Human beings are in communities helping each other every day. Many emerge in the immediate aftermath of disaster when an opportunity for them to help arises. It is clear that differences exist. However, it is even clearer that community empower-ment, and the integration and encouragement of organizing spontane-ous volunteers and emergent leaders, is the key to disaster response and long-term recovery.

GLOSSARY

WCC	World Cares Center
WMD	weapons of mass destruction

TERMS

accreditation: Empowerment provided to an organization through legislation, statute, or regulation from an appropriate local, state, tribal, or federal government agency authorizing the organization to credential personnel for incidents in which the organization participates.

action plans: Plans that reflect the overall incident goal and incident strategy, objectives for the operational period, specific tactical actions and assignments, and supporting information for the operational period. Provides personnel with knowledge of the objectives to be achieved and the strategy and steps to be used for achievement.

activate: To begin the process of mobilizing a response team, or to set in motion an emergency response or recovery plan, process, or procedure for an exercise or for an actual hazard incident.

advisory: A notification category that provides urgent information about an unusual occurrence or threat of an occurrence, but no activation of the notified entity is ordered or expected at that time.

affiliated volunteer: An individual who is associated with an organization and voluntarily performs services and often is trained by that organization.

after-action assessment: The document that describes the incident response and findings related to system response performance.

alert: Advisory that hazard is approaching but is less imminent than implied by a warning message. See also *warning*.

all-hazards: A specific strategy for managing activities in an emergency management program in which management structure, processes, and procedures are developed so that they are applicable to every significant identified hazard.

all-hazards approach: A strategy that addresses the commonalities of incident identification, assessment, and response to natural, technological, and intentional hazards. It provides a common emergency operations plan for use in response to and recovery from all emergencies and disasters.

asbestos[1]: Any of several minerals (as chrysotile) that readily separate into long flexible fibers that cause asbestosis and have been implicated as causes of certain cancers, and that were formerly used as fire-proof insulating materials.

attribute: A quality, property, or characteristic inherent in or ascribed to somebody or something.

attrition: Reduction of work force due to resignations, retirement, sickness, or death.

briefing: A meeting at which detailed information or instructions are given.

business-continuity program: An ongoing process supported by senior management and funded to ensure that the necessary steps are taken to identify the impact of potential losses, maintain viable recovery strategies and recovery plans, and ensure continuity of services through personnel training, plan testing, and maintenance.

calamitous[2]: Being, causing, or accompanied by calamity.

calamity[3]: (1) A state of deep distress or misery caused by major misfortune or loss. (2) A disastrous event marked by great loss and lasting distress and suffering.

catastrophic disaster: An event that results in large numbers of deaths and injuries; causes extensive damage or destruction of facilities that provide and sustain human needs; produces an overwhelming demand on state and local response resources and mechanisms; causes a severe long-term effect on general economic activity; and severely affects state, local, and private-sector capabilities to begin and sustain response activities. (Note: the Stafford Act provides no definition for this term [FEMA 1992, FRP Appendix B].)

certification: Certification "entails authoritatively attesting that individuals meet professional standards for the training, experience, and performance required for key incident management functions." FEMA, "NIMS Basic Resource Management." http://www.fema.gov/pdf/nims/NIMS_basic_resource_management.pdf.

chain of command[4]: Structure of decision-making responsibilities from the higher levels of authority to the lower levels.

check-in: The process through which resources first report to an incident. Check-in locations include the incident command post, resources unit, incident base, camps, staging areas, or directly on the site.

Citizen Corps: A community-level program, administered by the Department of Homeland Security, that brings government and private-sector groups together and coordinates the emergency preparedness and response activities of community members.

Through its network of community, state, and tribal councils, Citizen Corps increases community preparedness and response capabilities through public education, outreach, training, and volunteer service.

civil defense: The system of measures, usually run by a governmental agency, to protect the civilian population in wartime, to respond to disasters, and to prevent and mitigate the consequences of major emergencies in peacetime.

client[5]: (1) A person who engages the professional advice or services of another. (2) A customer. (3) A person served by or utilizing the services of a social agency.

climate change: Change observed in the climate on a global, regional or subregional scale caused by natural processes or human activity.

combustion[6]: (1) An act or instance of burning. (2) A usually rapid chemical process that produces heat and usually light.

command post (CP): An ad hoc location established at or as near as possible to a disaster site, from which the incident commander (IC) functions. It contains the command, control, coordination, and communications elements necessary to direct and manage the initial response to the event.

community-based organization (CBO)[7]: A private nonprofit organization that is representative of a community or significant segments of a community and that provides educational or related services to individuals in the community.

community leader: An individual who represents a community. Such persons often do not possess any legal power and are not appointed by the community.

community volunteer: A member of a community who voluntarily offers his or her services.

compassion fatigue[8]: The emotional residue of exposure to working with suffering, particularly those suffering from the consequences of traumatic events.

competency: A specific knowledge element, skill, or ability that is objective and measurable (i.e., demonstrable) on the job. It is required for effective performance within the context of a job's responsibilities, and leads to achieving the objectives of the organization.

contamination: The undesirable deposit of a chemical, biological, or radiological material on the surface of structures, areas, objects, or people.

convergent volunteers: Untrained community members who come out of their homes following a disaster.

credential: To supply with evidence or testimonials concerning one's right to credit, confidence, or authority, such as a letter or certificate.

danger[9]**:** Exposure or liability to injury, pain, harm, or loss.

debriefing: A semistructured conversation with an individual after a work shift or an event to gather details of his or her experience and to provide guidance and feedback.

declaration: A formal action by the president to make a state eligible for major disaster or emergency assistance under the Robert T. Stafford Relief and Emergency Assistance Act, Public Law 93-288, as amended.

decontamination: The reduction or removal of a chemical, biological, or radiological material from the surface of a structure, area, object, or person.

demobilization: The phase that transitions management, operations, and support functions and elements from the incident activities back to normal operations or to their baseline standby state.

disaster[10]**:** A sudden calamitous event bringing great damage, loss, or destruction.

disease control: All policies, precautions, and measures taken to prevent the outbreak or spread of communicable diseases, from limitation of occurrence to eradication.

disqualifier: A quality, behavior, or action that would make one unfit or unqualified for a duty or privilege.

domestic emergency: "Any natural disaster or other emergency that does not seriously endanger national security, but which is of such a catastrophic nature that it cannot be managed effectively without substantial Federal presence, or which arises within spheres of activity in which there is an established Federal role" (FEMA Disaster Dictionary 2001, 36; cites Domestic Emergencies Handbook, U.S. Army Forces Command, March 15, 1999).

drill: A training application that develops a combination or series of skills (for example, a drill of mobilizing the decontamination area). It can also be referred to as an "instructional drill" for clarity. A drill conducted primarily for evaluation rather than training should be referred to as an "evaluative drill."

emergency[11]**:** (1) An unforeseen combination of circumstances or the resulting state that calls for immediate action. (2) An urgent need for assistance or relief.

emergency assistance: Assistance that may be made available under an emergency declaration. In general, this is in the form of federal support to state and local efforts to save lives, protect property and public health and safety, and to lessen or avert the threat of a catastrophe. Federal emergency assistance may take the form of coordinating all disaster relief assistance (including voluntary assistance) provided by federal agencies, private organizations, and state and local governments. Or the federal government may provide technical and advisory assistance to affected state and local governments for the performance of essential community services; issuance of warnings of risks or hazards; public health and safety information, including dissemination of such information; provision of health and safety measures; management, control, and reduction of immediate threats to public health and safety; debris removal; temporary housing; and distribution of medicine, food, and other consumable supplies (Stafford Act).

emergency manager[12]**:** Individuals who are trained to support communities throughout the emergency life cycle. Their training is provided by local, state, federal, and private organizations and ranges from public information and media relations to high-level incident command and tactical skills, such as studying a terrorist bombing site or controlling an emergency scene.

emergency operations center (EOC): A location from which centralized emergency management can be performed during response and recovery.

emergency operations plan (EOP): An all-hazards document that specifies actions to be taken in the event of an emergency or disaster event; identifies authorities, relationships, and the actions to be taken by whom, what, when, and where, based on predetermined assumptions, objectives, and existing capabilities.

emergency support function: Mechanisms for grouping functions most frequently used to provide federal support to states and federal-to-federal support, both for declared disasters and emergencies under the Stafford Act and for non-Stafford Act incidents.

empathy: The capability to share and understand another's emotions and feelings. It is often characterized as the ability to "put oneself into another's shoes."

epidemic: (1) An unusual increase in the number of cases of an infectious disease that already exists in the region or population concerned. (2) The appearance of a significant number of cases of an infectious disease introduced in a region or population that is usually free from that disease.

evacuate[13]: (1) To remove from a military zone or dangerous area. (2) To withdraw from a place in an organized way, especially for protection.

evacuation: Organized, phased, and supervised withdrawal, dispersal, or removal of civilians from dangerous or potentially dangerous areas, and their reception and care in safe areas.

exposure: The condition of being subjected to a source of risk.

faith-based organization (FBO): (1) A religious congregation (church, mosque, synagogue, or temple). (2) An organization, program, or project sponsored/hosted by a religious congregation (may be incorporated or not incorporated). (3) A nonprofit organization founded by a religious congregation or religiously motivated incorporators and board members that clearly states in its name, incorporation, or mission statement that it is a religiously motivated institution (Americorps Guidance 2003).

Federal Response Plan (FRP): (1) The plan designed to address the consequences of any disaster or emergency situation in which there is a need for federal assistance under the authorities of the Robert T. Stafford Disaster Relief and Emergency Assistance Act, 42 U.S.C. 5121 et seq. (2) The FRP is the federal government's plan of action for assisting affected states and local jurisdictions in the event of a major disaster or emergency. As the implementing document for the Stafford Act, the FRP organizes the federal response by grouping potential response requirements into twelve functional categories, called Emergency Support Functions. The FRP was completed in April 1992, and twenty-nine federal departments and agencies are signatories to the plan (FRERP).

firewarden[14]: Officer who has authority to direct in the extinguishing of fires, or to order what precautions shall be taken against fires.

first aid: The immediate but temporary care given on site to the victims of an accident or sudden illness in order to avert complications, lessen suffering, and sustain life until competent services or a physician can be obtained.

first responder: Refers to individuals who, in the early stages of an incident, are responsible for the protection and preservation of life,

239

property, evidence, and the environment, including emergency response providers as defined in Section 2 of the Homeland Security Act of 2002 (6 U.S.C. 101). It includes emergency management, public health, clinical care, public works, and other skilled support personnel (e.g., equipment operators) who provide immediate support services during prevention, response, and recovery operations.

forecast: Statement or statistical estimate of the occurrence of a future event. This term is used with different meanings in different disciplines, as well as "prediction."

Geographic Information System (GIS): A computerized database for the capture, storage, analysis, and display of locationally defined information. Commonly, a GIS portrays a portion of the Earth's surface in the form of a map on which this information is overlaid.

goal[15]: The end or aim toward which effort is directed.

Good Samaritan law: Any person who, in good faith, renders emergency medical care or assistance to an injured person at the scene of an accident or other emergency without the expectation of receiving or intending to receive compensation from such injured person for such service, shall not be liable in civil damages for any act or omission, not constituting gross negligence, in the course of such care or assistance.

hazard[16]: (1) Source of danger. (2) Chance, risk. (3) Chance event: accident.

hazard assessment (also hazard analysis/evaluation): The process of estimating, for defined areas, the probabilities of the occurrence of potentially damaging phenomena of given magnitudes within a specified period of time. Hazard assessment involves analysis of formal and informal historical records, and skilled interpretation of existing topographical graphical, geological, geomorphological, hydrological, and land-use maps (Simeon Institute 1998).

hazardous material (hazmat): A substance or material that has been determined by an appropriate authority to be capable of posing an unreasonable risk to health, safety, and property.

hazmat team: Term used to describe a team of highly skilled professionals who specialize in dealing with hazardous material incidents.

humanitarian assistance: Rapid assistance given to people in immediate distress by individuals, organizations, or governments to relieve suffering during and after human-made emergencies (like wars) and natural disasters.

incident commander (IC): The individual responsible for all incident activities, including the development of strategies and tactics and the ordering and the release of resources. The IC has overall authority and responsibility for conducting incident operations and is responsible for the management of all incident operations at the incident site (NIMS).

Incident Command System (ICS): A management system designed to enable effective incident management by integrating a combination of facilities, equipment, personnel, procedures, and communications operating within a common organizational structure.

Integrated Emergency Management System (IEMS): A strategy for implementing emergency management activities that builds upon those functions common to preparedness for any type of occurrence and provides for special requirements of individual emergency situations.

interoperability: (1) The ability of emergency management/response personnel to interact and work well together. (2) In the context of technology, refers to having an emergency communications system that is the same, or is linked to the same, system that a jurisdiction uses for nonemergency procedures, and that effectively interfaces with national standards as they are developed. The system should allow the sharing of data with other jurisdictions and levels of government during planning and deployment.

jurisdiction: A range or sphere of authority. Public agencies have jurisdiction at an incident related to their legal responsibilities and authority. Jurisdictional authority at an incident can be political or geographical (e.g., federal, state, tribal, and local boundary lines) or functional (e.g., law enforcement, public health).

just-in-time training: Training given as needed for immediate application, without lag time and the usual loss of retention.

logistics: The range of operational activities concerned with supply, handling, transportation, and distribution of materials; also applicable to the transportation of people.

Military Support to Civil Authorities (MSCA): Those activities and measures taken by Department of Defense components to foster mutual assistance and support between DoD and any civil government agency in planning or preparedness for, or in the application of resources for response to, the consequences of civil emergencies or attacks, including national security emergencies. MSCA is described in DoD Directive 3025.1. The secretary of the army is designated as the DoD executive agent for MSCA (Title 32 CFR 185).

mission: An overarching objective that defines the end goal of an organization and is embraced by all relevant constituencies. It must demonstrate the difference an organization will make for those it serves, rather than merely describing what it does.

mitigation: (1) Measures taken in advance of a disaster aimed at decreasing or eliminating its impact on society and on the environment (IDNDR/DHA, 1992, 4). (2) Structural and nonstructural measures undertaken to limit the adverse impact of natural hazards, environmental degradation, and technological hazards (U.N. ISDR 2002, 25).

mobilization: The transition of elements from inactivity or normal operations to their designated response state. This may occur well into the response phase, as assets are brought online or as surge-capacity processes are instituted.

mutual aid and assistance agreement: Written or oral agreement between and among agencies/organizations and/or jurisdictions that provides a mechanism to quickly obtain emergency assistance in the form of personnel, equipment, materials, and other associated services. The primary objective is to facilitate rapid, short-term deployment of emergency support prior to, during, and/or after an incident.

National Incident Management System (NIMS): System that provides a proactive approach guiding government agencies at all levels, the private sector, and nongovernmental organizations to work seamlessly to prepare for, prevent, respond to, recover from, and mitigate the effects of incidents, regardless of cause, size, location, or complexity, in order to reduce the loss of life or property and harm to the environment.

National Response Framework (NRF): Guides how the nation conducts all-hazards response. The framework documents the key response principles, roles, and structures that organize national response. It describes how communities, states, the federal government, and private-sector and nongovernmental partners apply these principles for a coordinated, effective national response. And it describes special circumstances where the federal government exercises a larger role, including incidents where federal interests are involved and catastrophic incidents where a state would require significant support. It allows first responders, decision makers, and supporting entities to provide a unified national response.

National Voluntary Organizations Active in Disasters (NVOAD): An umbrella organization of established and experienced voluntary organizations that serve disaster-affected communities (FEMA 1995).

nongovernmental organization (NGO)[17]: An organization that is not part of the local or state or federal government.

objective[18]: Something toward which effort is directed; an aim, goal, or end of action.

pandemic influenza: Virulent human flu that causes a global outbreak, or pandemic, of serious illness. Because there is little natural immunity, the disease can spread easily from person to person.

posttraumatic growth: Perception of positive change and increased strength that an individual may feel in responding to a disaster.

posttraumatic stress disorder (PTSD)[19]: A psychological reaction occurring after experiencing a highly stressing event (as wartime combat, physical violence, or a natural disaster) that is usually characterized by depression, anxiety, flashbacks, recurrent nightmares, and avoidance of reminders of the event.

preparedness: Activities, programs, and systems developed and implemented prior to a disaster/emergency that are used to support and enhance mitigation of, response to, and recovery from disasters/emergencies.

prevention: Refers to activities undertaken by the first-responder community during the early stages of an incident to reduce the likelihood or consequences of threatened or actual terrorist attacks.

protocol: A set of standardized procedures that will assist you in objectively and consistently selecting and managing volunteers.

public health: The art and science that addresses the protection and improvement of community health by organized community effort, including preventive medicine and sanitary and social science.

public information: Processes, procedures, and systems for communicating timely, accurate, accessible information on an incident's cause, size, and current situation; resources committed; and other matters of general interest to the public, responders, and additional stakeholders (both directly affected and indirectly affected).

qualification: A term indicating that an individual has met all the requirements of training plus the requirements for physical and medical

243

fitness, psychological fitness, strength/agility, experience, or other necessary requirements/standards for a position.

reconstruction: Actions taken to reestablish a community after a period of rehabilitation subsequent to a disaster. Actions would include construction of permanent housing, full restoration of all services, and complete resumption of the predisaster state (OFDA).

recover[20]**:** (1) To get back; regain. (2) To bring back to a normal position or condition.

rehabilitation: The operations and decisions taken after a disaster with a view to restoring a stricken community to its former living conditions while encouraging and facilitating the necessary adjustments to the changes caused by the disaster.

relief: Assistance or intervention during or after disaster to meet the life preservation and basic subsistence needs. It can be of emergency or protracted duration (IDNDR/DHA, 992, 5).

resettlement: Actions necessary for the permanent settlement of persons dislocated or otherwise affected by a disaster to an area different from their last place of habitation.

resilience[21]**:** An ability to recover from or adjust easily to misfortune or change.

resource tracking: Supervisors must record and report resource status changes as they occur.

response: Activities to address the immediate and short-term effects of an emergency or disaster. Response includes immediate actions to save lives, protect property, and meet basic human needs. Based on the requirements of the situation, response assistance will be provided to an affected state under the federal response plan using a partial activation of selected emergency support functions (ESFs) or the full activation of all twelve ESFs to meet the needs of the situation (FEMA FRP, Appendix B).

risk[22]**:** The potential losses associated with a hazard and defined in terms of expected probability and frequency, exposure, and consequences (FEMA 1997, Multi Hazard Risk Assessment, xxi).

risk analysis: Risk analysis is the most sophisticated level of hazard assessment. It involves making quantitative estimates of the damage, injuries, and costs likely to be experienced within a specified geographic area over a specific period of time. Risk, therefore, has two measurable components: (1) the magnitude of the harm that may result (defined through vulnerability assessment), and (2) the likelihood or probability of the harm occurring in any particular location within any specified period of time (risk = magnitude × probability). A comprehensive risk analysis includes a full probability assessment of various levels of the hazard as well as probability assessments of impacts on structures and populations (Deyle, French, Olshansky, and Paterson 1998, 134).

role: A responsibility or function required or expected of an individual or an organization in order to fulfill its mission.

search and rescue: The process of locating and recovering disaster victims and the application of first aid and basic medical assistance as required.

secondary hazard: Those hazards that occur as a result of a primary hazard or disaster, e.g., fires after an earthquake or landslides after flooding rains.

secondary survivor: One who grieves the loss of primary victims, e.g., a mother who lost her child, or a man who lost his friend.

secondary trauma: (1) Trauma that occurs to those who care for, or are involved with, those who have been directly traumatized. (2) A condition caused by indirect exposure to trauma through a first-hand account or narrative of a traumatic event.

security: Security, in the traditional sense, refers to monitoring and reducing the risk of human-induced events that adversely affect people or property (intrusion of unauthorized personnel, theft, sabotage, assault, etc.) to some acceptable level (Shaw 1999).

self-care: Activities that individuals, families, and communities undertake with the intention of enhancing health, preventing disease, limiting illness, and restoring health. They can be undertaken by lay people on their own behalf or in collaboration with professionals.

severe weather: Any atmospheric condition potentially destructive or hazardous to human beings. It is often associated with extreme convective weather (tropical cyclones, tornadoes, severe thunderstorms, squalls, etc.) and with storms of freezing precipitation or blizzard conditions.

shelter: Physical protection requirements of disaster victims who no longer have access to normal habitation facilities. Immediate postdisaster needs are met by the use of tents. Alternatives may include polypropylene houses, plastic sheeting, geodesic domes, and other similar types of temporary housing.

simulation drill: Decision-making exercise and disaster drills within threatened communities in order to represent disaster situations to promote more effective coordination of response from relevant authorities and the population.

situation analysis: The process of evaluating the severity and consequences of an incident and communicating the results.

social networking: The building of online communities of people who have common interests. LinkedIn, Facebook, and MySpace facilitate these interconnected systems.

span of control: The number of individuals a supervisor is responsible for, usually expressed as the ratio of supervisors to individuals.

special-needs population: Populations whose members may have additional needs before, during, and after an incident in functional areas, including but not limited to maintaining independence, communication, transportation, supervision, and medical care. Individuals in need of additional response assistance may include those who have disabilities, who live in institutionalized settings, who are elderly, who are children, who are from diverse cultures, who have limited English proficiency or are non-English speaking, or who are transportation disadvantaged.

spontaneous[23]: Proceeding from natural feeling or native tendency without external constraint.

spontaneous volunteer: Individual who arrives without affiliation to an organization following a disaster. These individuals are not associated with any part of the existing emergency management team.

Stafford Disaster Relief and Emergency Assistance Act: The system by which a presidential disaster declaration of an emergency triggers financial and physical assistance through the Federal Emergency Management Agency (FEMA), and through which FEMA is given the responsibility for coordinating government-wide relief efforts.

standard operating procedure (SOP): Complete reference document or an operations manual that provides the purpose, authorities, duration, and details for the preferred method of performing a single function or a number of interrelated functions in a uniform manner (FEMA).

stress: A physical, mental, or emotional response to events that causes bodily or mental tension. Simply put, stress is any outside force or event that has an effect on our body or mind.

subject-matter expert: An individual or organization that can perform a job or a selected group of tasks to standards, whose experience and knowledge of the job designates them as a technical expert. They must know what is critical to the performance of the task.

sunsetting: A decline or final phase in preparation for the termination of a program or project.

surge-capacity management: Decision making and decision implementation that directs and coordinates activities to achieve a common goal. In ICS, this is accomplished by establishing objectives, assigning resources to the objectives, and delineating the parameters within which the resources are to achieve the objectives.

survivor: One who lives through an affliction.

tabletop exercise: A scenario-based discussion that permits evaluation of the emergency operations plan (EOP) or recovery plan, or elements thereof, through oral interaction and application of plan guidance. This is accomplished using minimal or no physical activity, hence the descriptor *tabletop*. It is used to have individuals and teams describe their roles and responsibilities through a presented scenario, and to evaluate the performance of these roles and responsibilities in a relatively low-stress environment. Through the use of simulation techniques, emphasis is placed on collaboration and cooperation, decision making, and team building in the context of a specified scenario. This format allows a significant amount of comment and coaching from the facilitators.

task: An action or set of actions required to complete a role or responsibility. Multiple *tasks* may be needed to complete one *role.*

template: Predesigned examples that serve as a guide.

terrorism: The unlawful use of force or violence against persons or property to intimidate or coerce a government, the civilian population, or any segment thereof, in furtherance of political or social objectives (FBI definition).

threat[24]: (1) An expression of intention to inflict evil, injury, or damage. (2) An indication of something impending.

tools: Those instruments and capabilities that allow for the professional performance of tasks, such as information systems, agreements, doctrine, capabilities, and legislative authorities.

training: Specialized instruction and practice to improve performance and lead to enhanced emergency management capabilities.

trauma: Any injury, whether physically or emotionally inflicted. In the mental health field, an experience that is emotionally painful, distressful, or shocking, which often results in lasting mental and physical effects.

Unified Command (UC): An Incident Command System (ICS) application used when more than one agency has incident jurisdiction or when incidents cross political jurisdictions. Agencies work together through the designated members of the UC, often the senior person from agencies or disciplines participating in the UC, to establish a common set of objectives and strategies and a single incident action plan (FEMA).

unity of command: Each individual involved in incident operations will be assigned to only one supervisor.

vicarious trauma: Cumulative impact of distress that clients' trauma-content stories have on the professional. It is defined as indirect exposure to trauma through a client's firsthand account or narrative of a traumatic event (Vicarious Trauma Institute, http://www.vicarioustrauma.com/blog.html).

victim[25]: (1) One who is injured, destroyed, or sacrificed under any of various conditions. (2) One who is subjected to oppression, hardship, or mistreatment.

volunteer[26]: A person who voluntarily undertakes or expresses a willingness to undertake a service.

volunteerism: (1) The principle or system of doing something by or relying on voluntary action or volunteers. (2) The act or practice of doing volunteer work in community service.

Volunteer Protection Act: A federal law that states that no volunteer shall be liable for harm caused by an act or omission of the volunteer on behalf of the organization or entity, as long as the volunteer is acting within the scope of his or her responsibilities, if the harm was not caused by willful or criminal misconduct, or the harm was not caused by the volunteer operating any vehicle or craft for which the state requires the operator or owner of the vehicle or craft to have an operator's license or insurance.

vulnerability: The susceptibility to being affected by hazards, and susceptibility to the impact and consequences (injury, death, and damage) of the hazard.

vulnerable[27]: Open to attack or damage.

warning: Dissemination of message signaling imminent hazard, which may include advice on protective measures. See also *alert*.

watch: A watch is a notification issued by the National Weather Service to let people know that conditions are right for a potential disaster to occur. It does not mean that an event will necessarily occur.

worried well: A person in a low-risk population who is concerned about having acquired or contracted a disease.

END NOTES

1. Merriam-Webster Online.
2. Merriam-Webster Online.
3. Merriam-Webster Online.
4. *Dictionary of Business Terms.* Barron's Educational Series. 2007.
5. Merriam-Webster Online.
6. Merriam-Webster Online.
7. State of New Jersey, Department of Education. http://www.nj.gov/education/grants/glossary.shtml.
8. ACE Network. http://www.ace-network.com/cfspotlight.htm#WhatIs%20CF.
9. Merriam-Webster Online.
10. Merriam-Webster Online.
11. Merriam-Webster Online.
12. Wikipedia. http://en.wikipedia.org/wiki/Emergency_management#As_a_profession.
13. Merriam-Webster Online.
14. *Webster's Revised Unabridged Dictionary.* http://machaut.uchicago.edu/?action=search&resource=Webster%27s&page=562&quicksearch=on.
15. Merriam-Webster Online.
16. Merriam-Webster Online.
17. http://wordnet.princeton.edu/perl/webwn.
18. Merriam-Webster Online.
19. Merriam-Webster Online.
20. Merriam-Webster Online.
21. Merriam-Webster Online.
22. Merriam-Webster Online.
23. Merriam-Webster Online.
24. Merriam-Webster Online.
25. Merriam-Webster Online.
26. Merriam-Webster Online.
27. Merriam-Webster Online.

APPENDIX A: FORMS

CHAPTER 2

Table 2.1 Worksheet: Organizational Challenges

	Gaps in human resources	Will affect agency's ability to provide following services
Public challenges		
❑ Public apathy	❑	_____
❑ Diverse demographics	❑	_____
Specify:	❑	_____
❑ Communications	❑	_____
Specify:	❑	_____
❑ Others: _____	❑	_____
Internal capacity challenges		
❑ Lack of staff	❑	_____
❑ Partner expectations	❑	_____
❑ Liability	❑	_____
Traditional challenges/natural hazards		
❑ Hurricanes/coastal storms	❑	_____
❑ Tsunamis	❑	_____
❑ Landslides	❑	_____
❑ Floods	❑	_____
❑ Tornadoes and windstorms	❑	_____
❑ Wildfires	❑	_____
❑ Earthquakes	❑	_____
❑ Ice storms	❑	_____
❑ Other: _____	❑	_____

Continued

Table 2.1 (*Continued*)   Worksheet: Organizational Challenges

	Gaps in human resources	Will affect agency's ability to provide following services
Human-made challenges hazards		
❏ Terrorism	❏	_____
❏ Cyberterrorism	❏	_____
❏ Pandemic	❏	_____
❏ Transit of hazardous materials	❏	_____
❏ Chemical and industrial hazards	❏	_____
Specify:	❏	_____
❏ Other: _____	❏	_____

Challenge conclusion

CHAPTER 3

Table 3.1   Worksheet: Identify Your Agency's Mission and ESF

Agency name:

Agency mission:

(If not disaster organization, your mission in disaster response):

Emergency support functions supported		Comment
1. Transportation	❏	_____
2. Communications	❏	_____
3. Public works and engineering	❏	_____
4. Firefighting	❏	_____
5. Emergency management	❏	_____
6. Mass care, emergency assistance, housing and human services	❏	_____
7. Logistics management and resource support	❏	_____
8. Public health and medical services	❏	_____
9. Search and rescue	❏	_____
10. Oil and hazardous materials response	❏	_____
11. Agriculture and natural resources	❏	_____
12. Energy	❏	_____
13. Public safety and security	❏	_____
14. Long-term community recovery	❏	_____
15. External affairs	❏	_____

CHAPTER 4

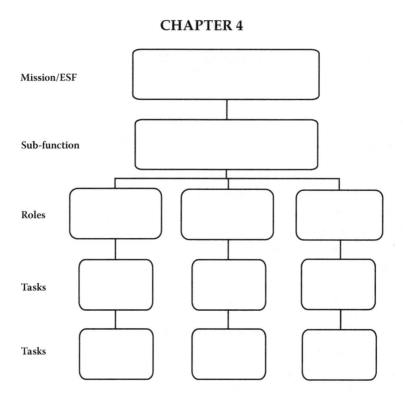

Mission/ESF

Sub-function

Roles

Tasks

Tasks

Figure 4.2 Worksheet: From agency mission to roles and tasks.

Mission/ESF:	
Sub function:	
	Role:
Task	
Task	
Task	
Task	
Task	
	Role:
Task	
Task	
Task	
Task	
Task	

Figure 4.3 Worksheet: Agency roles and tasks in list form.

Table 4.1   Worksheet: Assigning Roles and Tasks within Your Agency

		Staff	Affiliated volunteer	SUCV
Role	_____	_____	_____	_____
Task	_____	_____	_____	_____
Task	_____	_____	_____	_____
Task	_____	_____	_____	_____
Task	_____	_____	_____	_____
Task	_____	_____	_____	_____
Task	_____	_____	_____	_____
Task	_____	_____	_____	_____
Task	_____	_____	_____	_____

Table 4.3   Worksheet: Pros and Cons of Agency Subfunctions and SUCV Positions

Subfunction	SUCV	Pros	Cons
SUCV Role	_____	_____	_____
SUCV Task	_____	_____	_____
SUCV Task	_____	_____	_____
SUCV Task	_____	_____	_____
SUCV Task	_____	_____	_____
SUCV Task	_____	_____	_____
SUCV Task	_____	_____	_____

MEMORANDUM OF UNDERSTANDING

Between

YOUR AGENCY

And

PARTNER AGENCY

* Note : All italicized text in this template must be specified.

Purpose: This MOU establishes procedures and policies regarding the following function area(s):_____

Parties to the MOU

YOUR AGENCY Organizational background:
Mission:
Address:
Phone:
PARTNER AGENCY Organizational background:
Mission:
Address:
Phone:

Duties and Responsibilities

- *YOUR AGENCY* agrees to:

- *PARTNER AGENCY* agrees to:

Communications

YOUR AGENCY Main point of contact will be: _____

Phone: _____ Cell: _____

Figure 4.5   Memorandum of Understanding.   *Continued*

Emergency or after-hours contact: _____

Phone: _____ Cell: _____

PARTNER AGENCY Main point of contact will be: _____

Phone: _____ Cell: _____

Emergency or after-hours contact: _____

Phone: _____ Cell: _____

Terms of the Memorandum

This agreement is in effect starting ____/ ____/ _____.

It may be terminated by either party given _____ days written notice.

The agreement will be reviewed and updated __*annually*___ .

All changes to the agreement must be written and agreed to by both parties.

The personnel of *YOUR AGENCY* deployed for these duties and responsibilities will be in good standing with the agency.

The personnel of *PARTNER AGENCY* deployed for these duties and responsibilities will be in good standing with the agency.

The personnel of *YOUR AGENCY* will abide by all federal, state, and local laws.

The personnel of *PARTNER AGENCY* will abide by all federal, state, and local laws.

Method of Reimbursement?

The following services will be reimbursed: _____ by *YOUR AGENCY* to *PARTNER AGENCY* if all requirements for reimbursement have been met.   The rate of reimbursement will be:_____.

Requirement: The *PARTNER AGENCY* must provide detailed records of expenses and/or time spent by deployed staff or volunteers.

Liability Release and Covenant Not to Sue

YOUR AGENCY and PARTNER AGENCY understand the risks and hazards inherent in acting within these duties and responsibilities, and will assume all risk of loss, damage, and injury, including death, in

Figure 4.5 (*Continued*)   Memorandum of Understanding.   *Continued*

connection to performing the duties and responsibilities outlined in this Memorandum of Understanding.

YOUR AGENCY and PARTNER AGENCY will not bring a suit, claim, action or charge against the other party arising from fulfilling the duties and responsibilities outlined in this Memorandum of Understanding.

Activation

This agreement may be activated only by _____.

_____   _____
(Printed name)   (Printed name)

_____   _____
(Signed name)   (Signed name)

_____   _____
(Title)   (Title)

_____   _____
(Agency name)   (Agency name)

_____   _____
(Date)   (Date)

Figure 4.5 (*Continued*)   Memorandum of Understanding.

CHAPTER 5

Table 5.1 Example of Span of Control

Task: Registration	☐ Staff _____
	☐ Affiliated volunteer _____
	☑ SUCV __5–6__
Supervision	☑ 1 staff to __5–6 SUCVs__
	☑ 1 affiliated volunteer to __5 SUCVs__
	Teaming

Table 5.2 Example of Span of Control

Task: Childcare	☑ Staff ____2____
	☑ Affiliated volunteer ____6____
	☐ SUCV _____
Supervision	☑ 1 staff to 3 affiliated volunteers
	☐ Affiliated to Volunteer

Table 5.3 Post-shift Report

Date: _____ Shift: _____

Agency: _____ Location: _____

Volunteer name: _____ Contact info: _____

Supervisor: _____

Tasks	What worked	What needs improvement	Responsible team	Follow-up actions
_____	_____	_____	_____	_____
_____	_____	_____	_____	_____

Table 5.4   Worksheet: Disqualifier Chart

Role/task	Disqualifiers (please list)

Table 5.5   Worksheet: Core Attributes of a Disaster Volunteer

Role/task	Core Attributes

TEMPLATE
SUMMARY of Internal Protocols for ALL SUCV positions

SUCVs can be utilized in the following categories in the following positions
Sub-function
Role:_____
Role: _____
Role:_____
Role:_____
Sub-function
Role:_____
Role: _____
Role:_____
Role:_____
Sub-function
Role:_____
Role::_____
Role:_____
Role:_____
We do not use SUCVs for 1. 2. 3.
General attributes and disqualifiers related to all positions:
General guideline of supervision for all SUCVs
Code of conduct: All SUCVs must be treated equally to all others
An SUCV may be disqualified immediately for:
All SUCVs are responsible for:
SUCVs will not have the same access and responsibilities as:
All SUCVs should be allowed the opportunity to:
☐ Confidentiality agreement signed by volunteer
☐ Code of conduct signed by volunteer
☐ Self-care guidelines shared with volunteer
☐ Family preparedness training and guidelines offered to volunteer

Figure 5.4 Template: Summary of internal protocols for all SUCV positions.

Protocols for each SUCV Role/Task

FOR INTERNAL DISTRIBUTION ONLY

Sub-function:	
Emergency support function supported:	
Position:	
Position description:	
Number of SUCVs needed:	
Supervision: ___ ☐ Staff ☐ Affiliated volunteer ☐ SUCV	

Disqualifiers	
Immediate:	Two Strikes
☐ Criminal record	☐ No show
☐ Mental illness	☐ Lone ranger
☐ Substance abuse record	☐ Refuses supervision
☐ No transportation	☐ Overzealous
☐ Limited physica ability	☐ Others:_____
☐ Others:_____	

Attributes	
☐ Humble	☐ Compassionate
☐ Grounded	☐ Aware of self and other
☐ Effective listener	☐ Other:_____
☐ Culturally sensitive	

Specific Skills	*List here*
Qualifications:	☐ Licensed in _Expiration: ☐ Credentials_____Expiration: ☐ Other_____
Experience	
Equipment	
Debriefing	☐ Before shift ☐ End of shift
Length of shift	☐ 4 hours ☐ 6 hours ☐ 8 hours
Training provided	
Breaks	Every ☐ 2 hours ☐ 4 hours
Meals	Every ☐ 4 hours at _____ (time)

Figure 5.5 Template: Protocols for each SUCV role/task. *Continued*

Agency Protocols Cont'd

Length of commitment	_____ Weeks ☐ Option to renew ☐ NO renewals

Volunteer responsibilities	☐ Responsibilities at home/work ☐ Fulfilling delegated responsibilities ☐ Schedule, shift, hours committed or required ☐ Length of time commitment ☐ Self care ☐ Others: _____

Agency responsibilities

☐ Orientation	☐ Shift brief/debrief
☐ Training	☐ Shelter
☐ Reimbursement of expenses	☐ Insurance
☐ Medical Coverage	☐ Food
☐ Supplies	☐ Others:_____

Informational tools	☐ Volunteer role/task summary ☐ Volunteer self-assessment ☐ Volunteer self-care guidelines ☐ Site description ☐ Agency Incident Command System (ICS)

Liability	☐ Validate ☐ Credential ☐ Agency's insurance policy ☐ Volunteer release form

Figure 5.5 (*Continued*) Template: Protocols for each SUCV role/task.

Volunteer Self-Assessment
FOR EXTERNAL DISRTIBUTION

Please fill out in order to assess your readiness to volunteer.

1. Do my work/familial responsibilities leave time and energy to volunteer?

   ☐ Yes   ☐ No

2. Are my family responsibilities taken care of and my home secured?

   ☐ Yes   ☐ No

3. Does my family support my volunteer responsibilities?

   ☐ Yes   ☐ No

4. Do I feel confident I can manage the risks?

   ☐ Yes   ☐ No

5. Am I a good listener and a clear communicator?

   ☐ Yes   ☐ No

6. Do I have the personal discipline to practice effective self-care?

   ☐ Yes   ☐ No

7. Do I deal well when working in stressful conditions?

   ☐ Yes   ☐ No

8. Do I have the personal discipline to be punctual and to manage time well?

   ☐ Yes   ☐ No

9. Will I be comfortable and collegial working with people who are of different socio-economic backgrounds than me?

   ☐ Yes   ☐ No

10. What role(s) am I interested in and do they fit my skills?

11. What role(s) wouldn't I want and how will I feel if I'm asked to assume that role?

Figure 5.6   Template: Volunteer self-assessment.

TEMPLATE
Site Description
FOR EXTERNAL DISTRIBUTION

Location:
Date/time:
Site supervisor:
Contact info:
Site description:
☐ **Area map: (Attach)** ☐ **Directions**

Hazardous conditions:	**Weather conditions:**	**Environmental conditions:**
☐ Falling debris		
☐ Fire	☐ Sunny	☐ Mountainous
☐ Flooding	☐ Cloudy	☐ Forest
☐ Infected waters	☐ Slight rain	☐ Urban
☐ Other	☐ Heavy rains	☐ Suburban
	☐ Heavy winds	☐ City
	☐ Snow	☐ Country
		☐ Other:
	Daytime temp _____	
	Evening temp _____	_____

Location Requirements & Limitations

☐ Limited cell phone coverage
☐ No internet connectivity
☐ Food Provided
☐ Food not provided, bring your own
☐ Shelter provided, bring your onw sleeping bag, etc....
☐ Shelter (not provided) make own arrangements
☐ Safety gear provided: _____
☐ Safety gear: bring your own: _____
☐ Recommended clothing: _____

Figure 5.7   Template: Site description.

TEMPLATE

Agency Outreach Flyer
FOR EXTERNAL DISTRIBUTION

Organization name: _____

Address: _____

Contact person: _____

Phone number: _____

E-mail address: _____

Website: _____

Twitter: _____

Background
information: _____
Mission: _____

Open volunteer opportunities:

    Sub-function: _____
    Volunteer Position 1. _____
                      2. _____
                      3. _____
    Sub-function: _____
    Volunteer Position 1. _____
                        2. _____
                      3. _____
    Sub-function: _____
    Volunteer position: 1. _____
                        2. _____
                      3. _____
    Sub-function: _____
    Volunteer position: 1. _____
                        2. _____
                      3. _____

Figure 5.8   Template: Agency outreach flyer.

Agency Outreach Flyer Version 2
FOR PUBLIC OUTREACH

World Cares Center

Collaborate, Prepare, Recover

World Cares Center works within communities to foster sustainable, locally-led disaster preparedness,

response and recovery initiatives.

Name
Contact Info

Position: Community Trainer
Qualifications (possesses one or more of the following): comfortable in public speaking*, interpersonal skills*, training or teaching experience, able to travel in the greater New York City Metropolitan Area, detail oriented, bi-lingual a plus.
*These may be considered Attributes rather than skills!

Job Summary: As a community trainer, you will be facilitating World Cares Center's Grassroots Readiness and Response training program which includes Disaster Volunteering I, II, and III. This program addresses comprehensive disaster and emergency preparedness as it pertains to the specific needs of the community. As a representative of World Cares Center, it is important that you are culturally sensitive to the needs of the community as we work with all different constituencies. As the trainer you may also help with the community outreach and follow-up as well as the distribution of flyers.

Roles/Responsibilities:
- Facilitate Grassroots Readiness and Response – Disaster Volunteer I, II, and III
- Research information about community population and possible disasters affecting them
- Guide participants through activities and discussion
- Distribute surveys to participants
- Assist participants with any questions regarding their preparedness plan

Reports to: DPTM Training Associate

Steps to become Facilitator:
- Complete World Cares Center Train the Trainer Program
- Co-facilitate with Grassroots Readiness and Response
- Become Lead Facilitator

Hours:
Hours vary, however most of the actual training will be delivered after work hours and on the weekends.

Figure 5.9   Template: Job description for an SUCV position.

CHAPTER 6

Volunteer Reception Center Floor Plan

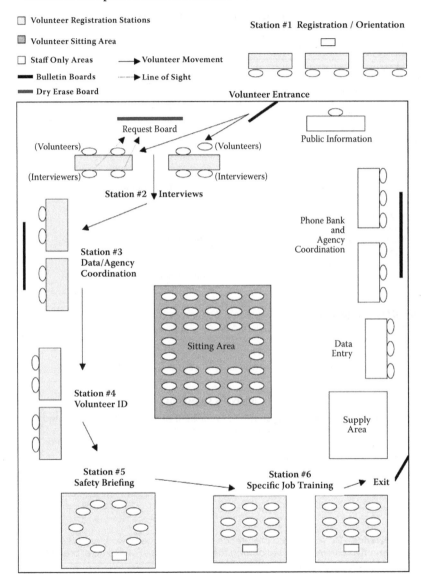

Figure 6.1 Mid-size VRC or VRA. (Source: World Cares Center.)

CHAPTER 7

Spot Screening Checklist

FOR INTERNAL DISTRIBUTION ONLY

Date:_____/ _____/_____

Name: _____

Identification: _____

Address: _____

Phone/cell: _____

Place of employment/school: _____

Emergency contact name: _____

Emergency contact phone/cell: _____

Interviewer: _____

Location: _____

Disqualifiers	Attributes
Immediate Disqualifiers: ☐ Criminal record ☐ Mental illness ☐ Substance abuse ☐ No transportation ☐ Cannot lift heavy items ☐ Other _____ **Two-Strike Disqualifiers** ☐ No Show ☐ Overzealous ☐ Lone Ranger ☐ Refuses Supervision ☐ Other:	☐ Humility ☐ Grounded ☐ Effective listener ☐ Compassion ☐ Awareness ☐ Cultural sensitivity ☐ Others _____

Interview Questions

☐ **Lifetime** – What has happened in your life that has made you interested or prepared to volunteer with us? Share a story about yourself.

Notes:_____
_____
_____
_____
_____

☐ **Preference**—Do you have a preference as to what type of work you take on? *(Name two different choices among the roles or tasks—For example: prefers working with people or quiet office work).*

Figure 7.1 Worksheet: Spot-screening checklist. *Continued*

Notes:_____

☐ Preference response aligned with lifetime response
☐ If not, explanation:

☐ **Strength** – What are your strengths, based on your current or past work or volunteering experiences, that would also apply to volunteering with us?

Notes:_____

☐ Strength response aligned with lifetime and preference response
☐ If not, explanation:

☐ **Specific** – Do you have specific details that show evidence of the strengths you just mentioned?

Notes:_____

☐ Specific response aligned with previous responses
☐ If not, explanation:

☐ **Proof** – Please tell me a few accomplishments that demonstrate evidence of your competence.

Notes:_____

☐ Proof response aligned with previous responses
☐ If not, explanation:

Other questions: _____
_____
_____

Additional notes: _____
_____

Recommendation:
☐ Selected for: _____   ☐ Decline   ☐ Refer to: _____
☐ Other:

Figure 7.1 (*Continued*)   Worksheet: Spot-screening checklist.

VRC Director/ICS Commander

Description: Oversee and manage all aspects of the VRC.

Responsibilities:

- Activate call list for all staff and affiliated volunteers who are signed up to help
- Create initial incident action plan
- Brief and assign tasks to staff and volunteers at the center
- Appoint executive-level officers and captains of VRC stations as needed
- Monitor operations and make staffing changes/add human resources if necessary
- Conduct debriefings of staff at end of shift
- Meet and thank volunteers
- Authorize release of information by public information officer
- Review and approve requests for procurement and release of resources
- Approve plan for demobilization

If the VRC operations are large-scale, then the director will additionally

- Oversee executive-level team, including operations, planning, logistics, finance, public information, and safety officers
- Ensure that the executive-level team meets to debrief and update

If the VRC operations are small-scale, then the director will directly be responsible for

- Coordinating operations, planning, logistics, finance, public information, and safety responsibilities, based on staff resources

Qualification/requirements:

- Staff or affiliated volunteer only
- Extensive managerial experience

- Trained in disaster response
- Has experience managing volunteers
- Organized
- Friendly

Supplies/equipment needed:

- ID badge
- VRC plan: operations, safety policies
- Phone
- Computer and printer
- Desk
- Display board, markers

Manages: All executive-level staff, other staff, and volunteers

Operations Officer
Description: Manage and coordinate all staff and volunteers, assigning them to appropriate tasks to maintain VRC operations.

Responsibilities:

- Manage all operations applicable to VRC mission
- Brief staff and volunteers as outlined in your plan
- Develop operations section of the plan
- Notify director if additional resources are needed
- Coordinate all operations staff and volunteer functions
- Monitor work progress and maintain time records of staff and volunteers

Qualifications/requirements:

- Staff or affiliated volunteer only
- Trained in managing volunteers in disaster response
- Detail-oriented and organized
- Responsible
- Good communication skills

Supplies/equipment needed:

- ID badge
- Operations plan
- Time sheets
- Record storage/file storage
- Phone
- Tables, chairs
- Display board, markers

Manages: All staff and volunteers

Planning Officer

Description: Responsible for collection, evaluation, and use of information about the VRC

Responsibilities:

- Collect all data to assess current operations, including records of safety and job training provided to volunteers and hours worked in the VRC by employees and volunteers
- Establish reporting guidelines for all stations
- Prepare action plans based on information collected
- Identify needs for use of specialized resources
- Submit plans for approval
- Disseminate plans
- Implement plans

Qualifications/requirements:

- Staff or affiliated volunteers only
- Experience in evaluation and action planning
- Detail-oriented
- Database and data assessment experience

Supplies/equipment needed:

- ID badge
- Tables and chairs
- Orientation and safety training records
- Reporting guidelines for each station
- Clipboards, pens
- Phone
- Computer and printer

Manages: Data entry staff

Logistics Officer
Description: Ensure that the VRC facility and its operations are running effectively.

Responsibilities:

- Provide the facility and all materials needed to run the VRC
- Set up and assign work locations and preliminary tasks
- Identify service and support requirements for operations
- Ensure that all needed equipment is in place and that it is in working condition
- Advise on communications capabilities or limitations
- Coordinate safety and feeding needs
- Coordinate medical emergency needs
- Establish sleeping facilities if needed
- Oversee sanitation, maintenance, and cleanup

Qualifications/requirements:

- Staff or affiliated volunteers only
- Detail-oriented
- Reliable
- Ability to multitask
- Experience with inventory/maintenance/multifunction institutions
- Good communication skills

Supplies/equipment needed:

- ID badge
- Agreements pertaining to facility
- Agreements pertaining to supplies, materials, equipment
- Supply inventory list
- Equipment list
- Storage space/secure area for supplies and equipment
- Phone
- Log of donations
- Sanitation/maintenance policy and schedule

Manages: Food/water/first-aid services

Finance Officer
Description: Manages and oversees all financial matters for the VRC.

Responsibilities:

- Track all expenses and maintain all receipts for expenses
- Handle all contracts for goods and services
- Log all injuries and claims
- Handle all compensation claims

Qualifications/requirements:

- Staff or affiliated volunteers only
- Responsible
- Detail-oriented
- Experienced at handling financial contracts, tasks, accounts receivables

Supplies/equipment needed:

- ID badge
- Table, chair
- Computer and printer
- Secure storage for receipts and financial records
- Injury claim forms
- Compensation and reimbursement forms

Public Information Officer
Description: Responds to external requests for information, including from the general public and the media

Responsibilities:

- Provide accurate and relevant information to the general public
- Brief staff and volunteers about who is authorized to speak to the press
- Establish and maintain single contact point with media
- Develop public information tools for staff and volunteers, including a FAQ form
- Coordinate release of information
- Update information on Web site or through other medium

Qualifications/requirements:

- Staff or affiliated volunteers only
- Experience handling media and communications
- Excellent communication skills, both oral and written

Safety Officer
Description: Ensures safety of VRC location and all staff, personnel, and volunteers

Responsibilities:

- Monitor daily operations of the VRC to assess that the environment is safe and that the VRC is being run in a safe manner
- Develop staff and volunteer safety policies
- Conduct safety briefings for staff and volunteers
- If there is damage, conduct damage assessment and determine impact and risks of damage for staff and volunteers
- Manage security team

Qualifications/requirements:

- Staff or affiliated volunteers only
- Experience with security and safety trainings in disaster response

Supplies/equipment needed:

- ID badge
- Other apparel marking security/safety role
- Walkie-talkie system to communicate with security team
- Phone
- Safety briefing log
- Facility blueprint/layout
- Safety policy and handouts

Manages: Security team

CHAPTER 9

VOLUNTEER SELF-CARE GUIDELINES

For External Distribution

Self-Care while Volunteering

- **Briefing and De-briefing Time is Your Time:**
  - Do you understand your responsibilities? If you have any uncertainty, ask your supervisor in your briefing.
  - Talk about your questions, your experiences and your concerns.
  - If you feel overwhelmed or exhausted, please tell your supervisor.
- **Having a "buddy" is helpful**
  - Find a buddy who is also a volunteer or responder. Meet on a regular basis to discuss your experiences, what you achieved, and what is bothering you.
- Wear the required safety equipment.
- Drink plenty of fluids and eat healthily.
- Take regular breaks and rest when you need to.
- Practice relaxation techniques (see note on Relaxation Techniques below).

Self-Care outside of Volunteering

- Manage time away from volunteering to recharge yourself.
- If needed, get support from friends and family. Remember that the people around you (family, friends, spiritual advisors, or coworkers) are a wonderful source of support. Give them permission to tell you when they notice signs of stress in your behavior.
- Find your local volunteer support center and register for support groups or programs.
- Engage in sixty minutes of moderate-intensity physical activity and movement daily.
- Eat a balanced and nutritious diet.
- Stay hydrated with water and fluids with electrolytes, like sports drinks.

- Get seven to eight hours minimum of sleep per night (more if you wake up tired).

Additional Self-Care Notes

Relaxation Techniques: Deep breathing
1. Sit or lie in a comfortable position.
2. Close your eyes and breathe deeply (three seconds in, three seconds out)
3. Focus all your attention on your breathing; notice the movement of your chest and abdomen in and out.
4. When you feel your attention wandering, briefly focus your attention on wherever it goes. Then, gently return your attention to your breathing.
5. Continue for five to ten minutes.

Keeping a Journal
1. Keep a notebook that details your experiences with a beginning and an end.
2. Spend fifteen to twenty minutes writing in your journal at the end of each day or when you take a break.
3. Pay attention to
   - How much you've done and experienced
   - Signs of stress

Other Relaxation Techniques
- Running
- Massage
- Yoga
- Acupressure
- Singing
- Stretching
- Kickboxing
- Acupuncture
- Prayer
- Your Own Preference: _____

Be Aware: Some Signs of Stress
- Exhaustion
- Difficulty sleeping
- Inability to focus

281

- Making simple mistakes
- Short-tempered or easily agitated
- Decrease in quality of work
- Change in general attitude or in health
- Forgetfulness
- Shortness of breath or tight chest
- Change in appetite

INDEX

For more information about
World Cares Center and its programs visit:

http://worldcares.org/

T - #0109 - 101024 - C0 - 234/156/17 [19] - CB - 9781439818336 - Gloss Lamination